*Friends,*
*Guests,*
*and Colleagues*

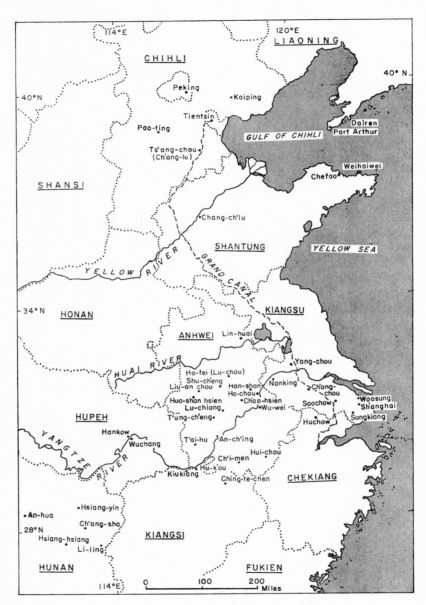

*Area of Li Hung-chang's Major Influence*

# Friends, Guests, and Colleagues

## THE MU-FU SYSTEM IN THE LATE CH'ING PERIOD

### Kenneth E. Folsom

*University of California Press / Berkeley and Los Angeles, 1968*

University of California Press
Berkeley and Los Angeles, California

Cambridge University Press
London, England

*In memory of*
*Li Kuo-ch'ao*

# Preface

In the study of Chinese history, the events, institutions, and personalities involved too often exude an aura of cold impersonality. The intense warmth and humanity of the Chinese world are lost in a welter of official titles, memorials, and imperial edicts. One could almost transpose the names of the famous officials, it seems, without materially affecting the historical narrative. The formidable language barrier is a partial cause. More important, however, is the nature of the traditional Chinese histories and biographies, which, although our primary sources of information, are usually devoid of intimate, personal references. A Chinese statesman's political achievements were recorded in detail, but his date of birth was generally absent. Chinese historical records were written from the viewpoint of the state, and, therefore, any attempt to ferret out personal feelings and desires is usually a frustrating venture. Only by piecing together bits of personal information gleaned from private letters, diaries, and memorials can the researcher begin to see the Chinese as living, breathing human beings with weaknesses and strengths, desires and hates.

This study is an attempt to get below the surface of Chinese history to the world of human feelings and personal relationships and, in the process, to breathe some life into an important historical figure of the late nineteenth century. Although I was already interested in Li Hung-chang as a subject of research, and had begun to feel that he had not been placed in his proper perspective by modern Chinese historians, it was not until I spent nine months in Taiwan on a Ford Foundation Foreign Area Training Fellowship that I became aware of the importance of the *mu-fu* system and of its effect on Li Hung-chang's career. While in Taiwan I also began to realize how deeply personal relationships permeate Chinese society and how little foreigners really know about them. "Fools rush in . . . ": I decided to attempt to penetrate the world of Chinese personal relationships through a combined study of Li Hung-chang and the *mu-fu* system. Time and space have made it necessary to limit the scope of this study, but I hope it will suggest to others new avenues of approach to a fascinating phase of modern Chinese history.

A great many people have come to my aid in the course of my research; to acknowledge my debt to each of them by name would make for rather tedious reading. At the risk of contradicting myself, however, I would like to single out a few individuals whose efforts on my behalf deserve special mention.

My greatest debt is to Professor Li Ting-i, formerly of the National Taiwan University, who introduced me to the *mu-fu* system and gave me freely of his time and ideas. Without his help this study would never have been possible. To the members of the Li family, Li Kuo-chan, Li Chia-huang, Li Chia-wei, and, above all, the late Li Kuo-ch'ao, I am indebted for personal information about Li Hung-chang and his family. I would like to thank Professors J. R. Levenson, W. Eberhard, and H. F. Schurmann, all of the University of California, Berkeley, for their suggestions, criticisms, and general guidance throughout the course of this study; Professor K. C. Liu, University of California, Davis, for reading the manuscript and for his many helpful suggestions; and the members of the Inter-University Research Colloquium on Modern China, and particularly its Chairman, Professor Franz Michael, Institute for Sino-Soviet Studies, George Washington University, for discussing some of the basic concepts. Needless to say, however, I am solely responsible for any errors of fact, omission, or interpretation.

I would further like to acknowledge the financial assistance of the Ford Foundation Foreign Area Training Fellowship Program, and the General Research Board of the University of Maryland. Finally, I would like to express my gratitude to George Allen and Unwin, Ltd., for their permission to quote the poem by Yüan Mei, which originally appeared in *Yuan Mei, Eighteenth Century Chinese Poet* by Arthur Waley.

K. E. F.

# Contents

# I. The Milieu

During the fourth decade of the nineteenth century, there began for China a traumatic experience which was to have repercussions up to the present day — the invasion and conquest of Chinese civilization by a totally foreign culture. This culture, from the other side of the world, was not wholly unknown to China; there had been varying degrees of contact for the previous several hundred years. But the Chinese had always considered it just another barbarian culture. However, in the nineteenth century, the European nations began to follow more aggressive policies. These were based on a competitive drive for trade, were backed up by advanced military techniques and equipment, and sprang from economic, scientific, political, religious, and social thinking that was completely alien to the Chinese. This change of policy was imperceptible to the Chinese. They still regarded the Westerners as barbarians and insisted on dealing with them in the time-honored manner of dealing with all barbarians — keep them at a distance but treat them with the benevolence that the only truly civilized culture in the world could afford to bestow on such benighted souls.

As the nineteenth century wore on, the Chinese suffered military defeat after military defeat, with accompanying forced economic and territorial concessions. A few of the more discerning Chinese began to realize that these were a new kind of barbarian. Unlike previous conquerers, they did not come to conquer and then rule in a Chinese way. Rather they remained physically on the territorial fringes of China and were content with an economic, religious, and intellectual conquest of the country. Such barbarians could not be dealt with in the usual manner through the tributary system, especially since they refused to acknowledge China's natural position of superiority, and to accept with humble gratitude whatever the emperor deigned to grant them. Instead, they insisted on being treated as equals and on gaining access to all of China for their trade and religion, with little or no restrictions. In addition they brought their own standards of conduct, their own laws, and a wholly new set of rules by which the game of international relations should be played. And even more, if their wishes were not granted, they started a war which they easily won with their superior guns and ships! Where in all of Chinese history had anything like this occurred?

It was not enough that China should be faced with such a baffling question in her external relations, but internally the Ch'ing government in the 1850's and 60's was embroiled in one of the greatest rebellions in Chinese history — the Taiping Rebellion. This rebellion, which was to threaten the very existence of the Ch'ing Dynasty before it was suppressed in 1864, also had ideological and religious connections with the Western world and was a graphic demonstration to the supporters of the state of the dangers of the Western invasion.

In the midst of this seemingly hopeless situation — external invasion and internal rebellion — a few Chinese leaders in their desperation turned to an unofficial and informal system, which had long existed as an adjunct to the rigid institutional structure of the Chinese government, as a means of providing the men and ideas with which they hoped to suppress the rebellion and repulse the invaders. The system was known as the *mu-fu* system and involved the use of advisers, who were recruited on a personal and unofficial basis by the provincial officials, and who supplied them with the technical knowledge they needed in order to cope with the problems of governing.

The governmental policy of the Ch'ing, as under the Ming and earlier dynasties, was to recruit its officials through the examination system. The series of examinations for the three successive degrees, which a candidate had to pass in order to qualify for government service, tested only the candidate's literary knowledge and style. Once having succeeded in the examinations, the newly appointed official, if assigned to a post in the provinces, was expected to handle all problems that arose, even those of a highly technical nature, such as flood control, tax collection, and legal decision. With his literary education, which had taken years of intensive study to acquire, the official knew little or nothing of the technical requirements of his office and, normally, had little inclination or opportunity to learn them for a number of years to come. In the meantime, because of the extensive rules and regulations governing his conduct in office, he was literally in danger of losing his head if he made a mistake. As a result the provincial official sought the advice of technical experts. The regular governmental system made no provision for either training or recruiting technical assistants, and so, of necessity, the official was forced to seek such personnel wherever he could find them.

If the government did not provide experts in tax collection and legal decision, the two most important aspects of local government, there would certainly be no provision for experts in foreign weapons of war and foreign rules of international relations. Yet, under the Ch'ing system of delegated and decentralized authority, a local official might very well be responsible for such new problems, especially if he were assigned to a treaty port where the foreign barbarians lived or to a coastal area which they threatened.

Many of the provincial officials, as well as the local gentry, who were either charged with or involved in the suppression of the Taiping Rebellion and the pacification of the foreign barbarians, appeared to be more aware of the problems the country faced and showed more independence of thought than their contemporaries. Nevertheless, despite their progressive ideas, they were still the products of Chinese civilization and held a deep conviction as to its superiority over that of the West. They felt that once China overcame the superior military power of the West, her otherwise superior civilization would be able to cope with these new barbarians. The logical conclusion was to borrow the superior military weapons of the West in order to defeat the West, and, at the same time, to use these new weapons to hasten the defeat of the Taiping rebels. To learn something about Western rules of diplomacy, on the other hand, would help China at the conference table.

Because the regular bureaucracy was rather rigidly structured and not particularly concerned with the problem of supplying technically qualified personnel, the provincial officials relied on the *mu-fu* system to enlist the services of experts in foreign weapons of war and foreign diplomacy. These technicians could easily be added to their existing staffs of experts in domestic affairs, and the system also was flexible enough to provide for the training of others. Another advantage was that the relationship between the official and his advisers was a personal one, which was in keeping with the social system, and was, therefore, not subject to the whims of the central government. Although the official governmental structure was not

flexible enough to meet the new demands, the informal confedera-
tions of the officials, which were the products of the society, were.

The Chinese society of the Ch'ing period (1644–1912) was the
product of centuries of development. During the course of this development, various conflicting forces and ideals had gone through
a process of modification and fusion, but the main themes, which
had been set in motion during the Warring States Period (403–221
B.C.), were still very much alive in the nineteenth century. The
Confucian *Classics* had encountered many reinterpretations but were
still regarded as the orthodox standard by which men governed their
lives. China's past was still very close to her present.

Out of the chaos of the Spring and Autumn (722–481 B.C.) and
the Warring States periods, various schools of thought arose, each
with its own solution of the evils created by the disintegration of
Chou (1027–256 B.C.) feudalism. Of all these schools, however, only
two were to survive the test of time and become constructive forces
of the future — Confucianism and Legalism.

The Confucianists advocated a system of social and political organization which was based on morality, human relationships, and
the hierarchical pattern of nature. At the apex of society would be a
sage ruler whose basic function was to provide the proper moral
guidance for his people; it was through his moral example, rather
than through the use of force, that men would be educated in the
proper conduct, and thus be able to retain their innate goodness.
Moral conduct was predicated on the two concepts of *jen* and *li*. *Jen*
was the quality of human heartedness, the feeling of concern for
one's fellow men. It was most succinctly expressed in the Confucian
maxim: "What you do not want done to yourself, do not do unto
others."[1] The concern was with human feelings on a person-to-person
basis, and the individual was supposed to look to himself and order
his own life in such a way as not to hurt others. *Li* is usually translated as "rites" or "ceremonies"; however, a more lucid translation
of this term would be "the proper conduct under any given social
situation." In a hierarchical society there would be an unending
number of possible social relationships, with infinite shadings. *Li*
was the generic term for all such relationships. A man who had
*li* would conduct himself properly no matter what the situation.

The family was the basic unit of Confucian society, and the

[1] James Legge, *The Chinese Classics* (Taiwan reprint, 1962), I, 301.

familial relationships served as the model for proper conduct, or *li*. Although only three of the Five Confucian Relationships (sovereign to subject, father to son, husband to wife, elder brother to younger brother, and friend to friend) dealt directly with the family, the other two, nonetheless, had familial overtones: the ruler was the Son of Heaven and the father of his people; and friends would almost unconsciously assume an elder brother-younger brother relationship.

The aim of the Confucianists was to achieve harmony and order in society in accordance with the natural harmony and order of the universe. Their society was to be one of human relationships and human feelings, where men, not impersonal systems of government, were the most important element. What Confucius proposed was not a break with the past, but merely a return to the idealized feudal structure of the early Chou. Chou feudalism had relied on custom, personal allegiance, and familial relationships rather than on any clearly defined body of law, and the Chou aristocracy had lived in accordance with an elaborate but, at that time, unwritten code of politeness and honor known as *li*.[2]

The Legalists, however, felt that the problems of the present could not be solved by clinging to the ideals of the past. Conditions were different and practical methods were needed if the prevailing anarchy was to be eradicated. What they proposed was an all-powerful state which would forcibly curb man's evil nature through a system of strict laws, backed up by harsh punishments and few rewards, to which all persons were subject on the basis of equality. Only the ruler was exempt from the laws; it was he who made them, and only he could alter them as changing conditions required. The proposal for a written law code was not a Legalist innovation, since there had been such codes in China as early as 536 B.C.,[3] but to make the law supreme and all men equal under it was new.

In the Western world, law has not only been an integral part of the culture for as far back as written records exist,[4] but in almost all instances it has been regarded as having some sort of supernatural sanction which places it above men. The laws of the Sumerians,

[2] Derk Bodde, "Authority and Law in Ancient China," *Journal of the American Oriental Society*, Supplement No. 17 (July/Sept., 1954), p. 47.

[3] *Ibid.*, p. 52.

[4] Samuel Noah Kramer, *History Begins at Sumer* (Garden City, N.Y.: Doubleday Anchor Books, 1959), pp. 51–55.

Babylonians, and Jews were believed to be gifts from their gods; in the Christian era it was God who sanctioned the laws of the state; and in more recent times it was "the people." This supernatural sanction gave Western law its strength. In China, however, during the historical period at least, law was never considered divinely inspired, nor was it associated with magic or curses.[5] It was man-made and, as such, had to rely on the strength of men to enforce it. The laws of the Legalists were all encompassing and were to be enforced to the letter; such totalitarian devices as "state rewards for public informers, the use of secret police, [the] institution of group responsibility for crime and [the] suppression of allegedly seditious literature"[6] were advocated to ensure compliance. The Legalists even went so far as to believe that privately performed acts of public welfare should be punished if they had not been specifically authorized by the state.[7] Under the Legalist system, the ruler would not depend on the efficacy of moral example in order to rule, but instead would rely on "establishing objective criteria for judging men and policies so as to make the rules independent of flattery and corruption, arbitrariness and personal foibles. Rewards and punishment were the two 'handles of the ruler.'"[8]

In the verbal battle that raged between Confucianists and Legalists, the latter did not deny many of the former's contentions, but rather took the position of hardheaded realists. They did not deny the reality of social differentiation as proclaimed by the Confucianists, but refused to allow such differences to have any bearing on the law and maintained that all must be equal before it.[9] They admitted that there were sage kings and good people, but held that, since a sage king appeared only once in every few thousand years, and since the number of truly good people in a state was minute in relation to the total, it was necessary to have laws that would make it impossible for the common kings and the majority of the people to do wrong. They were concerned with the majority, not the minority. In retaliation the Confucianists cited the Master's

---

[5] Ch'ü T'ung-tsu, *Law and Society in Traditional China* (The Hague: Mouton and Co., 1961), pp. 207, 220.

[6] Bodde, p. 53.

[7] *Ibid.*, p. 53.

[8] Sybille van der Sprenkel, *Legal Institutions in Manchu China*, London School of Economics Monographs on Social Anthropology, No. 24 (London: The Athlone Press, 1962), p. 32.

[9] Ch'ü, *Law and Society*, p. 242.

words: "If the people be led by laws, and uniformity sought to be given them by punishments, they will try to avoid the punishments, but have no sense of shame. If they be led by virtue, and uniformity sought to be given them by the rules of propriety, they will have the sense of shame, and moreover will become good."[10]

The Confucianists felt that it was men, not laws, that made society, and therefore moral training was more essential than legal machinery. "Let there be men and the government will flourish; but without the men, their government decays and ceases."[11] The moral man was versed in human relationships, which in turn were based on the degree of intimacy between relatives. He who cared for his relatives and old friends was considered virtuous. "Confucius said, 'When those who are in high stations perform well all their duties to their relations, the people are aroused to virtue. When old friends are not neglected by them, the people are preserved from meanness.' "[12] On the other hand, the Legalists believed, because the law should be above personal relationships, that a ruler should never change the laws for his relatives, old acquaintances, or the nobles.[13] In the minds of the Legalists, the private affections had no place in government because when one loved his relatives, he would show discrimination, and when one loved his friends, he would be partial, and this in turn would lead to disorder.[14]

The Legalists put the welfare of the state above that of private individuals in order for the state to survive. With threatening neighbors on all sides, the realities of the chaos of the Warring States Period had to be faced. Idealists could look back to the simpler times of the ancients for inspiration, but a realist would look to the present and institute harsh measures.

The conflict between Confucianism and Legalism moved from the realm of the abstract into the world of reality when the feudal state of Ch'in adopted Legalist policies and then went on to conquer and unify all of China by 221 B.C. Under the new empire, Confucianism, even as a philosophy, was thrown on the defensive and forced to fight for its very existence. Legalist policies, however, soon proved to be too radical a break with the past; the ex-nobles and peasants broke out in revolt, and the Ch'in was brought to a

[10] Legge, I, 146.                     [11] *Ibid.*, I, 401.
[12] Ch'ü, *Law and Society*, p. 245.
[13] *Ibid.*, pp. 242–243. Quoted from *Kuan-tzu*, 17, 5b.
[14] *Ibid.*, p. 245. Quoted from *Shang-chün shu*, 2, 10a.

sudden end (206 B.C.). Despite its early demise, the dynasty had done its job well and had established a structure of government that became the pattern for all future dynasties. The founder of the Han (206 B.C.–220 A.D.), maintained Ch'in institutions almost intact, and his law code was in essence Legalistic.[15] Thus, although Legalism as a formal school of thought had losts its preeminent position, it had not been knocked out of the fight; and it was not until the reign of the Han Emperor Wu-ti (140–87 B.C.) that Confucianists were finally able to acquire positions of trust in the government and get the emperor to implement their ideas.

In their struggle to become the dominant element in Chinese imperial society and government, the Confucianists were forced to accept the *fait accompli* of a Legalistic type of government; but they could attempt to modify it in a Confucian way. Legalistic law codes hit at the heart of their ideas and became therefore, a major area of concern. Imperial law was basically penal in nature and consisted of two parts, the *Lü* and the *Li*. The *Lü*, or Fundamental Laws, were set down by the founder of a dynasty and out of filial respect could not be altered by later emperors. The *Li*, or Supplementary Laws, were appended modifications, extensions, and revisions of the Fundamental Laws; in effect, they were a practical device to by-pass considerations of filial piety — the *Lü* could not be altered, but they could be amplified.[16] Even though the original Han law code made no provisions for the Confucian principles, nonetheless the Confucianists, by gaining the support of Han Wu-ti, were able to get their ideas incorporated into the Supplementary Laws.[17]

Confucius had never opposed punishment that was properly meted out, and the belief that punishments were a supplement to virtue and moral influence became very popular among the Han Confucianists.[18] What Confucianists, with their memories of the Ch'in excesses, refused to do was to magnify law to a degree where moral influences became secondary. If a man conducted himself in conformity with the principle of *li*, then he should be given special consideration and not be subject to the punishments of the law. Only those benighted souls who refused to be educated and who, as a result, were considered to be nothing more than animals should

---

15 *Ibid.*, pp. 9–10.
16 van der Sprenkel, p. 59.

17 Ch'ü, *Law and Society*, pp. 270–271.
18 *Ibid.*, pp. 271–272.

be made subject to the law and its punishments. As Confucian ethical principles gained greater acceptance, they became more respected than the legal authority, and the Confucian principle of *li* became incorporated into the law codes. This gradual process of "Confucianization of the law," which began in Han times, continued through the Six Dynasties Period (220–589) and reached its fullest development in the Sui (589–618) and T'ang (618–907). After that time there was very little fundamental change in the law codes of China until the advent of modern law.[19]

A fundamental issue in the struggle between Legalists and Confucianists was the question of the role of man in relation to the state. Chinese emperors, such as Han Wu-ti, who in many ways were amenable to Confucian principles in theory, nevertheless tended to rule in an autocratic manner and to accept the Legalist point of view that the end of man was to serve the state.[20] Legalists from the time of Shang Yang (d. 338 B.C.) had stressed the need to select men for government service on the basis of a rigid set of standards determined by law, merit, and ability,[21] and had ridiculed the Confucian standards of morality, virtue, personal relations, and literary knowledge.[22] Under a Legalist state, Shang Yang had stipulated that the people should concentrate on just one avocation. He further specifically provided for a group of special officials who would be trained in the law and would act as its interpreters.[23] That government officials should be specialists, that they should be promoted only on the basis of their achievements, and that government service was an end in itself were concepts basic to the Legalist point of view. These ideas were vehemently refuted by Confucianists, who believed in the rule of virtue, the importance of personal relationships, and that man, not government, was the ultimate end. Shortly after the end of the reign of Han Wu-ti, the conflict between these two points of view reached a climax in the famous *Debate*

[19] *Ibid.*, pp. 280–281.

[20] W. T. DeBary, ed., *Sources of Chinese Tradition* (New York: Columbia Univ. Press, 1960), pp. 256, 259, 235.

[21] Kung-sun Yang, *The Book of Lord Shang*, transl. with an introduction by J. J. L. Duyvendak (Chicago: Univ. of Chicago Press, 1963), pp. 97, 218; Han Fei Tzu, *Han Fei Tzu, Basic Writings*, transl. by Burton Watson (New York and London: Columbia Univ. Press, 1964), p. 24.

[22] Kung-sun Yang, pp. 64, 220, 225, 239–240, 252, 308, 326; Han Fei Tzu, pp. 23–24.

[23] Kung-sun Yang, pp. 235, 122–123, 327–330.

*on Salt and Iron.* In this debate, the professional administrators of the government monopolies, who were staunch supporters of the Legalist philosophy, were pitted against the Confucian literari, who attacked the validity of the monopolies. The basic issue at stake, however, was whether the Legalists or the Confucianists would control the government. The Confucianists were on the whole successful, even though the monopolies were not abolished, and Confucianist ideals gradually achieved the ascendancy.[24]

The Han Confucianists, under the leadership of scholars such as Tung Chung-shu, gradually created through borrowings and accommodations a new philosophical basis for imperial government. The end result was a syncretic philosophy which reflected elements of both Legalism and Confucianism and provided a new interpretation of and justification for imperial power. At the same time, the Confucianists began to create institutions which would act as a check on Legalistic, autocratic power and its abuses.[25]

Even though formal Legalism and the excesses of the Ch'in were anathema to Confucianists, imperial government nevertheless evolved as a blending of these two schools of thought, and Legalism remained a force to be reckoned with throughout imperial Chinese history — sometimes under the guise of good Confucianism. The writings of Han-fei-tzu (d. 233 B.C.), the leading Legalist philosopher, although shocking to many later Confucian scholars, were read in all ages, and the text appears to have come down to us intact.[26] In the later T'ang Dynasty there was a revival of Legalism under the name of Neo-Legalism,[27] and Wang An-shih of the Sung, with his demands for specialists in government, for impartial selection of officials on the basis of merit, and the like, was accused by some scholars of being a Legalist.[28] The impartial functioning of the examination system, which was basic to the Confucian bureaucracy from T'ang onward, and the specialist nature of the *mu-fu* system, which relied so heavily on personal relationships, seemed to

[24] DeBary, *Sources of Chinese Tradition*, pp. 235–236.

[25] *Ibid.*, pp. 257, 100, 199.

[26] Han Fei Tzu, p. 14.

[27] See Edwin G. Pulleyblank, "Neo-Confucianism and Neo-Legalism in T'ang Intellectual Life," *in* Arthur F. Wright, ed., *The Confucian Persuasion* (Stanford: Stanford Univ. Press, 1960), pp. 77–114.

[28] See H. R. Williamson, *Wang An-shih* (London: A. Probsthain, 1935–1937), I, 48–84; James T. C. Liu, *Reform in Sung China* (Cambridge: Harvard Univ. Press, 1959), p. 55.

reflect Legalist rather than Confucian ideas. Yet, despite the accommodations effected so that a Legalistic monarchy and a Confucian bureaucracy could work together to govern the empire, the tension between the two was never removed, and the basic point of conflict remained: was man an end in himself, or merely a tool of government? During the Sung period (960–1279) the Confucian point of view triumphed and held the field until the coming of the West, despite the occasional revivals of interest in Legalist theories by practical Confucian statesmen.

The Manchu semi-barbarians entered China in 1644 as conquerors and stayed to rule in a Chinese way. As rulers they assumed the Legalist position held by previous Chinese emperors which put the interests of the state above those of the people. They were interested in maintaining the state, and their position as rulers. In order to do this they took over most of the Ming policies and institutions and merely adapted them when necessary to fit their special needs. The government they inherited was the product of centuries of development, but its basic structure was Legalist. The *Lü* of the Ming law code was taken over almost *in toto*, and, as many of its provisions dated back to Ch'in and Han times, it too was fundamentally a Legalist instrument. The governmental structure of the state, as in previous ages, was thus oriented to Legalist principles of authority.

The society which the Manchus had conquered and ruled was, however, basically Confucian, guided by the principles of family loyalty and moral conduct (*jen* and *li*), rather than by laws and institutions. The upholders of these Confucian mores were the gentry. This was a distinct social group with special political, economic, and social privileges, which they earned by passing one or more of the imperial examinations. Despite their relatively small number, they were the upholders and arbiters of Confucian virtue and moral conduct for the rest of Chinese society, primarily because of their intensive education in the Confucian *Classics*. It was from this group that the officials were chosen. Membership in the gentry group was not hereditary, however, as each man had to pass the examinations for himself.[29] These gentry-officials were the ones who had "Confucianized the law" and had instructed the emperors in the moral teachings of Confucius.

[29] Chang Chung-li, *The Chinese Gentry* (Seattle: Univ. of Washington Press, 1955), pp. xiii, xvii.

The Ch'ing rulers, like their predecessors, realized that in order to secure their rule they must "take the gentry into camp." The state upheld the law, but the gentry upheld the moral teachings, and for the society at large the moral teachings, *li*, were more important than the law.[30] The Ch'ing rulers were in an even more unfavorable position in relation to the gentry than the previous dynasty had been because, as Manchus, they were considered barbarians. Ming loyalists resisted the Manchu take-over because they were foreigners — an incipient form of Chinese nationalism, but to the vast majority of Chinese it was not ethnic or geographic origins that legitimatized rule, but rather the barbarian's willingness to adopt Confucian culture. As a result, the Ch'ing tried to "out-Chinese the Chinese" in their support of Confucianism. They could not alter Confucian doctrine to suit their own needs, as it was the gentry who were its keepers and arbiters, but the Ch'ing rulers could and did use this doctrine as a device to gain acceptance, as well as control. They fostered the principle that a moral man would not do anything contrary to the interests of the state: "If everybody's filial and brotherly, nobody will oppose the law."[31]

In their determination to rule, the Manchus utilized every device, both moral and institutional, Confucian and Legalistic, to ensure the throne to themselves and their progeny. The most important weapon in their arsenal for control was the examination system, operated by the throne, but based on the Confucian *Classics* and accepted by the populace as the road to wealth, power, and prestige. In addition to controlling access to office and the benefits that office conferred, the examinations also provided a means of molding the gentry ideologically into a uniform, conservative pattern. Almost as soon as the Manchus entered Peking in 1644, the examinations were revived, and by 1679 the "first full-dress 'examination for scholars of wide learning and great literary attainment'" was held by the K'ang-hsi Emperor (1662–1723).[32]

When the Ch'ing rulers took over political control, they also claimed moral authority. The emperors themselves paid reverence

30 Marc van der Valk, *An Outline of Modern Chinese Family Law*, Monumenta Serica Monograph Series II (Peiping: H. Vetch, 1939), p. 10.
31 Olga Lang, *Chinese Family and Society* (New Haven: Yale Univ. Press, 1946), p. 18.
32 Hsiao Kung-ch'üan, *Rural China* (Seattle: Univ. of Washington Press, 1960), p. 184.

to Confucius, and canonized scholars of the past whose works and conduct were compatible with their ideas. Sung Confucianism of the Ch'eng-Chu school, with its stress on social duties and human relationships, was an excellent tool for maintaining a firm ideological control of the society, and the emperors from Shun-chih (1644–1662) to Ch'ien-lung (1736–1796) wrote commentaries on the Confucian *Classics*, as well as learned essays on Sung Confucian philosophy, and published editions of the works of Chu Hsi (1130–1200). The imperial power was creating an "imperial Confucianism."[33]

The acceptance of "imperial Confucianism" by the masses depended, in the final analysis, upon the reaction of the scholar-gentry class (*shih-ta-fu*), the clans, and the families, especially since the total number of officials in relation to the population was microscopic (in the *chou* and *hsien* hierarchy there were only about 1,500 posts).[34] Therefore, the Ch'ing rulers revitalized the local examination and school system which they had inherited from the Ming, and fostered academies, community schools, and charity schools. They also instituted a system of public lectures on Confucian morality which were held twice a month and which all the elders, scholars, and commoners of the neighborhood were expected to attend; they utilized the principle of "instruction through worship" by building temples and shrines in the capital and provinces, by personally conducting sacrificial rites, and by instituting various sacrifices in every *chou* and *hsien* in the empire.[35]

The emperors also issued moral injunctions to the people, such as *The Sacred Edict* of the K'ang-hsi Emperor, which was a collection of sixteen moral maxims which glorified piety to the father and submission to the elder brother. In 1724, the Yung-cheng Emperor (1723–1736) amplified this *Edict* in a dissertation of about 10,000 words, called *The Amplified Instructions of the Sacred Edict*, in order to make it more comprehensible to "ignorant rustics."[36] Such admonitions had become a recognized facet of imperial rule through the partial "Confucianization" of the emperor institution, and the Ch'ing rulers were merely following the pattern set by earlier Ming injunctions:

[33] *Ibid.*
[34] Hsiao Kung-ch'üan, "Rural Control in Nineteenth Century China," *Far Eastern Quarterly*, XII, No. 2 (Februay, 1953), 174.
[35] *Hsiao, Rural China*, pp. 235, 185, 220.
[36] *Ibid.*, p. 185; Lang, p. 18. The Chinese title of *The Amplified Instructions of the Sacred Edict* is *Sheng-yü Kuang-hsün*.

Render filial piety to parents;
Show respect to seniors by the generation-age order.
Remain in harmony with clan members and the community;
Teach and discipline sons and grandsons.
Attend to one's vocation properly;
And do not commit what the law forbids.[37]

Despite their stress on Confucian morality, Ch'ing emperors were autocrats and, as such, also relied on Legalist measures in their determination to control every aspect of Chinese society. From the beginning of the dynasty, a strict and extensive legal system was used to ensure submission to imperial authority. In reading the Ch'ing code, one has the feeling that it was compiled by men who knew only too well the magnitude of human wickedness, and every effort seems to have been made to forestall the creativity of evil minds. The law, however, was primarily criminal and punitive, and what is known as contractual and property law in the Western world came under the province of local custom and personal agreement.

In their application of the law, as well as in maintaining peace and order, the Ch'ing rulers, however, were once again dependent upon the cooperation of the leading elements in the society. As a result, the legal structure recognized and supported the existing system of head men and elders in the villages and the position of the old men in the families and clans. Thus, the rule of the conservative elements in society, which were more amenable to authority than the younger, hotter bloods, was preserved and perpetuated. In addition, the clans and families, through clan rules and social and economic pressures, could more effectively inculcate and enforce moral training than the central government could, and that area of social behavior pertaining to the family and human relationships was left largely in private hands. "When the Ming Code was formulated, the grandson of Emperor Tai-tsu (1368–1398) requested that 'all laws which were concerned with the five human relationships should give more consideration to human factors even at the expense of the law.'"[38] The law was there, but it served merely to back up the authority of the family or clan head, who in turn relied on the clan rules, which were basically instructions of a moral

[37] Liu Wang Hui-chen, *The Traditional Chinese Clan Rules*, Monographs of The Association for Asian Studies, VII (Locust Valley, N.Y.: J. J. Augustin, Inc., 1959), p. 23.
[38] Ch'ü, *Law and Society*, p. 69.

nature. These rules were designed primarily to warn the offender to reform his ways so that there would be no need to resort to law.[39]

The Chinese attitude towards the law, even today on Taiwan, is that it should be called upon only as a last measure. For one to admit that he had to go to court was to admit that social intercourse had broken down. "The Master said, 'In hearing litigations, I am like any other body. What is necessary, however, is to cause the people to have no litigations.'"[40] When mediation and human relationships could not solve a problem, then men ceased to be human, which was an indictment of the Confucian system itself.

Aside from the moral aspect of resorting to law, there was also a very practical reason for not becoming enmeshed in the courts: to come in contact with the law usually meant disaster. The operation of Ch'ing law involved the incarceration of not only the defendant, but also the plaintiff and the witnesses. Such detention, which also involved "gifts" or "fees" to various policemen, runners, jailors, and so forth could easily result in financial ruin, illness, and death.

Li Keng Yun, a noted *hsün li* of the Ch'ing Dynasty, was the prefect of Chang Chou. The people of that region were notorious for their pugnaciousness and were frequently given to private wars in which many casualties often resulted. Li Keng Yun called in the villagers and asked them: "When you have disputes of any kind it is proper to appeal to the magistrate for a decision. Why resort to private wars?" To this question the villagers unanimously answered: "When we appeal to the magistrate it may take one or two years for a decision. And then we are not sure whether we can obtain justice. In the meantime we have to go through much suffering."[41]

The primary reason for the unsatisfactory conditions of the courts was that the district magistrates were habitually and grossly overworked and usually not familiar with the extensive laws and legal precedents. Because a mistake, whether intentional or not, could result in the loss of their jobs or even their heads, many magistrates were afraid to make any legal judgments. It was much easier and

[39] Liu Wang Hui-chen, "Analysis of Chinese Clan Rules: Confucian Theories in Action," in David S. Nivison and Arthur F. Wright, eds., *Confucianism in Action* (Stanford: Stanford Univ. Press, 1959), p. 64.

[40] Legge, I, 257.

[41] Chang Ch'un-ming, "The Chinese Standards of Good Government: Being a Study of the 'Biographies of Model Officials' in Dynastic Histories," *Nankai Social and Economic Quarterly*, VIII, No. 2 (July, 1935), 242–243. A *hsün li* was a model official.

safer to put off making a decision and thus not risk the censure of their superiors. Another reason why the courts did not function well was that the legal structure was permeated by corruption and favoritism; as a result, the people were not confident that they would receive justice. The Ch'ing rulers were not blind to the evils of the legal system, and in some instances even sanctioned them.

The K'ang-hsi Emperor (reigned 1662–1723) in replying to a memorial once gave it as his opinion "that lawsuits would tend to increase to a frightful amount, if people were not afraid of the tribunals, and if they felt confident of always finding in them ready and perfect justice. As man is apt to delude himself concerning his own interests, contests would then be interminable, and half of the Empire would not suffice to settle the lawsuits of the other half. I desire therefore that those who have recourse to the tribunals should be treated without pity, and in such a manner that they shall be disgusted with law, and tremble to appear before a magistrate. . . ."[42]

The Ch'ing rulers, by the use of legal institutions and Confucian morality, were attempting to secure and perpetuate their rule. However, it was the ruled who set the moral standards and in general preferred to rely on themselves for the settlement of disputes, performance of marriages, arrangement for the sale of goods and land, and all the other adjustments that are necessary in a complex society.

The basic unit of Chinese society was the family, but since no family is an entity unto itself, relationships of an "extra-familial" nature were equally important in carrying on the everyday functions of society. Anyone who has lived in a Chinese community, whether in Taiwan, on mainland China, or in the overseas Chinese communities, has been struck by the intense importance of friends. If there is a job to be secured, a contract to be arranged, a marriage to be performed, a favor to be asked, a gift to be sent, or a special errand to be run, the natural avenue of approach is to seek a friend who will help in the matter. Friendship among the Chinese is so complex that few Westerners are able to fully comprehend it. The extent to which it permeates Chinese society and the varying degrees of its intensity and obligations far surpass the connotations of the term in the West.

The fifth of the Five Confucian Relationships was "friend to

42 van der Sprenkel, pp. 76–77. Quoted from T. R. Jernigan, *China in Law and Commerce* (New York, 1905), at p. 191.

friend." Here it would appear that the Master provided a safety valve for human emotions in the heirarchical structure of Chinese society. Within the family all relationships were hierarchical, and this arrangement was carried over into society, especially in the form of elder to junior, based on generations. The formality and relative positions involved inhibited the free exchange of ideas and feelings. Few, if any, Chinese sons felt that they could talk out their problems with their father on a man-to-man basis. The senior had the authority, and the junior should listen respectfully to his teachings. But friends were equals and could say what they felt to each other. The term for an intimate friend, *chih-chi* ("knows me"), clearly conveys this idea of closeness and open mindedness. With a friend you could freely discuss your inner feelings, ambitions, desires, problems, and sorrows which you dared not discuss with family members, elders, or juniors. Friends were equals in the hierarchical Confucian world.

In the Western world, and especially in modern times, the great theme of literature and art has been love for members of the opposite sex; yet, in China it has been friendship. The great Chinese popular novels, *Romance of the Three Kingdoms* and *All Men Are Brothers*, take friendship as their central theme. The opening lines of the *Confucian Analects* are: "The Master said, "Is it not pleasant to learn with a constant perseverance and application? *Is it not delightful to have friends coming from distant quarters?*"" [43] In Chinese landscape paintings one of the main themes is that of two old friends sitting together quietly enjoying the harmony and splendor of nature. Over and over again the theme of friendship appears in Chinese poetry, literature, and art — the realms of personal expression.

The degrees of friendship were extremely varied. Perhaps the most intimate was that of sworn brothers. Young men in China liked to pattern themselves after the three heroes of the *Romance of the Three Kingdoms*, Liu Pei, Kuan Yü, and Chang Fei, who swore brotherhood in the Peach Orchard:

We three, Liu Pei, Kuan Yü and Chang Fei, though of different families, swear brotherhood, and promise mutual help to one end. We will rescue each other in difficulty, we will aid each other in danger. We swear to serve the state and save the people. We ask not the same day of birth but

[43] Legge, I, 137. Italics mine.

we seek to die together. May Heaven, the all-ruling, and Earth, the all-producing, read our hearts, and if we turn aside from righteousness or forget kindliness may Heaven and man smite us.[44]

This oath provided the pattern for most of those which young men used in swearing brotherhood. The oath was also usually sworn to in a temple, shrine, or some other place of significance to the participants.

The terminology for friendship is also illuminating: *chiao-ch'ing*, meaning extremely close friendship, is composed of characters meaning "to have intercourse or intimacy" and "the affections, feelings, or desires." What is translated as "a firm and noble-minded friendship," *tao-i chin-shih chih chiao*, carries the implications of public and private morality and the firmness of minerals and rock.

In addition to direct friendship, which one contracted for oneself, there was a whole range of indirect ones. The friends of friends would fall into this category, as would the friends of a father and the sons of friends. Although the relationship was originally created by others, friendships of this nature could become intimate and lasting, depending on the interests and personalities of the participants.

A special class of friendship was that of "*t'ung*-ism." The character *t'ung*, which means "together" or "the same," has been applied as an adjective to many nouns in Chinese to describe the various categories of this particularly Chinese brand of friendship — *t'ung-hsiang* (same village), *t'ung-sheng* (same province), *t'ung-hsüeh* (students together), *t'ung-nien* (same year [graduates], classmates), and so on. Probably the most important of these for the educated class was that of *t'ung-nien*.

Those successful candidates at any particular examination, whether it was prefectural, provincial, or metropolitan, considered themselves as classmates. Under the Ch'ing system of education much of the real work of preparation for the examinations was done under private teachers or tutors, despite the government-sponsored schools. Because of this, the criteria for "classmate" was not whether you had attended the same school and had graduated together, as we think of it today, but whether you had passed the same imperial examination. During the course of the preparation, friendships were formed on the basis of common experience and interests. Those who were

[44]Lo Kuan-chung, *Romance of the Three Kingdoms*, transl. by C. H. Brewitt-Taylor (Rutland, Vermont and Tokyo: Charles E. Tuttle Company, 1959), I, 5–6.

successful in the examinations had the further bond of common achievement. Of the literally thousands of students who took the examinations, only a small percentage passed and, as in any human situation, not all of them became real friends. Nevertheless, to have passed the examinations in the same year, even though no real friendship was formed, still created a special affiliation. As with other types of friendship these too were subject to proliferation. The sons of classmates had a special relationship to their fathers' classmates; and the near relatives of a successful candidate would not only share in his glory but also in his friendships.[45]

People from the same village or the same province, when out of their native area, felt a special affinity and loyalty to one another on the basis of their common nativity. As a result they would band together in special provincial clubs (*hui-kuan*) for mutual support and companionship. Candidates from the same province who went up to Peking for the examinations would lodge together in their respective provincial clubs; there they would receive help in preparing for the examinations and, if in need, financial assistance. Merchants on business in Peking would also lodge at these clubs. While the composition of the clubs in the capital was mainly of a scholarly nature, in the other major centers of China, such as the provincial capitals and commercial centers, the merchants predominated. However officials whose duties led them away from their home provinces would also participate in the activities of their provincial club.[46] This loyalty to and feeling of pride in one's home region permeated Chinese society and added one more facet to the complex world of human relationships.

At the local level, the members of the same profession or occupation would form guilds, as would strangers to the area who came from the same region and pursued the same occupation. Some of these guilds had branches in other parts of China and thus their members would create a network of friendships based on the ties of common occupation and regional affinity. The Shansi bankers, who practically monopolized the transfer of funds in China prior to the advent of Western-type banking, are only one example of this phenomenon.

[45] Arthur Waley, *Yuan Mei, Eighteenth Century Chinese Poet* (London: George Allen and Unwin, Ltd., 1956), p. 26.

[46] Hosea Ballou Morse, *The Gilds of China* (London: Longmans, Green and Co., 1909), pp. 35–37; van der Sprenkel, p. 90.

The secret societies were another example of the Chinese proclivity to organize life on the basis of friendship and human relations.
These societies bound together a group of men who, although not
blood relatives, accepted ties which were patterned after those of
the family. Their relationship was generally that of sworn brothers
in keeping with the traditions of the three heroes of the *Romance
of the Three Kingdoms*. Such a relationship often demanded a loyalty that transcended the normal familial ties and put the organization above one's family.[47]

In most friendships, despite the equality involved, the participants
almost invariably assumed an elder brother-younger brother relationship. The question of who was senior was determined by age,
scholarly ability, status in the examinations, or any other factor
which was mutually and silently agreed upon. Despite the terminology, however, the relationship was not characterized by the same
formality and rigidity that existed between blood brothers; the relationship was considered a form of courtesy more than anything else.

Not so informal though was the relationship between student
and teacher. A man's teacher was regarded, in many ways, as his
father. The teacher was stern but humane to the student, and directed and guided him not only in his studies but also in proper
conduct. The student, on his part, revered his teacher and showed
a loyalty and concern for his welfare and that of his family for the
rest of his life.

The relationship between candidate and examiner in the examinations was a special category of friendship, which, although small
in relation to the total society, still had a marked influence on the
bureacracy. In a poem of 1768, addressed to his examiner Teng Shih-
min (1712–1775), Yüan Mei, the eighteenth-century official and
poet, aptly described the agony he endured while waiting for the
results of the examination, the extreme joy he experienced on passing, and the eternal gratitude he felt for the examiner who passed
him:

> What agony it was thirty years ago
> At Peking, waiting for the lists to appear!
> I was staying for the night at Mr. Ni's house
> And was hurrying home, prancing along through the dark.
> On the way I met someone who told me I had passed;

47 Morton H. Fried, *Fabric of Chinese Society* (London: Atlantic Press, 1956),
p. 203.

I was bowled over by this thunderclap of joy and surprise.
I thought it was a mistake, thought it was only a dream;
I was in a sorry state of doubt and dread.
Yet it was true; that staunch master Teng,
His two eyes freshened by the autumn light,
Had written that my name was to figure on the list,
Had rescued me out of my dark abyss.
Do not say I had earned it by my literary powers;
When have letters ever had influence?
Do not say that my horoscope was good;
When have horoscopes said the last word?
*Parents, however much they love a child,*
*Have not the power to place him among the chosen few.*
*Only the examiner can bring the young to notice,*
*And out of darkness carry them to Heaven!* [48]

The successful candidate considered himself the "pupil" of the examiner who had passed him, and called the examiner his "patron." [49] The relationship was less formal than that of student-teacher and not as informal as friend to friend. As the above poem, which was written thirty years after the event, indicates, this relationship usually lasted a lifetime. As with friends and classmates, the relationship between candidates and examiner extended downward and outward. " 'Just now I saw the list of successful candidates. Your patron, Mr. Tang, was a pupil of my grandfather; so I feel very close to you.' " " 'Mr. Chu is the grandson of the Prefect Chu of Nanchang,' put in Lovely Yu. 'My father served as an examiner in Nanchang. So Mr. Chu and I are related.' " [50] Those students of a particular examiner, even when passed in different examinations, possessed a common bond and on occasion would look out for each other. [51]

In the interplay of human relationships, the Chinese believed in a reciprocity of actions. When he acted, he anticipated a response or a return. When a favor was done or a gift sent, one was expected in return. These were considered "social investments," and anyone who did not keep the social balance sheet in order was considered lacking in human feelings (*jen-ch'ing*), since gifts, congratulations, and condolences on special occasions were the outward expression of

[48] Waley, pp. 23–24. Italics mine.
[49] Wu Ching-tzu, *The Scholars*, transl. by Yang Hsien-i and Gladys Yang (Peking: Foreign Language Press, 1957), p. 36, footnote 1.
[50] *Ibid.*, pp. 76, 459.                    [51] *Ibid.*, pp. 122–123.

feelings. This concept is not foreign to the Western world, but it has had a longer history, a higher and wider degree of conscious application, and a greater influence on society in China.[52]

Friendship had its obligations in Chinese society, and they were recognized and accepted. A friend was expected to be your critic, and you were expected to receive his criticism in the light in which it was offered — as that of a friend. One Chinese scholar claims that the quarrels of Tseng Kuo-fan and Tso-Tsung-t'ang were not those of enemies, but those of friends offering helpful criticism.[53] The fact that a person was your classmate, even though you scarcely knew him, gave him the right to call on you for aid. Friends were expected to help each other, either financially or through influential friends. In the Chinese novels *The Dream of the Red Chamber* and *The Scholars (Ju-lin wai-shih)*, there are innumerable examples of a poor scholar being helped by his rich friend or patron, either by gifts of money to support his studies or by letters of introduction to influential people.[54] "Friends should put their property at each other's disposal."[55] If one's patron or friend, their children or the members of their families got into trouble, and you were in a position to do something about it, then it was your duty to do so. This practice is illustrated by an incident from *The Scholars* in which a Miss Shen had run away from a lecherous villain who had promised to marry her but instead had taken her as a concubine. On the villain's complaint she was finally captured in another county and brought before the local magistrate for extradition. "This magistrate had passed the examination in the same year as the magistrate of Chiangtu County [the cognizant official] and was a good friend of his, so he enclosed a confidential letter in his official report, asking his colleague to release Miss Shen and send her back to her father in order that she might marry again." In his examination of her, he had been so impressed with her poetic ability, her obvious high character, and her connections with influential people, that he had

---

[52] Yang Lien-sheng, "The Concept of *Pao* as a Basis for Social Relations in China," *in* John K. Fairbank, ed., *Chinese Thought and Institutions* (Chicago: Univ. of Chicago Press, 1957), pp. 291–292.

[53] Li Shao-ling, *Tseng Kuo-fan* (Kao-hsiung, Taiwan: Ta-yeh shu-tien, 1955), pp. 68–72.

[54] Tsao Hsüeh-chin and Kao Ngoh, *The Dream of the Red Chamber*, transl. by Florence and Isabel McHugh from the German transl. of Franz Kuhn (Taiwan reprint), Chapters I, II, and III; Wu Ching-tzu, p. 252.

[55] Wu Ching-tzu, p. 181.

taken pity on her and requested his friend to release her, which was done.[56]

To have no friends was in many cases worse than having no family. One so unfortunate was not only lonely but had no one to turn to in times of trouble, no one to help him along the road to success. Ku Hung-ming, a Western-educated scholar of the late nineteenth century, a member of Chang Chih-tung's *mu-fu*, and an exceedingly independent and caustic person, never achieved any great success. He explains why in the following incident:

In the *ting-wei* year [1907] I followed Chang Chih-tung to the capital and got to know Jui Chung-lan, *ching-ch'ing*, and we got along with each other very well. We were sorry to have met each other so late. The *ching-ch'ing* asked me, "Have you paid your respects to people in the capital?" And I said, "I don't pay my respects to people." The *ching-ching* said, "For a long time I have heard that your talent and knowledge greatly exceeded that of our contemporaries, and in my opinion you should have become prominent a long time ago, but today you are still an underling. I just could not quite understand it. Now that I have heard your words, it suddenly becomes clear. The reason is because you will not pay your respects. There is no one to blame for your not being prominent." Then we looked at each other and smiled.[57]

Friends, as well as the family, served as a source of employment. Even though the bureaucratic regulations and the examination system attempted to make official employment as impartial as possible, still the personal element did have a bearing of varying degrees on official jobs. As Robert Marsh has pointed out, advancement in the bureaucracy was by seniority and merit, and generally speaking these standards were successfully maintained.[58] However, kinship and friendship were never successfully eliminated when there was a choice to be made between two equally qualified candidates; this was true also in the judging of past performances and in the granting of promotions.[59] In the struggle between a universalistic bureaucracy and a particularistic society, the one could never be completely

[56] *Ibid.*, pp. 553–554.
[57] Ku Hung-ming, *Chang Wen-hsiang mu-fu chi-wen* (A Record of Chang Chih-tung's *Mu-fu*) (Taipei, Taiwan: Shang-wu yin-shu-kuan, 1956), *hsia*, p. 20b. A *ching-ch'ing* is an official serving in the capital.
[58] Robert M. Marsh, *The Mandarins, The Circulation of Elites in China, 1600–1900* (Glencoe, Ill.: The Free Press, 1961), p. 190.
[59] Marion Joseph Levy, Jr., *The Family Revolution in Modern China* (Cambridge: Harvard Univ. Press, 1949), p. 222.

divorced from the other because the same people dwelled in both worlds and normally followed the teachings of Confucius in preference to those of the Legalists. "The duke of Chow addressed his son, the duke of Loo, saying, 'The virtuous prince does not neglect his relations. He does not cause the great ministers to repine at his not employing them. Without some great cause, he does not dismiss from their offices the members of old families. He does not seek in one man talents for every employment.' " [60]

In government, just as in society, the man who did not favor his relatives and friends when it came to jobs was considered to be completely lacking in human feelings. And if he refused to help his close relatives then he was said "to be unfilial or to demonstrate *pei-te*, that is not loving those to whom one is bound by natural ties, both of which are extremes of inhumanity." [61] A mother threatened to curse her son for not appointing a favorite nephew to a post for which he was totally unfit. [62] The question was not whether the relative or friend was qualified for the job, or whether the business or organization needed extra help, but whether the individual in question was a friend or relative and needed the job. Jobs provided livelihood, and livelihood was more important than efficiency. This attitude was reinforced by the fact that "all work depended on personal relationships and involved personal loyalties. Employees served their chief and not the institution or the business enterprise he conducted. The chief felt that he had to have underlings personally related to him, persons he could trust." [63]

Aside from the aesthetic, emotional, and economic aspects of friendships, there was one other which seems to have been overlooked in most discussions of this phenomenon, and that is "protection." Despite the existence of a detailed and extensive system of law, the Chinese people by and large had an aversion to using it. " 'Don't talk like that,' he said, 'we're a respectable family, who've never picked quarrels with people or gone to court!' " [64] Because of this lack of faith in the law, and a training which emphasized human relations, each family or individual consciously or unconsciously built up a network of alliances of families and friends as a form of insurance against the depredations of the officials, their enemies, the

[60] Legge, I, 338.                    [61] Levy, p. 355.
[62] Paul King, *In the Chinese Customs Service* (London: T. Fisher Unwin Ltd., 1924), p. 201.
[63] Lang, pp. 22–23.                    [64] Wu Ching-tzu, p. 248.

ravages of nature, and the government itself. In the West, men have usually turned to law for this type of protection. Of course Western law has not always had the stature and importance it does today. One need only to think of the periods of lawlessness in Western history when family and friends were the only recourse; but generally speaking the law has always been there. In China, however, the tradition has been to stay away from law and to look to the family and one's friends for protection. An old Chinese adage says, "At home rely on parents, going away rely on friends." [65]

The family was the basic unit of society and the basic unit of protection. Despite internal conflicts, to the world the family presented a unified front, and interfamily relations were the first link in the chain of defenses with which an individual was forced to surround himself. Interfamily links were formed by marriage, business connections, social or official status, or through any other medium of mutual interest.

The next link in the chain, or, in reality, the next group of links, was formed through friendships. A family was a comparatively small unit, but through the friendships of its various members it could expand its influence so that it penetrated upwards to the heart of government, downwards into the dregs of society, and outward to encompass large portions of the empire. A high official, through the extension of his influence, could protect literally hundreds of people, who in turn could be relied upon in times of need. Actually, many Chinese felt that friends were much more important than relatives in times of stress.[66] The following story illustrates how an official could make social investments as a form of insurance against a time of need.

In the first years of the ninth century, Ts'ui Ch'ün was prime minister and very famous for his incorruptibility. Once he served as commissioner of examinations. Sometime afterward, when his wife advised him to buy some real estate to be left to children and grandchildren, he replied smiling, "I have thirty excellent manor houses with rich fields spreading all over the empire. Why should you worry about real estate?" His wife was puzzled and said she had not heard anything like that. The minister said, "You remember the year before last I served as examiner and passed thirty candidates. Are they not excellent estates?" [67]

[65] Lang, p. 325.  [66] Fried, p. 91.
[67] Yang Lien-sheng, p. 304.

Although the story is of the ninth century and the comparison of candidates to estates may seem to be a joke, the story could have been set in the Ch'ing period, for the successful candidates were still a form of insurance for the examiner.

Human beings, whether in China or the West, appear to fit Sigmund Freud's assertion:

> Men are not gentle, friendly creatures wishing for love, who simply defend themselves if they are attacked, . . . a powerful measure of desire for aggression has to be reckoned as part of their instinctual endowment. The result is that their neighbour is to them not only a possible helper or sexual object, but also a temptation to them to gratify their aggressiveness on him, to exploit his capacity for work without recompense, to use him sexually without his consent, to seize his possessions, to humiliate him, to cause him pain, to torture and to kill him.[68]

In the West we have built a wall around man's aggressive nature with laws, customs, and social pressures so that within our society there are not a great many outward signs of social conflict. We have been taught that heated arguments in public and open displays of emotion are not proper, and that to slander, cheat, falsely accuse, and so on is not playing the game according to the rules. Yet, to anyone who has lived in a Chinese community, it is clear that there is constant social conflict. An eminent sociologist maintains that social conflict can be neither a disruptive force in a society or a means of maintaining stability, depending on the social structure and the issues involved. If the conflicts center around goals, values, and interests that do not contradict the basic assumptions upon which the society is founded, then such conflicts tend to make possible the readjustment of norms and power relations within groups in accordance with the desires of its individual members and subgroups. However, when the participants in internal conflicts no longer share the same basic assumptions, then the social structure is threatened.[69] On the basis of this hypothesis, it would appear that for Confucian China social conflict had a stabilizing effect. The internal social conflict that existed to a marked degree never focused on the basic assumption of the society that the Confucian way of

---

[68] Sigmund Frieud, *Civilization and Its Discontents*, transl. by Joan Riviere (Garden City, N.Y.: Doubleday and Co., Inc., 1958), pp. 60–61.

[69] Lewis A. Coser, *The Functions of Social Conflict* (Glencoe, Ill.: The Free Press, 1956), pp. 151–152.

life was the only way, but focused rather on the immediate goals, values, and interests of the people — power, wealth and prestige. The Ch'ing rulers did not need to fear the overthrow of the system because the "have nots" had the opportunity of becoming "haves," not only through the examination system but also through social conflict and custom. A chief minister could be laid low through the machinations of his enemies, a rich landlord could become a pauper through false accusation or dissolute sons, and a lowly official could become one of the chief ministers of state through the right connections.

In this atmosphere of social conflict, the greatest need for protection was against false accusation, the depredations of officials, and the demands of the government. H. B. Morse, a longtime member of the Imperial Chinese Customs Service, claimed that in China in the nineteenth century there were three kinds of people: the law abiding, the lawless, and the falsely accused.[70] Despite laws against slander and false accusation, this was a common means of getting back at one's enemies. Even if the accusation was eventually proven false, the defendant usually was economically and physically ruined, if not dead. In addition, there were individuals known as the *sung-tu* (lawsuit worms), the Chinese term for pettifoggers, who made it their business to stir up trouble and incite people to go to court over some imagined grievance.[71] The best protection against this sort of accusation was to have friends in high places or friends who had friends in high places. They could also help one fend off the depredations of corrupt officials or the honest accusations of upright officials. Of course the best means of protection in a case of this nature was to be an official or a member of the gentry yourself or, lacking that, to be the close friend of one. "Having official rank, fairly won by examination, and not obtained by purchase, your status will exempt you from persecution by the minor officials and their subordinates, and no magistrate will dare to threaten you with personal indignities or corporal punishment."[72] In the Chinese novel, *The Dream of the Red Chamber*, a young official is advised to keep a "Protection List":

---

[70] Hosea Ballou Morse, *The Trade and Administration of the Chinese Empire* (Shanghai: Kelly and Walsh, Ltd., 1908), p. 72.

[71] Chang Ch'un-ming, p. 244.

[72] Hosea Ballou Morse, *In the Days of the Taipings* (Salem, Mass.: The Essex Institute, 1927), p. 10.

It is customary nowadays for government officials in the provinces to keep a secret list of the names of all the specially prominent, well-off, and influential citizens domiciled in their district, above all the "Wearers of the Belt," or former high officials who have important connections with government circles at the Court. A prudent provincial magistrate will take great care not to come into conflict with these important people, otherwise he endangers his position or in certain circumstances even his life. That is why it is called the Protection List.[73]

One of the basic reasons for the formation of provincial clubs and guilds was protection. The members were strangers in a foreign area and felt that they needed the protection of a group to make sure that the natives of the area did not take advantage of them. Also, in both types of organizations, the secretary was always someone with official and literary standing so that he could represent them at the official level.[74] He could talk to the local officials as an equal, write official documents in the proper style, and use his influence to intercede for a member who might become entangled with the law. In the guilds, whether local or regional, there was always the question of whether or not its members were getting their fair share of the business. The Chinese attitude towards business was that the total volume was constant and any increase on the part of one businessman must be offset by a corresponding loss on the part of the others. By joining together in guilds they could rely on the weight of numbers in order to insure that they would not be discriminated against by local customs, if they were strangers to the area; and to insure that interlopers, unfair practices, and substandard products would not siphon off their profits, if they were native to the area.

There were certain human relationships in Chinese society, such as that of tenant and landlord, which were distinct from friendships and from family, provincial club, or guild relationships. In a relationship of this nature, the concept of *kan-ch'ing* was called into play as a means of protection.[75] *Kan-ch'ing* simply means "affection" and, as the term implies, was a reciprocal relationship.[76] The tenant farmer tried to develop *kan-ch'ing* with his landlord so that in times

[73] Tsao and Kao, p. 36.
[74] Morse, *Gilds of China*, pp. 37–38; van der Sprenkel, p. 95.
[75] van der Sprenkel, p. 100.
[76] Verbal discussion with Professor Ch'en Shih-hsiang, University of California, November 21, 1963.

of crop failure or other misfortunes the latter would be lenient in the matter of the repayment of a loan and the like. On the other hand, to have a tenant on his lands whom he could trust not to cheat him and who would take care of the property was of great benefit to the landlord. A merchant would try to develop *kan-ch'ing* with the local officials in order to insure against misfortunes, and the support of the merchants made the officials' jobs easier and afforded them the opportunity of investing in local enterprises. This concept could be applied to innumerable situations, and to have a "good *kan-ch'ing*" was the ideal, whereas to have no *kan-ch'ing* often led to disaster. In all cases it was an attempt to turn what would normally be an impersonal situation into a personal one, as a means of protection.[77]

"We must count half on friendship, half on money."[78] As this quotation suggests, money was a key link in the chain of defense, since friendship and human relationships alone were usually not enough to guarantee adequate protection. Wealth was a sign of success and was greatly sought after by the Chinese. To have wealth, however, laid one open to exploitation by the officials; on the other hand, it could open many doors and help to ward off disaster. Wealth was a means of "greasing the wheels of human intercourse." As long as the use of money was not overdone, it was considered a natural part of human relationships. It was only when it was used to excess that it was considered bribery. The dividing line between what was normal and what was excessive was intangible and was more or less "played by ear." To use one's money to purchase office, secure a small favor, smooth out a disagreement, or even thwart the government seems to have been considered normal, but to bribe a magistrate to decide a case in your favor, and thus injure someone else, was considered excessive. The Chinese had a very practical appreciation for money and what it could do, and, as a result, took a keen interest in it. Money was indispensable in the acquisition of power and prestige and was a necessary adjunct to their continued existence.

The Ch'ing rulers of China had inherited the problem of how to govern a society whose values opposed those of the ruling institutions — the Confucian world of human relationships versus the Legalistic world of law and authority. Although both the society and

[77] Fried, pp. 224, 103–104.          [78] Wu Ching-tzu, p. 658.

the government had made concessions to each other, a basic tension still existed. The crux of this tension was the question of supreme loyalty.

The state insisted that one's first loyalty should be to it and tried to redirect Confucian morality to this end. The Yung-cheng Emperor (1723–1736) in 1724 claimed that there was nothing wrong with friendship, but that it must cease to influence one's acts once one had assumed office; he also claimed that the relationship of son to parent must give way to a higher loyalty should the son assume office because, "he gives himself to his prince, and can no longer consider himself as belonging to his father and mother!"[79] On the other hand, society felt that the family was an end in itself and that one should be loyal to it above all else.

Confucius had made the first of the Five Confucian Relationships that of ruler to subject. He had never considered the question of divided loyalty because if everyone ordered his life in conformance with the proper moral principles, there would be no cause for conflict. In the ideal Confucian state the ruler would rule in a Confucian way and the state and the people would be in harmony. However, Chinese civilization did not develop as Confucius envisaged it. Legalism gained control first and set the patterns of imperial rule. The Confucianists could only attempt to modify and control them wherever possible. Thus in the course of the centuries of development of the imperial state, the tension between Legalist ruler and Confucian society resulted in the society making the family an end in itself. Although the first of the Five Confucian Relationships was still cited as "ruler to subject," in actual practice the society put the other four, which dealt with family and friends in the paramount position. As a result, loyalty to the state, in the Western sense, never developed in imperial China.

The history of Western civilization shows a tradition of loyalty to something higher than oneself or one's family. The Greeks and Romans put the state above the family. In the Christian world the church demanded loyalties that far exceeded those of the family, and in Europe during the Middle Ages loyalty to a territorial chieftain, the head of a *patria* or a local county, was the forerunner of

79 David S. Nivison, "Ho-shen and His Accusers: Ideology and Political Behavior in the Eighteenth Century," *in* David S. Nivison and Arthur F. Wright, eds., *Confucianism in Action* (Stanford: Stanford Univ. Press, 1959), p. 227.

modern patriotism.[80] In Tokugawa Japan, loyalty to the lord was put above that to the family in much the same way as it was in Medieval Europe, with the accompanying growth of patriotism. Yet in China such loyalties never developed on a national scale. A feeling for the "nation" had existed as far back as the end of the Sung, but it was not until the twentieth century that true nationalism began to develop. The Chinese did not adopt a national flag until 1862, and this was done merely for diplomatic purposes.[81] Sun Yat-sen referred to the Chinese as "a sheet of loose sand," when it came to national feelings, implying that there was no cohesion or unity. Actually there was a unity, but it was a unity of group affiliations.

The purpose of a state is to protect the people, but when the people turn to their own devices for protection and distrust the state, any possible chance of loyalty to the state is nullified. The Chinese state was so large geographically and so superior in culture to its neighbors that the threat of foreign invasion came only once in several hundred years. Hence, the state's role of protecting the people from invasion and conquest was only occasionally put to the test. What the people wanted was protection from the machinations of enemies within their own society (which the legal structure failed to provide because of the evils of the system and the moral values of the society), protection from the horrors of rebellion (which imperial armies usually intensified rather than alleviated), and protection from the demands of the state itself. The people received this protection not from the state, but from a broad network of human relations that they were forced to construct themselves.

One might well ask, since the state did not provide protection and was based on a set of principles which were contrary to those of the society, why the people did not change the system of government to one that would give the needed protection and be more in keeping with the Confucian ideals. The answer is that the members of the gentry-literati-official class — those who upheld and decided what Confucianism was, who set the social values, and who were the leaders of the society — depended upon this imperial, Legalist, authoritarian system of government as the source of all

[80] Henri Pirenne, A History of Europe, transl. by Bernard Miall (Garden City, N.Y.: Doubleday Anchor Books, 1956), I, 134.
[81] U.S. Dept of State, Despatches from United States Ministers to China, June 27, 1843–August 14, 1906 (Washington, D.C.: The National Archives, 1946–1947), Vol. 20, Prince Kung to Anson Burlingame, October 22, 1862.

their honors, their wealth, and their privileged position in society. Even when their personal depredations at the expense of the state resulted in its destruction, they were the first to work for its reestablishment, since they stood to lose the most if the system were changed. Despite their personal depredations and loyalties, which the state recognized and sought to control, the state needed this class in order to govern the country. It was the educated class, and its education was in how to rule and handle human beings. Both sides needed each other but were opposed to each other. As a result, a balance of tension existed which oscillated in favor of one or the other depending on their relative strengths. There was never any question, however, on the part of either side of lack of loyalty to the system. This loyalty was most evident when the system itself was threatened in the nineteenth century by the Taiping rebels from within and the Westerners from without. In order to meet this dual threat, Chinese such as Tseng Kuo-fan, Li Hung-chang, and Tso Tsung-t'ang, who had a vested interest in the society, and the Manchus, who had a vested interest in the state, joined forces to oppose the common enemy. Because of the weakened condition of the state, the initiative lay with the Chinese. Unable to rely on the ossified government and flexible institutions, they turned to the *mu-fu* system in order to preserve the world in which they believed.

# II. The Traditional Mu-Fu

The term *mu-fu* is used to designate the system of privately hired provincial advisers which flourished at various periods in Chinese history, but which was most extensively used during the Ch'ing period (1644–1912). The first of these two characters, *"mu,"* is defined by the *Shuo-wen*, the earliest Chinese etymological dictionary, compiled about 100 A.D. as "a curtain above, or, a tent." The second character, *"fu,"* is defined as "a public documents storehouse."[1] The earlier and basic meaning of this character is simply "a storehouse," but in time it took on connotations of government and came to be used in reference to government buildings or provincial government. The term was never used in connection with imperial government.[2] The combination of the two characters thus meant "tent government." A further connotation was "military government," in that the "tent" was conceived of as a military one, and the term was originally used to designate a specific military situation.

One of the earliest extant passages in which the term *mu-fu* was used can be found in the *Shih-chi*. In speaking of Li Mu, a famous general of the State of Chao who died in 229 B.C., the *Shih-chi* says: "He regularly dwelt at Tai-yen-men and prepared for the Hsiung-nu. In order to establish the proper officials, the market rents were all

[1] *Tz'u-hai* (Taipei, Taiwan: Chung-hua shu-chü, 1959), *shang,* pp. 183, 202; Ch'üan Tseng-yu, "Ch'ing-tai mu-liao chih-tu lun" (On the *Mu-liao* System of the Ch'ing Period), *Ssu-hsiang yü shih-tai yüeh-k'an,* No. 31 (Feb., 1944), p. 29. The same two characters are used by the Japanese for the term "Bakufu" to designate the military government of the Shogun. The principal difference between the Japanese and the Chinese systems was that the former remained basically military and was the instrument of centralized military authority, while the latter was civil, as well as military, and remained provincial. See Conrad D. Totman, "The Struggle for Control of the Shogunate (1853–1858)," Harvard University, Center for East Asian Studies, *Papers on Japan,* Vol. I, pp. 42–88.
[2] Verbal discussion with Professor Ch'en Shih-hsiang, University of California, November 21, 1963.

paid to the tent government [*mu-fu*]."[3] This quotation indicates that the generals were responsible not only for military government, but often for civil administration as well, particularly if they were campaigning in the border regions. The *Shih-chi*, in its explanation of this passage, states: "The ancients when going out on an expedition served as generals and commanders, and when the army returned, then they relinquished their posts. Because there were no permanently established offices, they used the tent [*mu*] as the government [*fu*] office." And, "the general, when he went out on a campaign, did not have a regular location. The place from which he governed was therefore called '*mu-fu.*'"[4]

In order to meet the demands of civil government, as well as those of military strategy and logistics, the generals of the Warring States and Han practiced the custom of nourishing scholars (*yang-shih chih feng*). Pan Ku, the Later Han historian (d. 92 A.D.), says, "I have seen *mu-fu* established recently, and they widely invited a multitude of excellent men."[5] The custom of nourishing scholars had flourished during the late Chou and Warring States Period, when a prince or wealthy lord would support scholars in much the same fashion as the nobles of Renaissance Europe. Confucius had received the support of princes when as a wandering scholar (*yu-shih*) he had sought a patron to implement his ideas on government. In the *Book of Mencius* it says, "If a prince hates disgrace, the best course for him to pursue is to esteem virtue and honor virtuous scholars, giving the worthiest among them places of dignity, and the able offices of trust."[6] This custom continued to flourish under the Ch'in and Han and spread among the high officials as well as the generals. Lü Pu-wei, the possible father of Ch'in Shih Huang-ti, had 3,000 eating guests, and, in the time of the Han Emperor Wu-ti (140–87 B.C.), the General-in-Chief, Wei Ch'ing, had many scholars under him. It was because of this custom of nourishing scholars that

[3] Ssu-ma Ch'ien, *Shih-chi* (Peking: Chung-hua shu-chü, 1959), Vol. 5, *chüan* 81, p. 2449; Ch'üan Tseng-yu, No. 31 (Feb., 1944), p. 29. Tai-yen-men is the present Yen-men *hsien* in northern Shansi.

[4] Ssu-ma, Vol. 5, *chüan* 81, p. 2449; Ch'üan Tseng-yu, No. 31 (Feb., 1944), p. 29.

[5] *Hou-Han shu*, Pan Ku chuan, *chüan* 70, *shang*, p. 7a, *in Erh-shih-ssu shih* (Twenty-Four Histories) (Shanghai: T'ung-wen shu-chü, 1884); *Tz'u-hai, shang*, p. 1032.

[6] James Legge, *The Chinese Classics* (Taiwan reprint, 1962), II, 197.

the country "constantly look to the *fu* as a source of supply for talented people."[7]

The system of military government, combined with the custom of nourishing scholars, thus produced the *mu-fu* system of the Han period. What had started out as basically a military device was extended to the realm of civil administration, primarily because it enabled provincial officials to meet their governing needs. During the Han, all of the subordinate officials in the *chün* (prefecture) and *chou* (department), such as the *pieh-chia* (a subprefect), the *chih-chung* (a subordinate administrative official), the *chu-pu* (a registrar), and the *kung-ts'ao* (a public documents assistant), were personally appointed to office by the senior provincial official. Wang T'ang, who served as the prefect of a *chün* (*t'ai-shou*) in the reigns of the Han emperors An-ti (107–126) and Shun-ti (126–145),

> searched for the talented, respected scholars, and would not be self-indulgent. He instructed his subordinate officials, saying: "The ancients labored in seeking the worthy and excelled in performing the duties of their posts. Therefore they could purify matters above and serve below. They enacted the laws in the proper manner and sought out talented officials"; he assigned the *kung-ts'ao*, Ch'en Fan, to assist in governing and managing affairs, to repair omissions, and to mend deficiencies; he employed the *chu-pu*, Ying Ssu, in order that he might follow the proper path, be responsible for actually carrying out matters, and examine the words and see the results.[8]

Prior to the Ming, the existence of the *mu-fu* system seemed to depend on whether or not the provincial officials, or military commanders, were permitted by the central authority to hire privately their own advisers and/or subordinate officials.[9] In a centralized gov-

[7] Ssu-ma, Lü Pu-wei lieh-chuan, Vol. 5, *chüan* 85, p. 2510; T'ien Shu lieh-chuan, Vol. 6, *chüan* 104, p. 2780; Ch'üan Tseng-yu, No. 31 (Feb., 1944), p. 29.

[8] *Hou-Han shu*, Wang T'ang chuan, *chüan* 61, pp. 12a–b; Chang Ch'un-ming, "Ch'ing-tai te mu-chih" (The *Mu* System of the Ch'ing Dynasty), *Ling-nan hsüeh-pao*, IX, No. 2 (June, 1949), 30.

[9] The provincial officials referred to here included, at one time or another, all levels of the provincial bureaucracy, from the governor of a province down to a district magistrate. In Han there is specific reference to *mu-fu* at the *chün* (prefecture) and *chou* (department) levels. By Sung the *mu-fu* system included the *hsien* (district) or lowest level. The same was true of the military, in that in Sung some of the lower ranks (*fang-yü-shih*) had their *mu-fu*. Ch'üan Tseng-yu, No. 31 (Feb., 1944), pp. 29–30; Chang Ch'un-ming, pp. 30, 31–32; Hsüeh Fu-ch'eng, "Hsü Tseng Wen-cheng-kung mu-fu" (A Discussion of the

ernment, the central administrative bodies normally hire all the government officials and are responsible for their salaries, promotions, and demotions. However, under the *mu-fu* system, prior to the Ming, the central authority recognized as valid the private appointments of the provincial officials. By permitting such a phenomenon to exist, however, the center was relinquishing some of its authority to the provincial and private sectors of the country and hastening its own destruction. The *mu-fu* system arose because the central government was unable or unwilling to provide provincial officials with the necessary personnel, and, up to the Ch'ing period, the system flourished more under a weak government than it did under a strong one.

During much of the Han, and especially in the Later Han, it was possible to achieve office through either public or private selection. The method of public selection (the examination system had not yet been firmly established) was for the local areas to nominate qualified persons, and the center would then appoint officials from those who were recommended. Under this process, however, promotion was slow, and the official derived little prestige from his appointment. The road to quick promotion, fame, and fortune lay in private selection. If a worthy and talented scholar was brought to the attention of a provincial governor by his friends or through his reputation, it was possible for him to receive a high official post almost immediately. As a result, to be selected privately was considered a high honor.[10]

The division and turmoil that followed the downfall of the Han were conductive to the amplification of the custom of nourishing scholars and the accompanying *mu-fu* system. The power and wealth of the military leaders and provincial authorities, as well as the growth of vast private estates that could afford to support large groups of followers, made the provincial areas attractive to the scholars. Consequently, there was an exodus of talented scholars from the capitals to the provinces, and provincial governors had large followings of guests and scholars whom they assigned to posts as prefects and magistrates.[11]

Members of Tseng Kuo-fan's *mu-fu*), reprinted in Tso Shun-sheng, comp., *Chung-kuo chin-pai-nien shih tzu-liao ch'u-pien* (Taipei, Taiwan: Chung-hua shu-chü, 1958), p. 134.

[10] Chang Ch'un-ming, p. 32.

[11] Ch'üan Tseng-yu, No. 31 (Feb. 1944), p. 29.

With the reunification of the empire under the Sui Dynasty and the strengthening of central power, the *mu-fu* system disappeared from the scene; all officials, from top to bottom, big and small, were hired by the imperial government.[12] The establishing of the examination system as the orthodox means of selecting officials in the T'ang further strengthened the imperial control over personnel, but the institution of military governors in the border regions (*chieh-tu-shih*) permitted the *mu-fu* system to raise its head again. By the time of Han Yü (768–824), private selection was again current. Ts'ao Yen-yüeh, a *chin-shih* of the Sung Emperor Ch'un-hsi's reign (1174–1190) and later President of the Board of War,[13] said, in regard to the selection of officials in the T'ang:

As to selection, it was according to the examinations, but in reality it depended on a good reputation. A person could be an official either from the examinations or from the private selection of the border commanders [*fan-chen*]. The border commanders could either choose an officer from among the common people or promote one of their own subordinates of lower rank on the basis of his behavior and achievements. Therefore those who were scholars knew how to behave themselves. At first they had to learn to be useful men. Once they had been selected, then they certainly worked with a good sense of responsibility; and after a long time in the *mu-fu* they were familiar with all the affairs. When they were appointed to an important position in the office, then within they knew how to get everything well organized, and without they knew how to defend the territory from the barbarian invasions. There was nothing they could not do.[14]

During the Five Dynasties Period (907–960), as might be expected, the *mu-fu* system flourished, and the various military leaders vied with each other to secure the services of scholars.[15] However, although the *mu-fu* continued to exist under the Sung, it was curtailed and lost a great deal of its strength; as a result, it was no longer the most important avenue of advancement.[16] The reasons behind this decline were the upsurge of bureaucratic power and the strengthening of Confucianism and the examination system that took place

[12] Chang Ch'un-ming, p. 30.
[13] *Chung-Kuo jen-ming ta-tz'u-tien* (Taipei, Taiwan: Shang-wu yin-shu-kuan 1960), p. 988.
[14] Chang Ch'un-ming, p. 31. Quoted from Ts'ao Yen-yüeh, *Ch'ang-ku chi.*
[15] Chang Ch'un-ming, p. 31.
[16] *Ibid.*, p. 32.

in the Sung. A further factor in the decline of the *mu-fu* system was the absence of nobility and the large estates of the earlier dynasties which had kept alive the custom of nourishing scholars. The Mongol conquest of China ended the *mu-fu* system as it had existed for well over a thousand years. What was reborn in the late Ming and early Ch'ing was something new.

The *mu-fu* system of the Ming–Ch'ing period differed from its earlier counterparts in that it was purely private and had no legal connection with the government. The principle of private hiring still existed, but the members of the *mu-fu* were only hired as personal advisers by the provincial officials and could not be appointed by them to any government office. Throughout the Ming and Ch'ing the power of appointment remained in the hands of the central authority. In addition, the resurrected *mu-fu* system was a civil device and had little or no connection with the military during the Ch'ing until the Taiping Rebellion. The most provocative feature of this new system was that, unlike the earlier system, it became firmly established and was extensively used at a time when the central authority had firm control — that is, during the early periods of the Ch'ing Dynasty. Strangely enough, the strengthening of the *mu-fu* can be attributed in part to the increase in central authority that took place during the Ming and Ch'ing, as well as to the position of the Manchus vis-à-vis the Chinese, and to the conflict between "expertise" and "amateurism."

Throughout much of Chinese imperial history there was a conflict between the clerks (*li*) and the scholars (*shih*) over the proper training for government service. The clerks were the experts in government who had learned their trade through practical experience. They served the same function in government as the members of a *mu-fu*, and occasionally both groups existed at the same time. Yet the conditions of service of the two groups differed: the clerks served in the capital, and, during periods when the *mu-fu* system did not exist, they served in the provinces as well, although they were not hired personally by the provincial officials. The clerks were degraded in official and social status in the Ming, and as a result a vacuum was created between clerk and official, which was filled by the *mu-fu* system. During their earlier periods of ascendancy, some clerks had been able to graduate from clerkships and become officials, and a few even rose to ministerial rank. Those that did achieve fame and position also became scholars in the process, although some may have been scholars all along. For the clerks as a group, practical experience served as the means of access to official position, just as it did for members of the *mu-fu*.

The scholars, on the other hand, chose the path of Confucian learning as their way of achieving office and the resulting fame and fortune. The *Classics* embodied certain truths, they felt, which encompassed the whole of life and which, when applied to any contemporary problem, offered a means of solution. Any solution which did not evolve from these truths was doomed to failure. Literature and writing were pursued as a means of communicating and preserving these truths.[17] The approach of the Confucianist scholars to government was at a higher and more moralistic level than that of the clerks; the scholars were not concerned with bureaucratic detail, but with the larger picture in relation to life itself.

Confucius had said, "The accomplished scholar is not a utensil."[18] However, the exponents of practicality and expertise were trying to do just that, make the scholar a utensil of government. The Ch'in ruler had tried this and has been vilified by Confucianists ever since. Wang Mang (33 B.C.–A.D. 23) and Wang An-shih (1021–1086) had both failed in their attempts to change Confucian standards and to make the scholar an expert in government. They failed because the scholars whom they sought to change were the real arbiters of Confucianism, and the policies that Wang Mang and Wang An-shih espoused were in opposition to the scholar's belief that Confucianism was an end in itself. Confucian truths were applicable to all of life and were not just a guide to government policy, and, in applying these to government, the scholar performed as an amateur, assuming a role that was similar to that of the English amateur of the nineteenth century. The scholars governed, and many of them governed well, but governing for them did not become an end in itself.

The scholars, then, were amateurs in government, as opposed to the clerks and the members of a *mu-fu*, who were the experts or professionals. Yet when a member of one of the latter two groups became an official, despite his qualifications as an expert, he assumed the mantle of amateurism. The ideals of Confucianism still outweighed those of Legalism.

In the conflict between the clerks and the scholars, society gen-

---

[17] W. T. DeBary, "A Reappraisal of Neo-Confucianism," *in* Arthur F. Wright, ed., *Studies in Chinese Thought* (Chicago: Univ. of Chicago Press, 1953), p. 90.
[18] Legge, I, 150.

erally held the claim of the scholars to be basic and regarded it
with the most favor. However, up to the later years of the Ming,
it was still possible for a clerk to achieve high government office. The
two periods of imperial Chinese history in which the clerks had
the greatest opportunities for advancement were the Han and Yüan.
During the Han period the Confucian system was not yet fully entrenched as the orthodox road to office. Hsiao Ho (d. 193 B.C.), and intimate of Liu Pang, [19] Ts'ao Ts'an (d. 190 B.C.), a supporter of Liu
Pang,[20] Kung Sun-hung (d. 121 B.C.), a Privy Counselor under the
Emperor Wu-ti,[21] Chang Ch'ang (d. 48 B.C.), Governor of the Metropolitan District,[22] and Wang Tsun, a high official during the reign
of the Han Emperor Ch'eng-ti (32–6 B.C.)[23] all started out as clerks.[24]
With the institutionalizing of the examination system as the approved means of selecting official personnel during the T'ang, the
opportunities for clerks to rise became more circumscribed, and
it was not until the Yüan Dynasty that they again achieved a position of importance. The Yüan shih records that, at the time of the
T'ai-ting Emperor (1324–1329), "Those who entered officialdom
from the ranks of the chin-shih were scarcely one in a hundred, but
for those who rose up from the ranks of the clerks and became
eminent, it was constantly ninety percent."[25] This ratio reflected the
Mongols' policy of not using scholars in top administrative positions,
as well as the scholars' reluctance to join the Mongol government in
which they were treated as merely utensils and not as ends in
themselves.

Under the early Ming, the clerks and scholars were almost on an
equal footing in regard to their social and political status upon
graduating into the ranks of officialdom. According to the Ta-Ming
hui-tien (Statutes of the Ming), in the 26th year of Hung-wu (1393)
it was stated that a chü-jen who passed the metropolitan examination in 1st position would enter office with the 6th official rank, and
those who achieved the 2nd and 3rd positions would receive the 7th

---

[19] Herbert A. Giles, A Chinese Biographical Dictionary (Taiwan reprint,
1962), I, 279.

[20] Ibid., II, 761.                      [21] Ibid., I, 394.

[22] Ibid., I, 9.

[23] Chung-Kuo jen-ming ta-tz'u-tien, p. 125.4.

[24] Ch'üan Tseng-yu, No. 31 (Feb., 1944), p. 30.

[25] Yüan shih, Han Yung chuan, chüan 185, p. 10a, in Erh-shih-ssu shih
(Shanghai: T'ung-wen shu-chü, 1884); Ch'üan Tseng-yu, No. 31 (Feb., 1944),
p. 30.

rank. On the other hand, a 1st rank *ya-men t'i-k'ung* (an expert in the records of cases in a government bureau) was authorized to receive the 7th rank when being promoted into the ranks of the officials.[26] However, in the 7th year of Yung-lo (1409), the Emperor decided that all the censors (*yü-shih*) should come exclusively from the ranks of the scholars. His reasons were as follows: "Although there is more than one basis on which to employ people, still the censors uphold the proper conduct for the country; and, since knowledge must be based on studies in order to insure proper governing and to maintain complete impartiality, therefore, let the scholars assume this position. If the scribes seek profit and are not concerned with righteousness, are stingy and do not bother with morality, and still we permit them to be responsible for discipline, then the people will think lightly of the court."[27] This decision was the start of a gradual trend toward degrading the position of the clerks in relation to the scholars. It was still possible for clerks to rise to high official position — Hsü Hsi and Yü Heng became President of the Board of War and President of the Board of Revenue, respectively, during the reign of the Hsüan-te Emperor (1426–1436) — but it became increasingly difficult as the dynasty progressed.[28]

As long as the clerks could take pride in their position and hope to achieve fame and fortune by becoming more adept in their work, they would play the game according to the scholars' rules and even try to emulate them. But once they found the way restricted and their prestige waning, they lost pride in themselves and sought wealth through the various forms of corruption open to those who had a detailed knowledge of the files and the machinery of government. This in turn resulted in a greater loss of prestige and social, as well as political, position.

By the time of the late Ming, then, government officials and military leaders no longer respected the clerks as social equals or near-equals and ceased to use them as advisers. This, however, created a shortage of qualified personnel, and, because professional advisers had become almost indispensable for officials, the *mu-fu* system was

---

[26] Ku Yen-wu, *Jih-chih lu* (Shanghai: Shang-wu yin-shu-kuan, 1935), *chüan* 17, T'ung-ching wei li, p. 93; Ch'üan Tseng-yu, No. 31 (Feb., 1944), p. 30.

[27] Ku Yen-wu, *chüan* 17, p. 93; Ch'üan Tseng-yu, No. 31 (Feb., 1944), p. 30.

[28] *Ming shih*, Hsüan-chü chih erh, *chüan* 70, pp. 14a–b, *in Erh-shih-ssu shih* (Shanghai: T'ung-wen shu-chü, 1884); Ch'üan Tseng-yu, No. 32 (March, 1944), p. 35.

gradually reestablished. Prior to the late Ming, in the Hung-hsi period (1425–1426), clerks and high-ranking officials were sent from the central government to the military headquarters of the various generals. The job of these clerks was to supervise and put in order official documents and to discuss military problems, but they were not to take part in the actual military affairs.[29] However, approximately one hundred years later, during the reign of the Chia-ching Emperor (1522–1567), the Governor-General of Chekiang, Hu Tsung-hsien, was inviting famous scholars to enter his *mu-fu* to manage official documents and help in military strategy.[30]

The introduction of the "Eight-Legged Essay" as the focal point of the examinations during the Ming was another factor which contributed to the rise of the *mu-fu* system. This essay placed a new emphasis on literary style, and thus tended to make the scholars even more bookish and less practical. At the beginning of the Ming, a scholar who had ambition was not afraid to humble himself by being a clerk, as it was felt that this was a necessary step in one's training as an official.[31] But the requirements of the "Eight-Legged Essay" forced the scholar to forgo any considerations of the practical problems of government and, when combined with the degradation of the clerk's position, created a wide gap between the experts and the amateurs. The government could not, or would not, provide the personnel to fill this gap, and hence the resurgence of the *mu-fu* system.

Other policies of the Ming rulers contributed still further to the reappearance of the *mu-fu* system. In order to strengthen their hold on the empire, the Ming rulers had increased the importance of law. Extensive and detailed laws were promulgated, which not only restricted the officials' flexibility in handling cases but also increased the amount of paper work involved. In order to make sure that the officials personally handled all the cases and did not leave them to their clerks, in the 4th year of Hung-wu (1371) the number of clerks was restricted by law, and any official who exceeded the prescribed number was to be punished.[32] However, as the cases accumulated,

---

[29] *Ming shih*, Chih-kuan chih ssu, *chüan* 75, pp. 15a–b; Ch'üan Tseng-yu, No. 31 (Feb., 1944), p. 31.

[30] *Ming shih*, Hsü Wei chuan, *chüan* 288, p. 3a; Ch'üan Tseng-yu, No. 31 (Feb., 1944), p. 31.

[31] Ch'üan Tseng-yu, No. 32 (March, 1944), p. 36.

[32] *Ibid.*, No. 31 (Feb., 1944), pp. 31–32. Cited from Ku Yen-wu, *Jih-chih lu*.

"layer upon layer," it became physically impossible for the officials to read them all. To complicate matters even further, towards the end of the dynasty there was a growing movement to commute the land taxes, which had been paid in kind, and the labor services into cash payments. This naturally resulted in an increase in accounting, but the number of clerks and officials was not increased accordingly.[33]

The Ch'ing inherited the government and society of the Ming, and with them the faults which had contributed to the widespread adoption of the *mu-fu* system. Instead of restricting the growth of this system, the early Ch'ing rulers intensified the policies of their Ming predecessors and hastened the day when every provincial official, from the governor-general of a province down to the lowest *hsien* magistrate, would have his own *mu-fu*.

The laws of the Ming were not only taken over by the Ch'ing but were further amplified by the dynasty in order to insure the complete control of the society. In the handling of legal cases, the magistrates were forced to base their decisions on the precedents (*Li*), instead of on the Fundamental Laws (*Lü*), which were of a more general nature. The precedents became so voluminous that it took a legal expert to keep them straight.[34] The officials, however, being the products of an examination system which stressed literature and the *Classics*, were not legal experts. Even if they had wanted to study law as a means of preparing themselves for official life, it would have been almost impossible because of social and family pressures against legal studies which did not prepare one for the examinations and because of government policies restricting the sale and distribution of books on law. In the 30th year of Ch'ien-lung (1765) it was memorialized and granted that books pertaining to law were not to be printed for or sold to the common people, and all such previously printed books were to be destroyed.[35] Thus, no family that did not have official rank was allowed to have a copy of the *Ta-Ch'ing lü-li* (Statutes of the Ch'ing). This meant that the

[33] C. John Stanley, *Late Ch'ing Finance: Hu Kuang-yung as an Innovator* (Cambridge: Harvard Univ. Press, 1961), p. 3; see Liang Fang-chung, *The Single-Whip Method of Taxation in China* (Cambridge: Harvard Univ. Press, 1956.)

[34] C. John Stanley, "The *Mu-yu* in the Ch'ing Dynasty" (MS, Harvard University, May 25, 1949), p. 11; Ch'üan Tseng-yu, No. 31 (Feb., 1944), p. 32.

[35] *Ta-Ch'ing hui-tien shih-li* (Shanghai: Shang-wu yin-shu-kuan, 1908), *chüan* 112, p. 2a; Ch'üan Tseng-yu, No. 31 (Feb., 1944), p. 32.

official was responsible for carrying out the law but was hindered
from acquiring any prior knowledge of it.

The officials were subjected to detailed regulations concerning
their conduct in office. There were two general categories of crimes:
malfeasance in office (*kung-tsui*) and personal crimes (*ssu-tsui*).
The personal crimes were those involving corruption and private
gain, such as bribery and embezzlement, and carried a harsher punishment; however, if a personal crime was unintentional, then it was
judged on the basis of malfeasance. When malfeasance was intentional and committed in the line of duty, then the more serious
penalties for personal crimes applied. Punishment could be the loss
of nominal salary, demotion, or dismissal, and, in the case of more
serious violations, it could be banishment or death. Because of the
complexity of the administrative regulations, it was almost impossible to avoid malfeasance in office, even though the official led an
exemplary life.[36]

The autocratic and, at times, tyrannical policies of the Shun-chih
(1644–1662) and K'ang-hsi (1662–1723) emperors provided yet another reason for the extensive establishment of the *mu-fu* system
by the middle of the eighteenth century. They frequently instigated
great trials and were abnormally petty. As a result, the officials trod
very cautiously and were very circumspect in their memorials. A
great deal of attention was paid to the correct phraseology, and the
memorials became highly stylized with very little content.[37] An
official was once again forced to hire the services of an expert, only
this time his job was to write documents and memorials.

In order for the *hsien* magistrate to carry out the multifarious
duties imposed on him, the central government was supposed to provide him with a few subordinate officials, such as an assistant magistrate (*hsien-ch'eng*), a registrar (*chu-pu*), a jail warden (*tien-shih*),
and the like.[38] In actuality, though, there were relatively very few
of them, and what few there were were usually insignificant. Their
duties were ill-defined, and they had less authority than the clerks.[39]
The only other official members of the magistrate's *yamen* were the
clerks, and through necessity he was forced to rely on them.

The role of the clerks in the Ch'ing provincial bureaucratic struc-

[36] Ch'ü T'ung-tsu, *Local Government in China Under the Ch'ing* (Cambridge: Harvard Univ. Press, 1962), pp. 32–33.
[37] Chang Ch'un-ming, p. 29.
[38] Ch'ü, *Local Government in China*, p. 8.        [39] *Ibid.*, pp. 9–13.

ture was a unique one. Their ratio in relation to the officials, on an empire–wide basis, was about thirty to one.[40] They were recruited locally and thus spoke the local dialect. Their families, relatives, and friends had lived in the area for generations and had built up a network of connections and vested interests which were the spawning grounds for corruption in matters related to taxation, labor services, and lawsuits. Because the clerks were not paid any salary, they made their money from the special fees which they extorted from the local populace and any special "deals" they could manipulate. The officials were often the victims of the clerks' evil machinations because they were not familiar with the files and the local situation, and usually did not speak the local dialect. In addition they often had little or no connection with the local people except perhaps with some of the members of the gentry.[41] Under the "Laws of Avoidance," the officials were normally shifted every three years, but the clerks stayed on in the local *yamen*. The clerks' term of office was set at five years, but they were usually able to find ways of getting around this, either by changing their names or by having their vacated post taken over by a relative or friend.[42] As a result the officials were caught in the middle. They had to rely on the clerks for the operation of the government, but they were also held accountable for the clerks' corrupt practices, and it was impossible for one man to root out such deeply entrenched habits.

The Ch'ing rulers had inherited the institutions and policies of a Chinese dynasty, and, because they were Manchus and not Chinese, they tried to be more Chinese than the Chinese in carrying on the forms of government in order to insure their rule. As a result, they were unwilling or unable to change the system they had inherited. Instead of modifying the institutions to provide a socially acceptable official class of experts in government, a modification which would probably have been strongly opposed by the bureaucracy and the gentry and might have resulted in their early downfall, they swam with the current and attempted to gain the support and control of the Chinese by intensifying the use of law and by giving imperial support to the Confucian ideals. In the process, learning and respectability were further divorced from practicality, and the officials were unable to cope with the problems of governing. Be-

[40] Karl Wittfogel, *Oriental Despotism: A Comparative Study of Total Power* (New Haven: Yale Univ. Press, 1957), p. 307.
[41] Ch'ü, *Local Governmnt in China*, p. 36.    [42] *Ibid.*

cause the imperial government did not provide technical advisers, the provincial officials, from governor-general down to *hsien* magistrate, in order to protect themselves, were forced to seek help on a private basis,[43] and the *mu-fu* system became firmly entrenched in a period of strong central government.

The personnel for the *mu-fu* system were recruited primarily from that group of scholars who, for one reason or another were in limbo: those who had not yet achieved office, those who were out of office, or those whose frame of mind was of a more practical bent and who, because of this, were unable to conform to the examination standards.[44] Of these, the largest number came from the unsuccessful candidates for the examinations. As members of a *mu-fu*, they could still engage in scholarly pursuits, take time out for the examinations, and not have to degrade themselves by becoming clerks in order to earn a living. They could still be a part of the world of the scholars, even though they were on the fringes of the world of the officials and the rich. Another group came from the "expectants."[45] These were scholars who had passed the examinations but had not been given a substantive office. Instead they were sent to a particular province where they waited for the first vacancy. Because the supply of officials always exceeded the demand, an "expectant" official could wait for years before a vacancy occurred. In the meantime they had to earn a living in a world which provided few opportunities for the official who was out of office or for the unsuccessful scholar. The *mu-fu* system by employing the unsuccessful or the unemployed was filling an economic need, and, in turn, it found a ready supply of candidates.

A special class of *mu-fu* personnel, and one which tended to monopolize the positions at the lower levels of the provincial bureaucracy, were the people from Shao-hsing Prefecture in Chekiang. For them being in a *mu-fu* was an hereditary occupation, and it was as natural for a Shao-hsing man to be in a *mu-fu* as it was for a Shansi man to be a banker.[46] For this group, their technical knowledge

[43] Hsieh Pao-chao, *The Government of China (1644–1911)* (Baltimore: The Johns Hopkins Press, 1925), pp. 297–298.

[44] Stanley, "The *Mu-yu* in the Ch'ing Dynasty," p. 17.

[45] Hosea Ballou Morse, *The International Relations of the Chinese Empire* (Taiwan Reprint), I, 16.

[46] Byron Brenan, "The Office of District Magistrate in China," *The Journal of the North China Branch of the Royal Asiatic Society*, New Series, XXXII (1897–1898), 45.

was their only means of livelihood, and they tried to keep "as secret as possible the forms of correspondence, the inner wheel of the accounts, and the bribery ledgers, and formed such a powerful combination that it was almost hopeless for a mandarin of merely average ability to work except under their guidance."[47]

A scholar seeking to enter a *mu-fu* would usually be recommended to an official by a friend or relative; sometimes he himself would be a friend of the official, or he would be invited to join on the strength of his reputation. If he had had no previous technical training, a scholar would enter the *mu-fu* as a trainee and gradually acquire technical competence. Once he had acquired experience, it was a fairly simple matter to find other jobs through recommendations. Most veteran members of a *mu-fu* had one or two protégés whom they were training, and who, in the course of time, would be recommended for employment to officials who were in need of personnel.[48]

Wang Hui-tsu is an excellent example of the type of person who enters a *mu-fu*. He was born in Hsiao-shan, Chekiang, on January 21, 1731. His father, who was a prison warder, died in 1741, forcing Wang to support the family. At the age of seventeen (*sui*) he became a *hsiu-ts'ai* and two years later, in 1749, was married. In 1752 he began his career in the *mu-fu* by becoming a secretary to his father-in-law, who was a magistrate in Kiangsu. The legal secretary of a *mu-fu* was the most highly paid, and it was purely for economic reasons that Wang began training himself in this field. For the next thirty-four years he worked at this profession, serving under sixteen different officials. During this period he took time out to compete in the examinations for the higher degrees. In 1768 he became a *chü-jen*, after having failed eight times, and in 1775, at the age of forty-six (*sui*), became a *chin-shih*, after having failed three times. Even though he had achieved the *chin-shih* degree, he continued working as a legal adviser for the next eleven years while awaiting an official appointment. Between 1786, when he was appointed as a magistrate in Hunan, and 1793, when he retired, he served in various official posts in that province. After his retirement, he devoted himself to scholarly pursuits until his death in 1807.[49]

[47] Edward Harper Parker, *China, Past and Present* (London: Chapman and Hall, Ltd., 1903), p. 246.

[48] Brenan, p. 45.

[49] U. S. Library of Congress, Asiatic Division, *Eminent Chinese of the Ch'ing Period (1644–1912)*, ed. by Arthur W. Hummel (Washington, D.C.: U.S. Gov't. Printing Office, 1943), II, 824.

Wang was also an accomplished scholar and historian. Two of his works, the *Tso-chih yao-yen* and the *Hsüeh-chih i-shuo*, were regarded as indispensable guides to local administrative officials up to the end of the imperial period (1912). The former work, with its supplement, the *Hsü tso-chih yao-yen*, consists of sixty-six articles which, in the words of the author, "record what I have done and said when I was a *mu-yu*."[50] Written as advice and encouragement, they provided an ideal of morality and proficiency for *mu-yu* at all levels to emulate.

The members of a *mu-fu* were referred to as *mu-yu* (tent friends), *mu-pin* or *mu-k'e* (tent guests), or *mu-liao* (tent colleagues). As these terms imply, the relationship between the official and his advisers was one of equality. The official was considered the host (*chu*) and was addressed as "*tung-weng*" (Mr. Host) or "*lao-tung*" (old host).[51] In accordance with Chinese etiquette, the guest is given the position of honor and the host assumes a lower position. To be a *mu-yu* was, therefore, not to be an underling but to hold a position of honor and respect.

The *mu-yu* were invited to enter a *mu-fu*, and the invitation, according to custom, had to exhibit the proper amount of solemnity and impressiveness as a sign of honor and respect.[52] Etiquette was an important part of the life within the *mu-fu*, and Wang Hui-tsu advised *mu-yu* to pay attention to the small ceremonies as a sign of the host official's sincerity. If the host ate good food and served his *mu-yu* poor food, then he was not being sincere.[53] Chang Chih-tung was criticized by his *mu-yu*, Ku Hung-ming, because he tried to be economical and asked all the *mu-liao* to prepare their own food.[54] However, once the sincerity of the host official had been established, the ceremonies could be dispensed with.

In addition to the host-guest relationship, there was also that of student-teacher. When the *mu-yu* was hired, his letter of appointment was written on a full-sized red card, and he was referred to as "*lao-fu-tzu*" (old master), a term of respect conventionally used for

---

[50] Wang Hui-tsu, *Hsü tso-chih yao-yen* (Additional Admonitions on Government) (Shanghai: Shang-wu yin-shu-kuan, 1937), p. 12.

[51] Ch'ü, *Local Government in China*, p. 108.

[52] Ch'üan Tseng-yu, No. 31 (Feb., 1944), p. 34.

[53] Wang, *Hsü tso-chih yao-yen*, p. 7.

[54] Ku Hung-ming, *Chang Wen-hsiang mu-fu chi-wen* (A Record of Chang Chih-tung's *Mu-fu*) (Taipei, Taiwan: Shang-wu yin-shu-kuan, 1956), *shang*, p. 10a.

teachers. In addition, instead of using his given name (*ming*), his *tzu*, or style, was used.[55] The *tzu* is only used in referring to equals or superiors as a sign of respect. Colloquially, the *mu-yu* were referred to as *shih-yeh* (teacher-master), and it was the host who humbled himself to receive their instructions. It was not an uncommon occurrence for the host to go to the rooms of the *mu-yu* to seek their advice and teaching.[56]

Because there were no set rules and regulations governing conduct within a *mu-fu*, social customs and right and honor were used as the guiding principles. For this reason, personal relationships were crucial, and a *mu-yu* was cautioned to be very careful in picking his host because if there was a clash of personalities and no sense of respect, then nothing could be accomplished.[57]

The *mu-yu* normally lived and worked within the host official's *yamen* and were constantly in contact with their host to whom they had access at all times and with whom they normally took their meals. Because of the physical and spiritual closeness of the association, it was not unusual for the host and *mu-yu* to become close friends; however, Wang Hui-tsu repeatedly warned against this because such intimacy could cause loss of confidence. The *mu-yu* was hired to give advice, and if the relationship was too close, then the advice would not be heeded. The key to being a good *mu-yu* was to maintain a certain degree of independence and distance from one's host.[58]

As an adviser, the *mu-yu* was expected to give moral as well as technical advice. In many ways he was a sort of unofficial censor and could serve as a check on the conduct of the official. Of course, the *mu-yu* himself had to lead a proper life and be competent in his work in order to gain the respect of his host and have his advice accepted. But above all, a *mu-yu* needed to have the courage and independence to say what he felt should be said, and, if his advice was not accepted, he should also have the courage and independence to quit. Only in this way would he be able to fulfill his role properly and justify his salary as an adviser.[59]

[55] Ch'ü, *Local Government in China*, p. 108.
[56] Ch'üan Tseng-yu, No. 31 (Feb., 1944), p. 34.
[57] Wang Hui-tsu, *Tso-chih yao-yen* (Admonitions on Government) (Shanghai: Shang-wu yin-shu-kuan, 1937), p. 16.
[58] Wang, *Hsü tso-chih yao-yen*, p. 6.
[59] Wang, *Tso-chih yao-yen*, pp. 1–3.

The *mu-yu* were hired privately by the host official and were paid out of his own pocket. Their earnings were not referred to as "salaries," but as "the money of the dried flesh." This was the conventional way of referring to the wages of a teacher and stemmed from the Confucian *Classics*. "The Master said, 'From the man bringing his bundle of dried flesh for my teaching upwards, I have never refused instruction to anyone.'"[60] The size of the retainer varied according to the job and from time to time and from official to official, but it was anywhere between 400 and 800 taels per year up to the nineteenth century, and after that it rose to as high as 2,000.[61] On the other hand, a magistrate's official income was only from about 450 to 2,500 taels per year.[62]

Within the average *mu-fu* the most important *mu-yu* were the legal *mu-yu* (*hsing-ming*) and the taxation *mu-yu* (*ch'ien-ku*).[63] Wang Hui-tsu advised prospective candidates not to go into the profession unless they could become one of these, because only these two posts paid well and were plentiful enough so that they would be easy to acquire.[64] These two posts, which were often combined in small *mu-fu*, were the chief administrative ones. The legal *mu-yu* was responsible for all cases involving "fighting, fraud, marriage, disputes over graveyards or the designation of an heir, and other cases in which family members were involved," plus cases of homicide and larceny. It was the duty of this *mu-yu* to receive the initial complaint, study the case carefully, and write up a rescript for the official's approval. The rescript was much in the nature of the findings of a grand jury, in that it announced whether or not the complaint would be accepted for trial. An astute *mu-yu* was able to dispose of many cases at this stage by seeing through the conflicting claims and getting to the heart of the matter. If the case was accepted, then the legal *mu-yu* set the dates of the hearing, advised the official before and after the hearings, and, if the case involved penal servitude, banishment, or death, prepared the detailed report

---

[60] Legge, I, 197; Chang Ch'un-ming, p. 36; Stanley, "The *Mu-yu* in the Ch'ing Dynasty," p. 4.

[61] Stanley, "The *Mu-yu* in the Ch'ing Dynasty," p. 4; Ch'üan Tseng-yu, No. 31 (Feb., 1944), p. 34; Chang Ch'un-ming, p. 37; Ch'ü, *Local Government in China*, p. 112.

[62] Ch'ü, *Local Government in China*, p. 22. The officials supplemented their official income by special fees and embezzlement, hence they were able to pay the salaries of several *mu-yu*.

[63] Wang, *Tso-chih yao-yen*, pp. 13–14.     [64] *Ibid.*, pp. 14–15.

which had to be sent to the superior officials for review and approval.[65]

The taxation *mu-yu* was responsible for helping the newly arrived official take over his post by checking all the tax records and determining how much had been embezzled by his predecessor or other *yamen* personnel. He determined the total amount of taxes required from the area of jurisdiction, kept track of what taxes had been paid, and in general supervised their collection. In addition he had jurisdiction over cases involving disputes over property, loans, and business transactions. He was also responsible for expenditures and the delivery of government funds.[66]

In addition to these two posts, there was usually a correspondence *mu-yu* (*shu-ch'i*) who prepared draft letters for the official's approval and either copied or supervised the copying of the letters in their final form; [67] a registration *mu-yu* (*kua-hao*) who registered all incoming and outgoing documents, official notices, and warrants and, thus, kept a check on the status of each document;[68] and a *mu-yu* in charge of the enforcement of taxation (*cheng-pi*). Depending on the size of the official's area of jurisdiction, there could also be a *mu-yu* of the red and black brushes (*chu-mo* or *hung-hei pi*) who copied in black the documents and rescripts prepared by the legal and taxation *mu-yu* and used red brushes to write the key words and add the red signs and flourishes,[69] and a bookkeeper *mu-yu* (*chang-fang*) who was more or less a cashier, in that he handled the actual receipt and disbursement of cash and kept track of gifts sent and received, of fees paid to gate porters of superior *yamen*, and of various expenses involved in entertaining visiting officials. This post was usually held by the host official's confidant or, in some cases, by one of his relatives.[70] In a few cases there was also a *mu-yu* in charge of land tax (*ch'ien-liang tsung*) and a *mu-yu* in charge of law suits (*an-tsung*).[71] The *mu-fu* of governors-general and governors followed the general pattern outlined above, as did those of the prefects and taotais (*tao-t'ai*), except that they had

---

[65] Ch'ü, *Local Government in China*, pp. 98–101; Chang Ch'un-ming, pp. 39–40.

[66] Ch'ü, *Local Government in China*, pp. 101–103, 98; Chang Ch'un-ming, pp. 39–40.

[67] Ch'ü, *Local Government in China*, pp. 104–105.

[68] *Ibid.*, p. 104.                    [70] *Ibid.*, pp. 103–104.

[69] *Ibid.*                             [71] *Ibid.*, p. 97.

literary *mu-yu* for drafting memorials to the throne and other documents, *mu-yu* for education and military affairs, and, after the establishment of the Tsungli Yamen in 1861 when all governors-general and governors were concurrently appointed to this new office, *mu-yu* for foreign affairs.[72]

The *mu-yu*, in addition to his regular duties, would also assist the host official in any one or all of his multifarious duties, such as suppressing pirates, administering disaster relief and water transport, and reading the preliminary examination papers which a magistrate set before candidates for the provincial examinations.[73] The legal *mu-yu* was normally considered the head *mu-yu* and, in addition to his normal duties, was responsible for running the *yamen* in accordance with his host official's wishes. Because of his position, the legal *mu-yu's* recommendation was usually necessary in order to get a job in the *mu-fu*.[74]

One of the chief functions of all *mu-yu* was to supervise the clerks and to try to prevent their corrupt practices.[75] Since the clerks received no salary and were in charge of the files, it was only natural that they would not be above changing a document, dropping someone's name from a tax list, marking someone's taxes paid, and the like in return for a monetary consideration. The *mu-yu* were experts in their fields and were much more aware of the ingenuity and multiplicity of clerical manipulations than the officials and were, therefore, in a better position to control them. It was an important part of the *mu-yu's* job to protect the host official from the wrath of his superiors, which was usually caused by clerical corruption.

As privately hired advisers, the *mu-yu* had no official relationship to the central government, could not be appointed to any official post by their host officials, and were not supposed to appear in public in any official capacity. When an official presided in court, his legal *mu-yu* was not allowed to be present.[76] In addition, the

---

[72] Hsieh, pp. 297–298.

[73] Ch'ü, *Local Government in China*, p. 105; Ch'üan Tseng-yu, No. 32 (March, 1944), p. 37.

[74] Ch'üan, Tseng-yu, No. 31 (Feb., 1944), p. 36.

[75] Stanley, "The *Mu-yu* in the Ch'ing Dynasty," p. 4; Mary C. Wright, *The Last Stand of Chinese Conservatism. The T'ung-Chih Restoration, 1862–1874* (Stanford: Stanford Univ. Press, 1957), p. 92; Ch'üan Tseng-yu, No. 31 (Feb., 1944), p. 32.

[76] Stanley, "The *Mu-yu* in the Ch'ing Dynasty," pp. 3–4; Mary C. Wright, p. 92.

*mu-yu* were supposed to remain within the *yamen* and within their quarters as much as possible.[77] These restrictions on their movements were to keep them from creating a network of local alliances that could be used for corrupt purposes.

The position of the *mu-yu* within the *yamen* gave them a tremendous amount of power over local affairs and in some cases over their host official. Since they could use this power for good or evil, the character of both the *mu-yu* and the official was of the utmost importance. A strong official could control morally weak *mu-yu*, and a morally strong *mu-yu*, such as Wang Hui-tsu, could go a long way in strengthening the backbone of a weak official; but when both the host official and his *mu-yu* were only concerned with their own selfish interests, corruption ran rampant.

The *mu-fu* system was a product of necessity and had not been officially sponsored or sanctioned by the central government. On the other hand, it was not considered illegal, nor did the imperial authority seek to eliminate it. The central government claimed the right of complete authority over everything and everyone in China and was determined to exercise that right, but when it was presented with a *fait accompli*, as it was in the case of the *mu-fu* system, it recognized the value of the system and only sought to control its corrupt features by regulations and admonitions to the officials. In the 7th year of Ch'ien-lung (1741), it was decreed: "Because the provincial officials' affairs are very heavy, they cannot help but invite some *mu-pin* to help them manage. But the *mu-pin* are not consistently virtuous. Therefore it is easy for corrupt practices to arise."[78]

The types of corruption against which the imperial authority inveighed were those which favored the private interests of family and friends at the expense of the government. The injunctions were aimed at the officials' relations with their *mu-yu*, the *mu-yu's* relations with the *yamen* clerks and the local populace, combinations of *mu-yu* in various provincial *yamen*, and the *mu-yu's* usurpation of the official's power. No official was permitted to hire members of his family, his relatives, or his friends as *mu-yu* (Ch'ien-lung 1st, 5th, 28th, and 34th years; Chia-ch'ing 5th year).[79] No person who came

[77] Ch'üan Tseng-yu, No. 31 (Feb., 1944), p. 34.
[78] Hsiao Kung-ch'üan, *Rural China* (Seattle: Univ. of Washington Press, 1960), p. 505; *Ta-Ch'ing hui-tien shih-li, chüan* 97, p. 4a.
[79] *Ta-Ch'ing hui-tien shih-li, chüan* 97, pp. 3b–4a, 4a, 5a, 5b.

from the province to which the official was assigned, or from the neighboring province within a distance of 500 *li*, was allowed to be hired as a *mu-yu*, nor were the *mu-yu* permitted to follow the host official from an old post to a new one; moreover, anyone who had been in a *mu-fu* for five years had to be replaced (Ch'ien-lung 37th and 41st years),[80] and a newly appointed official was not allowed to take over a *mu-yu* of his predecessor (Ch'ien-lung 28th year).[81] The governors-general and governors had to keep the Board of Civil Appointments informed at all times regarding their *mu-yu*, and the lesser officials in the province had to inform the governors-general and governors who their *mu-yu* were. At the end of the year the governors-general and governors were required to inform the board in regard to all the *mu-yu* of the lesser officials (Ch'ien-lung 37th year).[82] The officials were not permitted to recommend *mu-yu* to their subordinate officials, to choose their *mu-yu* from among their subordinate officials, or to allow members of their family to recommend *mu-yu* (Ch'ien-lung 32nd year; Chia-ch'ing 5th, 8th, and 12th years; Tao-kuang 8th, 13th and 27th years).[83]

The officials were also enjoined to take special precautions to prevent their *mu-yu* from creating alliances with *mu-yu* in other *yamen*, especially alliances with blood relatives, from marrying someone from the local area, from setting up private businesses, from using their privileged position in the *yamen* to bully and show-off, from giving friends and other officials privileged information, and in general from becoming too friendly with the local populace (Ch'ien-lung 6th, 28th, and 34th years; Chia-ch'ing 5th year).[84] "The *mu-yu's* friendliness causes corruption, and this is the beginning of injury to the government, so we must find ways to clear it up and severely prohibit it."[85]

The onus was on the officials, and the punishments for violation of these regulations varied from one year's loss of salary to dismissal. In some cases, a more serious punishment would be imposed by the board. However, if the violations occurred without the officials' knowledge, or if they were guilty only of not investigating thoroughly

[80] *Ibid., chüan* 97, pp. 5a–b.
[81] *Ibid., chüan* 97, p. 4b.
[82] *Ibid., chüan* 97, p. 5a.
[83] *Ibid., chüan* 97, pp. 5a, 5b, 6a.
[84] Ibid., *chüan* 97, pp. 4a, 4b, 4b–5a, 5a, 5b; Ch'üan Tseng-yu, No. 31 (Feb., 1944), p. 42; Wu Ching-tzu, *The Scholars,* transl. by Yang Hsien-i and Gladys Yang (Peking: Foreign Language Press, 1957), p. 150.
[85] *Ta-Ch'ing hui-tien shih-li, chüan* 97, p. 4a.

enough, then the punishment was lighter. On the other hand, in the case of a serious violation, the *mu-yu* concerned were also liable to punishment by the board.

On the positive side, the imperial government, in order to reduce the officials' reliance on their *mu-yu*, singled out for praise those officials who conducted their affairs without the aid of *mu-yu*. The K'ang-hsi Emperor praised Chao Shen-ch'iao for not having any *mu-k'e*, even though he had held posts ranging from magistrate to governor,[86] and in Ch'ien-lung 28th year (1763) the officials were admonished to handle everything themselves.[87]

As a further inducement to honest government, in the 1st year of Yung-cheng (1723), in a reply to the Board of Civil Appointments, it was decreed that the worthy *mu-k'e* should be reported to the board by the governors-general and governors for appointment as officials.[88] This decree was issued again in Yung-cheng 13th year (1735) and in Ch'ien-lung 1st year (1736), but it was encompassed by limitations: the *mu-yu* must be virtuous, must have served six years in one continuous period, and must be guaranteed by the recommending official. Moreover, they had to take an examination given by the governors-general or governors and then wait for all the papers from all the provinces to be forwarded to the board to be further examined and graded. Finally they were selected and assigned a rank by an imperial commissioner.[89] Because of the limitations and financial hardships involved, not many *mu-yu* took advantage of these decrees until the later years of the Ch'ing, when most of the restrictions were eliminated or overlooked.[90] These decrees, however, had given the officials the privilege of recommending *mu-yu* for office, and this privilege was never abrogated during the balance of the Ch'ing period. This was as close as the officials of the Ch'ing ever came to having the power of private appointment.

At the beginning of the Ch'ien-lung period it was proposed that the *mu-yu* be incorporated into the official bureaucratic structure. *Mu-yu* who had been working for a governor-general or a governor would be assigned to the 7th rank; those who had worked for a

[86] Chang Ch'un-ming, p. 29.
[87] *Ta-Ch'ing hui-tien shih-li, chüan* 97, p. 4a.
[88] Wang Hsien-ch'ien, ed., *Tung-hua lu*, Yung-cheng ch'ao (Shanghai, 1911), *chüan* 2, p. 15b; Chang Ch'un-ming, p. 47.
[89] *Ta-Ch'ing hui-tien shih-li, chüan* 97, pp. 3b–4a.
[90] Ch'üan Tseng-yu, No. 32 (March, 1944), p. 36.

provincial treasurer or judge, the 8th rank; and those who had worked in a *fu, chou,* or *hsien,* the 9th rank. Whether future *mu-yu* would be hired by the central government or continue to be hired by the provincial officials was not stated. However, the proposal was never carried out because the ranks assigned would have degraded the position of the *mu-yu* in relation to the host official, and the *mu-yu* would have suffered a sizable loss of salary.[91] The system was strong enough to protect the vested interests of the *mu-yu* and to stop this one attempt to make them government employees.

The imperial authority was well aware that the restrictions it sought to impose were in many cases not adhered to. In the 41st year of Ch'ien-lung (1776) it was officially acknowledged that the prohibition on hiring *mu-yu* from the same province and the five-year limit on service had merely "a name but no actuality." At the same time, the year-end reports of all the *mu-yu* to the board were done away with. Instead, the officials were almost beseeched to redouble their efforts to prevent the corrupt combinations and practices of the *mu-yu*.[92]

While the *mu-yu* served a necessary function in the operation of the government, and while, in their capacity as moral advisers, they appeared to support the government, their primary loyalty was to the officials who paid their salaries, and their primary purpose was to protect the officials from the government by making it possible for them to carry out their duties. The *mu-fu* was the official's family away from home and, as such, was feared by the government as an added source of depredation. The imperial authority had found it necessary to restrict the official in relation to his family, and it also found it necessary to restrict the official in relation to his *mu-fu*.

In any given social situation where a rigid or formal organization exists, people will instinctively set up an informal structure alongside it in order to get the work done.[93] Such informal structures are dependent on human relations, personalities, and a high degree of flexibility. Under the Ch'ing governmental system, the bureauc-

[91] Chang Ch'un ming, p. 47.

[92] *Ta-Ch'ing hui-tien shih-li, chüan* 97, pp. 5a–b.

[93] Chester I. Barnard, *The Functions of the Executive* (Cambridge: Harvard Univ. Press, 1956), pp. 123, 224–225, 286; Robert C. Sampson, *The Staff Role in Management. Its Creative Uses* (New York: Harper & Brothers, Publishers, 1955), p. 72; Herbert A. Simon, *Administrative Behavior,* 2nd ed. (New York: The Macmillan Co., 1958), pp. 148–149, 157, 160.

racy, with its detailed rules and regulations and its hierarchical relationships, was the formal structure, but the *mu-fu* system, with
its stress on personal relationships and technical competency, and
its freedom from rigid government control combined with the personal friendships of the officials themselves, was the informal structure. Each needed the other in order for the government to operate.

In times of peace and stability, the formal structure of the Ch'ing
government had been able to provide the necessary leadership and
to control its informal counterpart. The inherent tension between
emperor and bureaucracy, although diluted to a large extent by
"imperial Confucianism," was still a productive force; and the link
between society and government, which made the Confucian scholar-
official class a true elite, was still viable.[94] The goals and values of
the society were still Confucian, and the *mu-yu* remained subordi-
nated to the officialdom, with little or no desire to change the system
or to assume roles of leadership. Yet, by the mid-nineteenth century,
the social system was under serious attack, and foreign encroachments had resulted in a new polarization: the tension between the
throne and the bureaucracy was being overshadowed by that between China and the West. Emperor and officials joined ranks to
meet the threat from abroad, but the life had gone out of the
system, and the bureaucratic elite had lost its leadership qualities —
the ability to innovate and create.[95] Those few far-seeing Chinese
statesmen who could still be regarded as leaders turned to the traditional *mu-fu* system whose informal and flexible nature made it
possible for them to attempt to meet the West on its own terms.
Men who could innovate, create, and help China absorb the shock
of rebellion and invasion were recruited into the *mu-fu* system,
but, because of the new opportunities afforded by the crisis situation, many of them moved upward out of the ranks of mere advisors
and into the realm of active leadership. China was being forced to
change, and in the process the *mu-fu* system expanded in both scope
and importance.

[94] Franz Schurmann, *Ideology and Organization in Communist China* (Berkeley: Univ. of California Press, 1966), p. 5.
[95] *Ibid.*, p. xxxviii–xxxix, 5.

# III. The Mu-Fu System
## Under Tseng Kuo-Fan

In the 2nd year of Hsien-feng, the 12th month (January 9–February 7, 1853), the Governor of Hunan Province received a decree ordering Tseng Kuo-fan "to help and share in managing the said province's militia and to investigate the local bandit conditions."[1] This decree, which marks the beginning of Tseng's military operations against the Taiping rebels, also marks a turning point in the development of the *mu-fu* system. The implementation of the measures which Tseng devised to put down the rebellion and, later, to ward off the encroachments of the West was possible only within the informal, flexible, and personal structure of the *mu-fu* system. These measures also changed the composition and scope of the system itself. The basic criteria remained the same, namely, personal relationships, technical competency, and subordination to the provincial bureaucreacy, but the area of parochial responsibility was expanded. Provincial officials became involved in the problems created by the presence of the West, and they were just as responsible for negotiations with a foreign consul, maintenance of a multiprovincial defense system, or the operation of a steamship company to win back China's economic rights as they had been for the collection of local taxes. To accomplish these tasks they needed the technical advice of an increasing number of experts in Western methods and technology — men who would never have been mem-

---

[1] Li Fang-ch'en, *Chung-kuo chin-tai shih* (Modern History of China) (Taipei, Taiwan: Wu-chou ch'u-pan she, 1960), *shang*, p. 298; Tseng Kuo-fan, *Tseng Wen-cheng-kung ch'üan-chi* (The Complete Works of Tseng Kuo-fan) (Taipei, Taiwan: Shih-chieh shu-chü, 1952), Nien-p'u, p. 14 (hereafter referred to as *TWCK-NP*); Wang Hsien-ch'ien, ed., *Tung-hua lu*, Hsien-feng ch'ao (Shanghai, 1911), *chüan* 18, p. 9a.

bers of a traditional *mu-fu*. In addition, the heretofore clear-cut line of demarcation between the system and the bureaucracy gradually became indistinct. Through the privilege of recommendation, which had been granted to the governors-general and governors by the Yung-cheng Emperor (1723–1736) and was never rescinded by later emperors, *mu-yu* now began to enter the ranks of the bureaucracy in ever increasing numbers. The demands of the state, occasioned by internal and external threats, forced the central authority to relax the restrictions on the elevation of *mu-yu*, to rely on their knowledge of the West, and to authorize the creation of Western-style enterprises under provincial aegis. In the face of the common enemy, the informal *mu-fu* system and the government were becoming closely attached, and the bureaucracy (the realm of amateurs in politics) was beginning to take on a professional tinge. To compound the situation, the loyalties and interests of the *mu-yu* who were raised to official rank tended to strengthen, rather than break, the tie between *mu-yu* and host official. Recommendation by a high provincial official, who had similar interests, whether political or technical, made the climb up the bureaucratic ladder less arduous and the implementation of one's ideas more certain. Many ex-*mu-yu* who were serving as officials, therefore, continued to accede to the wishes of their former host officials, as well as to advise them on foreign affairs and commercial and military matters. These changes began with Tseng, but were copied and improved upon by others to the point where they became an integral part of the *mu-fu* system during the remainder of its existence under the Ch'ing Dynasty.

The Taiping Rebellion broke out in Kwangsi in 1850, and it was immediately apparent that the regular armies of the Ch'ing, the Eight Banners and the Green Standard, were completely inept. Armies are a reflection of the society which creates them, and the Manchu armies were no exception. Nurhachi (1559–1626), in keeping with the tribal origins of the Manchus, had established the Eight Banners as a system in which the various units were personally commanded by hereditary banner chiefs who were under his control but were forced to share the burdens of administration.[2]

[2] Lo Erh-kang, "Ch'ing-chi ping wei chiang-yu ti ch'i-yüan" (The Origin of the Personal Armies at the End of the Ch'ing), *Chung-kuo she-hui ching-chi shih chi-k'an*, V. No. 2 (June, 1937), 237; U.S. Library of Congress, Asiatic Division, *Eminent Chinese of the Ch'ing Period (1644–1912)*, ed. by Arthur W.

His eighth son and successor, Abahai (1592–1643), whose position at first was more one of *primus inter pares*, began the process of the centralization of power by gaining control of three of the eight banners and by depriving the other banner chiefs of their roles as co-rulers.[3] The process was completed by the Shun-chih Emperor (1644–1662), who, after the death of the Prince Regent, Dorgon (1612–1650), gathered all the power to himself and appointed his own representatives as banner chiefs to replace the hereditary ones. From this time on, the Eight Banners were the private army of the emperor.[4] What had started out as basically a decentralized tribal organization had been changed by the exigencies of conquest and imperial rule into a centralized military structure.

The other branch of the Manchu army, the Green Standard, which was originally composed of Chinese who had been loyal to the Manchus during the period of conquest, became the regular garrison army and was placed under the control of the Board of War. Its officers were career men who were promoted and transferred at the will of the board. The enlisted soldiers were registered in permanent army registers and considered their occupation to be hereditary. Between the officers and men there were no personal connections or ties of loyalty, as it was a centralized military organization owing its allegiance to the center and not to provincial or private commanders.[5]

Although the Ch'ing had created a highly centralized army, it was unable to maintain its fighting efficiency due to the enervating effect of peacetime garrison duty and the privileged position of the Manchus as conquerors. The decomposition of the Eight Banners as a fighting force began soon after the capture of Peking, and by 1796, during the White Lotus Rebellion, had reached the point where this branch of the Ch'ing army was considered useless. The decline of the Green Standard was not as rapid, but during the White Lotus Rebellion (1796–1804), it also showed signs of decay and had to be supported by militia units. The Opium War resulted in the complete discredit of the Green Standard.[6]

The Chinese proclivity for local loyalties and personal relation-

Hummel (Washington, D.C.: U.S. Gov't. Printing Office, 1943), I, 594 (hereafter referred to as Hummel).

[3] Lo Erh-kang, p. 237; Hummel, I, 1.
[4] Lo Erh-kang, pp. 237–238; Hummel, I, 215.
[5] Lo Erh-kang, pp. 238–239.       [6] *Ibid.*, pp. 239–240.

ships had undermined the concept of loyalty to the center, which is essential if a centralized army is to maintain its fighting efficiency. When the Taiping rebels arose in 1850, within the Imperial Army there was no sense of loyalty or cooperation between the troops and their commanders, or between the commanders of the various units. The army lacked any sense of cohesion and purpose. In victory, the various units were jealous of each other; and in defeat, there was no thought of rescuing those in distress. The Imperial Commissioner, who was in command of the army, and the Governor of Kwangsi Province, in whose territory the army was operating, were at odds with each other and gave conflicting orders.[7] Needless to say, when the Imperial Army came face to face with the rebels, it scattered and fled. As the rebellion progressed, it soon became evident that the only effective military units on the imperial side were the local militia units, which were composed of and created by the local populace for the purpose of defending their homes against the rebels and the local bandits. It was on these units that the Ch'ing was soon forced to rely.

At the time the above-mentioned decree was issued, the Taiping rebels were attacking Ch'ang-sha, the capital of Hunan, and the court, fully aware of the seriousness of the situation, was attempting to bolster the defenses of the province by creating more militia units. Tseng Kuo-fan was at his native place, Hsiang-hsiang, Hunan, mourning his mother.[8] At first he did not wish to undertake the job of organizing militia because he felt that while in mourning it was not proper to engage in public affairs. However, the emperor nullified this objection by stating that there was no higher form of filial piety than to come to the aid of the imperiled country, and that the deed would certainly satisfy his departed mother's spirit.[9] Nonetheless, Tseng still held back because he realized that his efforts would not be too well received by the local officials on whom he would be forced to rely. However, he listened to the arguments of his friends, principally Kuo Sung-t'ao, and finally agreed to go. Tseng set out from his home on January 26, 1853, for a conference with the governor, and Kuo followed him to become his first *mu-yu*.[10]

[7] *Ibid.*, p. 240.  [8] Li Fang-ch'en, *shang*, p. 298.

[9] William James Hail, *Tseng Kuo-fan and the Taiping Rebellion* (New Haven: Yale Univ. Press, 1927), pp. 148, 170.

[10] *Ibid.*, p. 148; Yü Yü-ti, "Tseng Kuo-fan mu-fu pin-liao nien-p'u" (A Chronological Record of Tseng Kuo-fan's *Mu-fu* and Its Members) (unpublished

Tseng Kuo-fan had seen the effectiveness of the militia in keeping down local rebels, and, he also recognized the reasons behind the dismal failure of the Green Standard. He proposed to use the militia bands of Chiang Chung-yüan and Lo Tse-nan as the hard core of a new army in which the element of personal loyalties would be the binding principle.[11] His aim was to create a force in which "the spirit of loyalty and righteousness" was paramount and "all the generals are of one heart, and the masses are of one spirit." In order to do this, he felt it necessary for every commander to recruit his own troops personally.[12]

The *Hsiang-chün*, as his new army came to be called, used the battalion (*ying*) of 500 men as its basic unit. The battalion was divided into four companies (*shao*) and controlled by the battalion commander (*ying-kuan*). Above the battalion commanders was a commander of detachments (*t'ung-ling*), who commanded anywhere from two to several tens of battalions, depending on his ability. The commanders of detachments were directly under the control of the generalissimo (*ta-shuai*), who was Tseng Kuo-fan. Under this system, Tseng selected the commanders of detachments who in turn selected their battalion commanders. They in turn would select their company commanders, who would recruit the actual "braves." In this way the officers and men of a battalion knew each other personally, were from the same local area, and had a feeling of loyalty and personal attachment. The battalion and company commanders looked to the detachment commanders, and the detachment commanders looked to the generalissimo "like sons and younger brothers who served their father and elder brothers."[13] In the words of Wang K'ai-yün, who was an off-and-on member of Tseng's *mu-fu*, "The value of the *Hsiang-chün* lies in the fact that it is based on familial relationships, and, therefore, the superiors and inferiors have a close bond. . . . If you follow the *Hsiang-chün* system, then the superiors and inferiors are personally connected with each other, the generals and soldiers have a personal friendship, and everyone protects his senior. If the general dies, then his

Bachelor's Thesis, National Taiwan University, Taipei, Taiwan, 1960), pp. 9, 47. Cited from *Ch'ing Shih-kao* and *Hsü pei-chuan chi, chüan* 15.

[11] Hail, pp. 147, 149; Li Chien-nung, *The Political History of China, 1840–1928*, transl. and ed. by Teng Ssu-yü and J. Ingalls (Princeton: D. Van Nostrand Co., Inc., 1956), p. 66.

[12] Lo Erh-kang, p. 242. Cited from *Tseng Wen-cheng-kung shu-cha, chüan* 2.

[13] Lo Erh-kang, p. 242.

army falls apart. If the general survives, then his army remains intact."[14]

Tseng Kuo-fan was especially adamant about the matter of personal recruitment. He insisted that if a commander of detachments had to be changed for any reason, then his entire army must be disbanded and recruited all over again by the new commander. This was necessary, he felt, in order to be certain that the "braves" would fight under the new commander. Subsequent events proved Tseng to be correct. In several instances when battalions were not personally recruited after the transfer of a commander of detachments, the negligent new commander lost his life because his troops would not fight for him, but scattered before the Taiping rebels.[15]

The personal loyalties between the officers and men of the *Hsiang-chün* were strengthened by the manner in which the "braves" were provisioned, supplied, and paid. Because the *Hsiang-chün* was outside the regularly established and traditional armed services, there was no way that its members could be paid through the regular bureaucratic channels. At first they were forced to live on the contributions of the local gentry, and the court ordered the Governor-General of Hupeh and Hunan and the Governor of Hunan to help Tseng in his efforts to secure funds. Later, when the army left Hunan to campaign in other provinces, the Board of Revenue promised to support it, but failed to do so.[16] For the most part, the various commanders were on their own, and the method of "going to the land to raise provisions" (*chiu-ti ch'ou-hsiang*) sprang up.[17] Each commander regarded the resources of the local areas as his private possessions. They assumed control of the *likin* barriers, instituted taxes on the production and transport of opium, and raised local contributions.[18] At the top level, Tseng Kuo-fan, in 1858, with the approval of the Board of Revenue, established a supply bureau at Hu-k'ou for receiving and forwarding supplies, gained permission to sell honorary official ranks from the 6th to the 9th grades in return for substantial contributions, and, in 1860, established *likin* stations

---

[14] *Ibid.*, p. 245. Cited from *Hsiang-ch'i lou jih-chi* and *Hsiang-chün chih ying-chih p'ien*.

[15] Lo Erh-kang, pp. 242–245.

[16] *Ibid.*, p. 245.

[17] *Ibid.*; Ralph L. Powell, *The Rise of Chinese Military Power, 1895–1912* (Princeton: Princeton Univ. Press, 1955), pp. 25–26.

[18] C. John Stanley, *Late Ch'ing Finance: Hu Kuang-yung as an Innovator* (Cambridge: Harvard Univ. Press, 1961), p. 11; Lo Erh-kang, p. 246.

all over Kiangsi.[19] Tseng's close friend and staunch supporter, Hu Lin-i, who was at this time the Governor of Hupeh, established the Hupeh General Commissary under his own direct control in order to help Tseng. All of the revenue from the province was collected by this bureau, which also made all the disbursements, and the centrally assigned provincial treasurer was bypassed and unable to question its policies.[20] Despite the above measures, the *Hsiang-chün* was always handicapped by a lack of supplies and money, which limited its size. The "braves," however, were well aware of the efforts of their commanders to pay and feed them. As a result, their loyalties were not to the state, but to their respective commanders, who also shared their hardships.

The creation of personal armies by Tseng Kuo-fan resurrected the military features of the *mu-fu* system. From this time until the end of the Ch'ing such armies were an integral part of the system, and one of the principal criteria for membership in a *mu-fu* was military competence.

The personal armies of the Ch'ing had arisen for basically the same reasons that they are arisen in pre-Yüan times: the central government was unable, or unwilling, to provide the money and the trained personnel needed to meet new situations. It also was unable to overcome the Chinese need to look to the family and friends, rather than to the central authority, for protection. Tseng had been assigned the task of raising a militia army to fight the Taiping rebels, but had not been provided with the necessary tools. In order to carry out his assignment he was, therefore, forced to rely on his friends.

Tseng Kuo-fan's position between the years 1853 and 1860 was ambiguous in that it did not fit into the regular provincial hierarchy, and, because of this, his *mu-fu* was forced to develop patterns which had not previously existed in the Ch'ing. When Tseng left Peking in 1852 to supervise the Kiangsi provincial examinations, he was concurrently a Senior Vice-President (*tso-shih-lang*) of the Board of Rites and an Acting Senior Vice-President of the Board of Punishments and the Board of Civil Appointments.[21] His official career

---

[19] Hail, p. 156, footnote 38, pp. 204, 208–209.
[20] Lo Erh-kang, p. 246.
[21] *TWCK-NP*, pp. 7, 11, 13; Tseng Kuo-fan, *Tseng Wen-cheng-kung ch'üan-chi* (The Complete Works of Tseng Kuo-fan) (Taipei, Taiwan: Shih-chieh shu-chü, 1952), Tsou-kao, *chüan* 1, pp. 15, 20 (hereafter referred to as *TWCK-TK*).

had begun in 1838 when he became a *chin-shih* and a member of the Hanlin Academy. Since that time, he had served in various capacities in the capital and had built up a network of friends. However, when he received word of his mother's death, while in Kiangsi in 1852, and went into mourning, he became officially "a Vice-President of a Board in mourning" (*ting-yu shih-lang*).[22] As such, he had no official power or salary, only honors, and was not supposed to engage in any government affairs. Although he was shortly thereafter ordered to assist the Governor of Hunan in militia defense and the investigation of the rebels, his position was still indefinite because he was never given provincial rank and was technically in mourning, first for his mother and later for his father, for three and a half of the next seven years.[23] In 1854 he was ordered to assume the post of Acting Governor of Hupeh but begged to decline it on the grounds that he felt his primary responsibility was the conduct of the war against the rebels and that all of his energies should be devoted exclusively to that end. His request was granted, and instead he was appointed a Junior Vice-President (*yu-shih-lang*) of the Board of War.[24] All during the seven year period from 1853 to 1860 Tseng was consistently referred to as a Vice-President of a Board (*shih-lang*) in official correspondence. He was serving in the provinces, but his official rank was one associated with the capital. To complicate matters even further, none of the five different seals of office which Tseng received during this period were clear enough to indicate definite authority and to beget from the provincial officials suitable respect for his commissions and orders. His first seal of office, which he received in 1853, read: "By Imperial Command to Assist in the Management of Militia Defense and to Investigate Rebel Affairs. The Seal of Office of the Former Board of Rites Senior Vice-President." Subsequent seals read: (1854) "By Imperial Command to Manage Military Affairs. The Seal of Office of the Former Board of Rites Vice-President"; (1855) "The Seal of Office of the Commissioner and Vice-President of the Board of War, the former Board of Rites Vice-President"; (1855) "The Seal of Office of the Commissioner and Junior Vice-President of the Board of War"; and (1858) "By Imperial Command to Manage

---

[22] Li Fang-ch'en, *shang*, p. 298.
[23] *TWCK-TK, chüan* 1, pp. 71, 105; *chüan* 2, pp. 274, 317.
[24] *TWCK-NP*, pp. 31, 32; *TWCK-TK, chüan* 1, pp. 84, 94.

Chekiang Military Affairs. The Seal of Office of the Former Board of War Vice-President." [25] Because of his ambiguous position, Tseng was openly flouted by the officials; the regular military officials opposed his army, and the civil officials, who had to help bear the expense of his army, scarcely gave him more than lukewarm support. The provincial revenues all passed through the hands of the regular officials, and all Tseng could do was to stand at the side and beg. [26] The ambiguity of his position also made it impossible for him to recruit civil officials through the regular government channels to govern the areas his army recaptured from the rebels.

Although his position as a Vice-President of a Board created many problems for Tseng in raising his army, still it helped him in his relations with the Hunanese gentry. Because he was sometimes in mourning, and not a regular provincial official, they considered him as one of themselves. He had come from a poor farmer's family, yet had already made a mark for himself in Peking, which attested to his above average intelligence and moral qualities. He also was young, and had bright prospects for the future. For these reasons he was acceptable to the gentry of Hunan and gained their support. He relied on them to man his army, to raise the necessary money and supplies to keep it going, and to staff his *mu-fu*. [27] It was also through his friends that Tseng eventually acquired the necessary power to successfully terminate the rebellion.

In 1860 through the efforts of Hu Lin-i, who was the Governor of Hupeh, Lo Ping-chang, the Governor of Hunan, and his friends in Peking who praised him highly before the emperor, Tseng was made the Liangkiang Governor-General and Imperial Commissioner (*ch'in-ch'ai ta-ch'en*) with full authority to wipe out the Taiping rebels, including the power to levy funds. [28] Up to this point Tseng had had to rely on his *mu-yu* to get the job done, but now he had a clearly defined and powerful position which, combined with the talents of his *mu-yu*, made it possible for him to become one of the most powerful men in China in the nineteenth century. In the process he also created a group of men who would be the mainstay of the dynasty long after his death in 1872.

25 *TWCK-NP*, pp. 57, 61; Hail, p. 201.
26 Hail, pp. 164, 149, 201.
27 Conversation with Professor Li Ting-i, National Taiwan University, Taipei, Taiwan, July 20, 1961.
28 Li Chien-nung, p. 75; Hail, pp. 220, 238; *TWCK-NP*, p. 76.

Power and its concomitant wealth were the two pillars which supported the *mu-fu* system. Without them the system could not exist. Tseng Kuo-fan is unique in that he was able to maintain and rely on his *mu-fu*, even though up to 1860 his power was ill-defined and his income uncertain. His high character and the nature of his cause made it possible for him to gain the support of equally dedicated men and to achieve a limited degree of success during the first seven years of his career as a military leader.

Tseng Kuo-fan was not a military man, nor had he had any previous military experience. Yet he undertook to create a new type of army which eventually became the mainstay of the dynasty and was able to suppress the Taiping rebels. In order to do this, he relied on the Confucian principle that it was men, not impersonal government institutions, that were important. He surrounded himself with capable advisers, listened to their advice, and tried to develop their latent talents to fit his needs. Although he relied principally on Hunanese, especially for his army, in matters of military administration, civil government, and the procurement of supplies he ranged far and wide in his solicitation of personnel. Hsüeh Fu-ch'eng, who joined Tseng's *mu-fu* in 1865, has left a list of eighty-four of the most important members of Tseng's *mu-fu*, from 1853 to 1872. Of this list, there were nineteen from Hunan, sixteen from Kiangsu, fourteen from Anhwei, eleven from Chekiang, six each from Hupeh and Szechwan, four each from Kiangsi and Kwangtung, two from Kweichow, one from the Green Standard, and one unknown. In addition, there were countless others of lesser importance who were not recorded.[29]

In the recruitment of personnel for his *mu-fu*, Tseng Kuo-fan made a conscious effort to find men of talent wherever they might be.

Tseng kept systematic lists of able men and encouraged them by writing to them, paying them visits, and lecturing them. His formula for the restoration of civil government was to recruit widely, employ cautiously, instruct diligently, and control strictly. The first step was to become widely acquainted, the second to note down the strengths and weaknesses of different men and their types of ability — Tseng's estimates were shrewd

---

[29] Hsüeh Fu-ch'eng, "Hsü Tseng Wen-cheng-kung mu-fu pin-liao" (A Discussion of the Members of Tseng Kuo-fan's *Mu-fu*), *in* Tso Shun-sheng, comp., *Chung-kuo chin-pai-nien shih tzu-liao ch'u-pien* (First Volume of Materials on the Last One Hundred Years of Chinese History) (Taipei, Taiwan: Chung-hua shu-chü, 1958), pp. 131–134.

and realistic. Although he believed that all talent rested ultimately on
moral training, he recognized that specific abilities varied, and that constant effort was needed to bring out particular latent talents and to use
them appropriately.[30]

While many members of his *mu-fu* were recruited on the basis of
personal friendship, such as Kuo Sung-t'ao, from among the members
of his family, such as his brothers Kuo-ch'üan and Kuo-pao, and
others were recommended to him by friends or belonged to militia
units which were incorporated into his army, such as P'eng Yü-lin,
T'ang Hsün-fang, and Liu Jung, still others were secured by me-
morializing to have them transferred to his *mu-fu* from official positions. Tseng followed this latter practice as early as 1854 when he
memorialized to have several "expectant" officials transferred to
his staff to assist him in military affairs; [31] and as late as 1869 when,
as the new Governor-General of Chihli, he compiled a list of eight
persons and memorialized that they be transferred to his *mu-fu*.
The eight persons were the Taotais Ch'ien Ting-ming and Ch'en
Nai, the Prefect Li Hsing-hui, the *chou* Prefects Yu Chih-k'ai and
Chao Lieh-wen, the District Magistrates Fang Tsung-ch'eng and
Chin Wu-lan, and the Assistant Department Director Ch'en Lan-
pin.[32] Although the normal procedure was for a *mu-yu* to leave the
*mu-fu* when he was appointed to an official position, in some cases,
when one of his more important *mu-yu* was assigned to an official
post by the Board of Civil Appointments, Tseng would memorialize
to retain him. This happened in the case of Chou K'ai-hsi, who was
appointed as a *chou* Prefect, but was retained by Tseng in Hupeh
in 1861.[33]

The early career of Tso Tsung-t'ang is an excellent example of
the circumstances which would lead a man to join Tseng's *mu-fu*
and of how important friends were in helping one along the road
to success. Tso was from Hsiang-yin, Hunan. He had passed the
examination for the *chü-jen* degree in 1832, but failed to pass the
metropolitan examinations and decided to give up the attempt in
1838 after his third failure. In 1837, while lecturing in Li-ling,
Hunan, he became acquainted with T'ao Chu, the Governor-General

[30] Mary C. Wright, *The Last Stand of Chinese Conservatism. The T'ung-chih
Restoration, 1862–1874* (Stanford: Stanford Univ. Press, 1957), p. 78.
[31] *TWCK-TK, chüan* 1, pp. 78–79.
[32] Yü, p. 109; *TWCK-NP*, p. 148.
[33] Yü, p. 85. Cited from *TWCK-NP* and *TWCK-TK*.

of Liangkiang (Kiangsu, Kiangsi, and Anhwei). When T'ao Chu died in 1839, he requested that Tso be his son's teacher. This son, T'ao Kuang, later became Tso's son-in-law. From 1840 to 1848 he taught in the T'ao family in An-hua, Hunan. One of T'ao Chu's daughters was married to Hu Lin-i, and Tso and Hu, who were of the same age, met and became fast friends. In 1852, on the recommendation of Hu Lin-i, Tso was invited to join the *mu-fu* of Chang Liang-chi, the Governor of Hunan, and was given full responsibility for military affairs. When Chang was transferred in 1853, Tso retired and went home. However in the next year, as a result of an interview with Tseng Kuo-fan, Lo Ping-chang, the new Governor of Hunan, sent for Tso to enter his *mu-fu* as chief military adviser. He served under Lo for five years, but because of his power in the *mu-fu* and his frankness and self-assurance, his colleagues became jealous and, in 1859, brought charges against him of corruptness and unruliness. However, Hu Lin-i came to his rescue and the charges were dropped. Hu Lin-i never lost an opportunity to recommend Tso and often tried to use his influence to get Tseng Kuo-fan to give him a position of command in the field. But Tseng was not keen about using Tso. The two men had such different personalities that Tseng was sure they would clash and, therefore, refused to invite Tso to join his *mu-fu*. Finally in 1860, when Tso had decided to try again for the metropolitan examinations and was on his way to Peking, a letter from Hu Lin-i intercepted him; Hu told Tso that he had been invited to join Tseng's *mu-fu* and that he should proceed to Tseng's camp in Anhwei. The entreaties of Hu Lin-i, the exigencies of the time, and the need for capable personnel had overcome Tseng's personal feelings regarding Tso, and under Tseng's sponsorship he began his rapid rise to fame.[34]

The caliber of Tseng's *mu-yu* was extremely high, which reflected the character of its host. Most of his military commanders were scholars before they became generals. They did not have the spirit of military men, and, in handling their troops, they used *jen* and *li* and treated their junior officers like younger brothers.[35] Tseng himself was a rigid Confucianist, puritanical, and a strict discipli-

[34] Hummel, II, 762; W. L. Bales, *Tso Tsung-t'ang: Soldier and Statesman of Old China* (Shanghai: Kelley and Walsh, 1937), pp. 71, 68, 107, 112, 125.

[35] Hsiao I-shan, *Tseng Kuo-fan chuan* (Biography of Tseng Kuo-fan) (Taipei, Taiwan: Chung-hua wen-hua ch'u-pan shih-yeh wei-yüan-hui ch'u-pan, 1955), p. 188.

narian, but in the sense of a strict father. When speaking of his subordinates, he once said: "During periods of decline, morality is weakened. I am only afraid of being too lenient and certainly am not afraid of being too severe. I constantly cherish the desire to be a father and a teacher. Whether I use punishment or encouragement, I certainly hope that the sons and younger brothers will acquire good names for themselves, and that I can make them become good men."[36]

In the recruitment of "braves," Tseng accepted only villagers, and especially farmers from the hill country. Each recruit had to have a good record in his village, and his family background was recorded in the battalion registers. Tseng established strict regulations in order to insure the proper deportment of his troops. Opium smoking and gambling were forbidden, and attacks on women were considered a capital offense.[37] Tseng also stressed the need for training his troops in the proper use of their weapons, because he felt that one of the main reasons why the Green Standard had failed was because its men had never been properly trained:

If you train one man, then you receive the benefit of one trained man, and if you train for one month, then you have the results of one month's training. . . . I have never heard of our troops [Green Standard] ever having had a bloody battle with them [Taipings]. Usually we only pursue them from the rear, as I have never heard of one battle where we have met them head on. We only use large cannons and fowling pieces to shoot at them from a distance. I have never heard of one case of hand-to-hand fighting or of the use of rifle-butts for infighting. What is the reason for this? Without exception it is because the soldiers have not been trained in the use of their weapons. There is no bravery, and there is no skill with their weapons. Therefore, no matter what they have had to face, the soldiers retreated and were cowards. Now I want to change the situation, and it is best that we consider the training of the soldiers to be the most important item.[38]

After 1860, Tseng Kuo-fan achieved an extremely powerful position, but instead of using this power for his own ends and to the detriment of the central power, he continued to abide by his policy of supporting the imperial government. What Tseng was really

[36] Li Shao-ling, *Tseng Kuo-fan* (Kao-hsiung, Taiwan: Ta-yeh shu-tien, 1955), p. 81.
[37] Powell, p. 24.
[38] Lo Erh-kang, p. 241; *TWCK-TK*, *chüan* 1, p. 22.

supporting was the Confucian way of life, and, since the Manchu rulers were ruling in a Confucian way, they had his support. The Taiping rebels were not Confucian but believed in an aberrant form of Christianity, and, because of this, they were anathema to Tseng. Instead of undermining the center, Tseng worked to achieve the return of the traditionally desired balance between the central and the provincial authority and, in the process, became the link between the court and the local gentry. Through him the gentry could make effective their support of the central government as the protector of their Confucian heritage, and, in reverse order, it was through him that the central government could make itself felt at the local level.[39] Tseng was not a solitary figure who was battling for the preservation of the Confucian order, but merely the most outstanding of many like-minded men. His army and his *mu-fu* were made up of men who considered the war against the Taiping rebels and, later, his policies against the Westerners as the best means of holding together and protecting the Confucian teachings.[40]

Despite his support of the Confucian order and the imperial system, Tseng was enough of a realist to recognize the inefficiency of the bureaucratic structure. He constantly advised his colleagues and subordinates to work out a problem at the local level and on a person-to-person basis. When Tseng had just become the Governor-General of Liangkiang, he wrote to the Kiangsi Governor, Yü K'o, saying: "In regard to the financial matters about which we ought to memorialize, we should be especially careful and use as few memorials as possible. Perhaps the best thing would be for you to draw up a draft letter and send it to me for discussion. Once we have satisfactorily settled things between ourselves, then we can respectfully present just one memorial to the Throne."[41] In another instance, when Tso Tsung-t'ang wished to memorialize to transfer Chiang I-li's army from Kwangsi to Anhwei in order to support Tseng's campaign, Tseng wrote to Tso as follows:

Whether or not Hsiang-ch'üan [Chiang I-li] will be able to come, depends entirely on whether or not the Governor Yin-ch'ü [Liu Ch'ang-yu] is determined to keep him. You and Yin-ch'ü are noble and firm friends (*tao-i chin-shih chih chiao*). If you can settle this matter through personal letters, then you need only send in one memorial to settle it. This is by far the

[39] Mary C. Wright, pp. 57–58.          [40] Hsiao I-shan, p. 187.
[41] Lo Erh-kang, p. 246. Cited from *Tseng Wen-cheng-kung shu-cha, chüan* 12.

best way to handle it. Otherwise, even though you received an imperial decree granting you permission, it would not be of any use, as long as Mr. Yin refused to permit it. Last year I memorialized to transfer Hsiao's army and, as a result, almost created a great deal of ill-will. Let this be an example for you.[42]

The upshot of this letter was that Tso followed Tseng's advice, and, by writing to Liu Ch'ang-yu as a close friend, he was able to get him to release Chiang I-li and his army. Tseng Kuo-fan had previously tried through official channels to force Liu into releasing these troops but had failed.[43]

The above incident indicates that Tseng's position after 1860 was not one of supremacy but rather one of *primus inter pares*. The generals and governors all considered their armies as their personal possessions and guarded them jealously. The same was also true of their source of supply. In the beginning of the T'ung-chih reign (1862–1875), Tseng Kuo-fan and Shen Pao-chen, the Governor of Kiangsi, carried on a running feud through the medium of memorials to the throne over the matter of provisions for their troops.[44] The court's position in relation to these feuds was two-fold. On the one hand, it assumed the role of mediator, rather than exercise its power of decision and risk losing the services of either party by antagonizing it. On the other hand, one has the feeling that the court was apprehensive of the growing regional power and that in order to control it, it even fostered these local feuds as a part of its policy of divide and rule. In view of the power and jealousy of the provincial leaders and the attitude of the court, imperial decrees were of little use in getting things done. What really kept the wheels turning was the use of intimate friendship (*chiao-i*).[45]

In addition to making the military an important part of the *mu-fu* system, a phenomenon which was new in the Ch'ing period but in reality only a reversion to an earlier condition in Chinese history, Tseng Kuo-fan practiced the custom of nourishing scholars. Compared with the *mu-fu* of a district magistrate or of a *chou* prefect, as described in Chapter II above, Tseng's *mu-fu* was more like those of the Han period in which there were collected all types of learned personnel. Yet, it was the character of the host which set

[42] Lo Erh-kang, p. 247. Cited from *Tseng Wen-cheng-kung shu-cha, chüan* 13.
[43] Lo Erh-kang, p. 247.
[44] *Ibid.*, p. 246.                       [45] *Ibid.*, p. 248.

the tenor of the *mu-fu*. As *The Doctrine of the Mean* says, "the administration of government lies in getting proper men. Such men are to be got by means of the ruler's own character. That character is to be cultivated by his treading in the ways of duty. And the treading those ways of duty is to be cultivated by the cherishing of benevolence."[46] It was Tseng's high Confucian character, his official position, his love of scholars and learning, and his interest in the methods of self-strengthening that drew to his *mu-fu* the outstanding men of his era. On the occasion of his interview with Tseng in 1863, Yung Wing has this to say about Tseng's *mu-fu*:

There were living in his military headquarters at least two hundred officials, gathered there from all parts of the Empire, for various objects and purposes. Besides his secretaries, who numbered no less than a hundred, there were expectant officials, learned scholars, lawyers, mathematicians, astronomers and machinists; in short, the picked and noted men of China were all drawn there by the magnetic force of his character and great name. He always had a great admiration for men of distinguished learning and talents and loved to associate and mingle with them.[47]

The existence of this type of *mu-fu* was not peculiar to Tseng Kuo-fan. Earlier in the Ch'ing, powerful provincial officials, such as Pi Yüan (1729–1797),[48] Chu Yün (1729–1780),[49] and Jüan Yüan (1764–1849),[50] had been fond of scholars and had gathered them into their *mu-fu*;[51] but Tseng had the power and influence after 1860, as well as the character, to develop his *mu-fu* into something really unique. In the waning days of the Ch'ing, other great men, such as Li Hung-chang and Chang Chih-tung, would be famous for their *mu-fu*, but theirs would follow a slightly different pattern and never attain such a noble stature.

The range of activities carried on in Tseng's *mu-fu* was wide and varied, with room for both the utilitarian and the scholarly. In an age of turmoil, cruelty and slaughter, self-sacrifice and soul-

[46] James Legge, *The Chinese Classics* (Taiwan reprint, 1962), I, 405.
[47] Yung Wing, *My Life in China and America* (New York: Henry Holt and Co., 1909), p. 148.
[48] Herbert A. Giles, *A Chinese Biographical Dictionary* (Taiwan reprint, 1962), II, 627.
[49] *Ibid.*, I, 194.
[50] *Ibid.*, II, 976.
[51] Ch'üan Tseng-yu, "Ch'ing-tai mu-liao chih-tu lun" (On the *Mu-liao* System of the Ch'ing Period), *Ssu-hsiang yü shih-tai yüeh-k'an*, No. 32 (March, 1944), p. 37.

searching, his *mu-yu* were called upon to exert themselves to the limit of their capabilities. Secretaries toiled around the clock to keep up with the flow of despatches,[52] and the strain took its toll in illness and death.[53] Relief of the human miseries occasioned by battles, famines, pestilence, and floods tested the ingenuity of his *mu-yu*,[54] as did the collecting of revenues and the weeding out of corrupt officials.[55] In his struggle to shore up a tottering world, Tseng was also concerned with the minds of men and actively supported the scholarly pursuits which were so vital to the Confucian ideal. His *mu-yu* prepared new editions of the *Classics* and the *Histories*,[56] which were published by Tseng's own book stores.[57] They also carried on the custom of joining with their host for informal and leisurely literary get-togethers.[58] His military *mu-yu* were called upon not only to train and command troops in the field, but also to solicit funds for the support of the army,[59] to organize, recruit, and construct ships for his inland navy,[60] to arrange for supplies and equipment, and to handle the voluminous paper work involved in running a major military operation.[61] Despite the press of work, which forced some *mu-yu* to hire their own *mu-yu*,[62] Tseng was still a Confucianist and included within the scope of his organization room for guests, who were not assigned any specific duties or responsibilities but could come and go as they chose.[63]

A roster of Tseng's principal *mu-yu* and their general areas of responsibility was as follows: In administrative affairs there were Li Tsung-hsi, Hung Ju-k'uei, Chao Lieh-wen, Ho Ching, Ni Wen-wei, Fang Tsung-ch'eng, and Hsiao Shih-pen. His writers were Hsü Chen-wei, Lo Hsüan, Ch'eng Hung-chao, K'o Yüeh, Hsiang Shih-ti, Sun I-yen, and Li Shu-ch'ang. For strategy Tseng relied on Kuo

[52] Yü, pp. 55–56. Cited from *Ch'ing-shih lieh-chuan*, Hsü Chen-wei chuan.
[53] Yü, p. 88. Cited from *TWCK-NP*, p. 97.
[54] Yü, p. 84. Cited from *Pei-chuan chi pu*, *chüan* 26, pp. 109–110; from *Ch'ing-shih lieh-chuan*, Li Hsing-jui chuan, p. 112; and from *TWCK-NP*.
[55] Yü, p. 79. Cited from *Yang-chün Li-shu hsing-shu*, pp. 87–88; and from *Ch'ing shih-kao*, Wang K'ai-yün chuan.
[56] Yü, p. 88. Cited from *Kan-ch'üan-hsiang jen kao ching shih fu-chün nien-p'u*.
[57] Yü, p. 96.
[58] *Ibid.*, pp. 98–99. Cited from *Pei-chuan chi pu*, *chüan* 51.
[59] Yü, p. 48. Cited from *Kuo Sung-t'ao shen-tao-pei*.
[60] Yü, pp. 48–50.
[61] *Ibid.*, p. 89. Cited from *Pei-chuan chi pu*, *chüan* 18.
[62] Yü, p. 94. Cited from *Hsü pei-chuan chi*, *chüan* 75.
[63] Yü, p. 58. Cited from *Lo Ju-huai mu-chih-ming*.

Sung-t'ao, Tso Tsung-t'ang, Ch'en Shih-chieh, Li Hung-chang, Li Hung-i, Ch'ien Ying-p'u, and Hsüeh Fu-ch'eng. In his navy he had P'eng Yü-lin and Yang Tsai-fu, and in his army there were Li Yüan-tu, T'ang Hsün-fang, Li Jung, Wu K'un-hsiu, and Huang Jun-ch'ang. To take care of military supplies there were Li Han-chang, Kan Chin, Kuo K'un-t'ao, and Li Hsing-jui. Wu Min-shu, Mo Yu-chih, Ch'en Ai, Yü Yüeh, Tai Wang, Wu Ju-lun, Chang Yü-chao, T'ang Jen-shou, and Liu Yü-sung were all engaged in literary pursuits, and Li Shan-lan, Hsü Shou, Hua Heng-fang, Feng Tsun-kuang, Ch'en Lan-pin, and Jung Hung devoted their energies to matters of self-strengthening.[64]

The problem of suppressing the Taiping rebels occupied most of Tseng Kuo-fan's attention until 1864, but as early as 1862 he began to devote some time to the question of how to strengthen the country in order to ward off the invasion of the West. His diary for June 3, 1862, records the following statement to his *mu-yu*: "If we wish to find a method of self-strengthening, we should begin by considering the reform of government service and the securing of men of ability as urgent tasks, and then regard learning to make explosive shells and steamships and other instruments as the work of first importance."[65] Tseng's plan was to use the weapons and scientific techniques of the West to strengthen the military power of the country. In keeping with this aim, he collected in his *mu-fu* those Chinese who were trained in Western mathematics, physical sciences, geography, and diplomacy, and who could establish and run machine shops, arsenals, and training schools.[66] His two greatest projects were the establishment of the Kiangnan Arsenal in 1865 and the Chinese Educational Mission. In both of these endeavors, Jung Hung, or as he is more commonly known, Yung Wing, played an important role.

Yung Wing began his Western education as a boy in the Morrison School in Macao and then went on to become, in 1854, the first Chinese to graduate from Yale University. He returned to China in the same year, but it was not until 1863 that the value of his

[64] Yü, pp. 117–118.

[65] Teng Ssu-yü and John K. Fairbank, *China's Response to the West, A Documentary Survey, 1839–1923* (Cambridge: Harvard Univ. Press, 1954), p. 62. Quoted from *Tseng Wen-cheng-kung shou-shu jih-chi, ts'e,* 13.

[66] Yü, p. 96. Cited from *TWCK-NP,* pp. 107, 108; from *Pei-chuan chi pu, chüan* 75, p. 109; and from *Ch'ing ch'i-pai ming-jen chuan.*

education was recognized by the Chinese authorities. In that year he was invited by two of his friends, Chang Ssu-kuei and Li Shan-lan, who were in Tseng's *mu-fu*, to present a plan to Tseng for the introduction of Western machinery into China. He was commissioned by Tseng to go to America to buy machinery for what subsequently became the Kiangnan Arsenal. For his efforts he was made an official of the 5th rank and soon after, in 1867, was decorated with the Peacock Feather and raised to the 4th rank. One of Yung Wing's favorite ideas was to send young Chinese boys to the United States for a period of ten years to acquire a technical education as a means of introducing Western technology into China. In 1870, with the aid of Ting Jih-ch'ang, who had befriended him and taken him to Tientsin as a *mu-yu* to help in the settlement of the Tientsin Massacre, his ideas were presented to Tseng, who had also been thinking along these lines. Tseng, with the aid of Li Hung-chang, perfected the details of the plan and presented it to the throne in 1871. The plan, known as the Chinese Educational Mission, was approved, and the first students sailed for America in the summer of 1872. The group was under the supervision of Ch'en Lan-pin, who had been a member of Tseng's *mu-fu* since 1869, with Yung Wing as his assistant.[67] Yung Wing was the first of the "returned students" who was forced to rely on service as a *mu-yu* in order to break into the ranks of officialdom because his foreign education had not prepared him for the traditional examinations.

The privilege of recommendation was the device by which such *mu-yu* were able to become officials. This was especially true during and after the Taiping Rebellion, when the situation in China called for a type of personnel that the examination system could not provide. Tseng Kuo-fan used this privilege to recommend many of his *mu-yu* for official position, and, because of his importance to the regime, his noble reputation, and a shortage of qualified personnel, even for civil administrative positions, his recommendations were usually granted. Many of the people he recommended, such as P'eng Yü-lin, Kuo Sung-t'ao, and Li Hung-chang, already held literary degrees, but had chosen to enter his *mu-fu* as a more tangible means not only of serving the country but also of achieving quick promotion.

Tseng Kuo-fan left to Ch'ing China a legacy of personal armies

67 Hummel, I, 402.

as well as a large group of capable men, many of them scholars whom he had nourished, who continued to support the throne after his death. In 1871, just a year before his death, of the ten governors-general in China, the highest provincial rank, three were graduates of his *mu-fu*: Li Hung-chang in Chihli, Tso Tsung-t'ang in Kansu and Shensi, and Li Han-chang in Hunan and Hupeh. He himself was the Liangkiang Governor-General.[68] In addition, the subsequent achievements of the eighty-four members of Tseng's *mu-fu*, as listed by Hsüeh Fu-ch'eng, included several governors and taotais, as well as prefects, magistrates, censors, presidents and vice-presidents of the Six Boards, provincial judges and treasurers, members of the Hanlin Academy, and foreign ambassadors.[69]

Of all the graduates of Tseng Kuo-fan's *mu-fu*, probably the most powerful and the most widely known in the Western world was Li Hung-chang. Li had played an active role in the establishment of the Kiangnan Arsenal and the Chinese Educational Mission, and it was he who carried on and developed Tseng's "self-strengthening" policies. Li also incorporated Tseng's military policies into his own army, the *Huai-chün*, which acted as the principal link between the personal armies of the nineteenth century and those of the twentieth. The relationship between Tseng and Li is a representative manifestation of the personal element in Chinese government and society, and it also serves as an illlustration of the effect that the *mu-fu* system had on the course of late Ch'ing history.

[68] *Ch'ing-tai cheng-hsien lei-pien* (Taipei, Taiwan: Shih-chieh shu-chü, 1961), *shang*, Tsung-tu nien-piao, *chüan* 3, p. 8b.
[69] Hsüeh, "Hsü Tseng Wen-cheng-kung mu-fu pin-liao," pp. 131 ff.

# IV. Tseng Kuo-fan and Li Hung-chang

"On the night of the 12th [March 20, 1872] I received an urgent report from the Provincial Commander-in-Chief Huang that my teacher's [Tseng Kuo-fan] headaches had reoccurred, but that after several days of nursing his health, he had recovered. However, on the 4th day of the 2nd month [March 12, 1872], after finishing a game of chess, he went for a stroll in the garden and summer house, and suddenly died." This description of Tseng's death is from a letter of condolence which Li Hung-chang wrote to Tseng's two sons, Chi-kang (Chi-tse) and Li-hsien (Chi-hung), on March 24, 1872. In the same letter Li also reviewed his long and intimate association with Tseng. "I followed him for almost thirty years. It seems that among all of his disciples, I was the first to receive his instruction and received it the most extensively. I was also the most intimate with him."[1]

Li Hung-chang's relationship with Tseng Kuo-fan was based on his being the son of one of Tseng's classmates (*nien-chia-tzu*). Li's father, Li Wen-an, and Tseng were both *chin-shih* of *wu-shü* (1838).[2] The affinity created by such a relationship was in itself, however, not necessarily enough to produce such a close friendship. It was only when Li became Tseng's student that the relationship began to flower into an association that was to last for "almost thirty years."

---

[1] Li Hung-chang, *Li Wen-chung-kung ch'üan-chi* (The Complete Works of Li Hung-chang), ed. by Wu Ju-lun (Nanking, 1908), P'eng-liao han-kao (Letters to Friends and Colleagues), *chüan* 12, pp. 5a–b (hereafter cited as LWCK-PL).

[2] Ch'üan Tseng-yu, "Ch'ing-tai mu-liao chih-tu lun" (On the *Mu-liao* System of the Ch'ing Period), *Ssu-hsiang yü shih-tai yüeh-k'an*, No. 31 (Feb., 1944), p. 34; Wu Ju-lun, "Li Wen-chung-kung mu-chih-ming" (Li Hung-chang's Tomb Inscription), *in Li Wen-chung-kung ch'üan-chi*, chüan-shou, p. 67b; Fang Chao-ying and Tu Lien-che, *Tseng-chiao Ch'ing-ch'ao chin-shih t'i-ming pei-lu* (A Ranking of the *Chin-shih* of the Ch'ing Dynasty), Harvard-Yenching Institute Sinological Index Series, Supplement No. 19 (Peiping: Harvard-Yenching Institute, 1941), p. 170.

Just how early in Li's career he became Tseng's student is not clear. As far as we know, Li did not visit Peking prior to 1843 or 1844, and, as Tseng had remained in the capital after he passed the *chin-shih* examinations in 1838, there would have been little opportunity for the two men to have met before that date. Undoubtedly, Li's father had written to his son about Tseng, and Li must have been well aware of Tseng's connections with his father before he arrived in Peking. Therefore, it is reasonable to assume that when Li did arrive in the capital, he had Tseng in mind as a possible teacher. The most widely accepted and authoritative source on this question is the *Tseng Wen-cheng-kung nien-p'u* (Biographical Sketch of Tseng Kuo-fan), which states that Li Hung-chang arrived in the capital in 1844 (*chia-ch'en*) after having passed the examination for the *chü-jen* degree, and that in the same year he became Tseng's disciple.[3] Despite the authenticity of this source, Li's own writings would appear to place the date a year earlier, in 1843. In the *Li Wen-chung-kung i-chi* (Posthumous Collection of the Writings of Li Hung-chang), there is a poem by Li entitled "Entering the Capital," which is dated 1843 (*kuei-mao*). In this poem he describes his feelings and ambitions on entering Peking for the first time.[4] Shortly after he entered the capital, Li must have become Tseng's student because in 1863, in a letter to Tseng, he said, "For twenty years I have been your disciple."[5] Assuming that Li went to Peking in 1843, then he did so as a senior licentiate (*yu-kung*) and not as a *chü-jen*.[6] He passed the former examination in 1843 and then became a provincial graduate in 1844.[7] For men of his rank,

[3] Tseng Kuo-fan, *Tseng Wen-cheng-kung ch'üan-chi* (The Complete Works of Tseng Kuo-fan) (Taipei, Taiwan: Shih-chieh shu-chü, 1952), Nien-p'u, p. 6 (hereafter cited as *TWCK-NP*); U.S. Library of Congress, Asiatic Division, *Eminent Chinese of the Ch'ing Period (1644–1912)*, ed. by Arthur W. Hummel (Washington, D.C.: U.S. Gov't Printing Office, 1943), I, 464 (hereafter cited as Hummel), corroborates this statement, but the evidence seems to come from Li Shu-ch'un, "Li Wen-chung-kung Hung-chang nien-p'u" (A Chronological Biography of Li Hung-chang), *Shih-hsüeh nien-pao*, No. 1 (July, 1929), p. 100, which in turn appears to be based on the account in *TWCK-NP*.

[4] Li Hung-chang, *Li Wen-chung-kung i-chi* (Posthumous Collection of the Writings of Li Hung-chang) in Li Kuo-chieh, ed., *Ho-fei Li shih san shih i-chi* ([no place]: The Li Family of Ho-fei, 1904), chüan 6, p. 1b (hereafter referred to as *LWCK-IC*).

[5] *LWCK-PL*, chüan 3, p. 23a. Letter to Tseng Kuo-fan, dated May 30, 1863.

[6] Wei Hsi-yü, *Li Hung-chang* (Shanghai: Chung-hua shu-chü, 1931), p. 1. This account states that Li was a senior licentiate when he entered the capital.

[7] Huang Yün-hsiu, *Hsü-hsiu Lu-chou fu-chih* (Revised edition of the Lu-chou Prefecture Gazetteer) (1885), chüan 31, p. 10a; Mrs. Archibald Little, *Li*

however, it was possible to take the latter examination in the capital.[8] Although the evidence is not conclusive, it would appear that Li became Tseng's student and was in close association with him shortly after he arrived in Peking in 1843, at the age of twenty.[9]

During his pre-*chin-shih* years in Peking, Li followed Tseng Kuo-fan as his master in order to study government and to improve his literary knowledge.[10] When Li became a *chin-shih* in 1847, however, his status gap, in relation to Tseng, narrowed, especially since he also became a member of the Hanlin Academy. Tseng was a Hanlin, and therefore the two men in theory became colleagues. Nevertheless, the student-teacher relationship remained, and he continued to seek instruction from Tseng.[11] This relationship existed for the next five years until 1852, when Tseng was sent to Kiangsi to supervise the provincial examinations. In the 2nd month (March 10–April 7) of the following year, Li also left the capital, returning to his native place, Ho-fei, Anhwei, to train local militia units. With both men away from Peking and engaged in militia operations in different provinces, their close association terminated, and there was little communication between them.[12] However, Tseng did not forget Li, and in 1853 he recommended him to Chiang Chung-yüan, the Governor of Anhwei and old friend of Tseng's, as "a useful man of talent"; he requested that Chiang use him in an administrative capacity and in the conduct of military affairs.[13] At the same

*Hung-Chang. His Life and Time* (London: Cassell and Company, Ltd., 1903), p. 5. Mrs. Little states that Li passed the provincial examination in Peking, but she places this event in 1845. She seems to be a year off in her dating in that she says he became a *chin-shih* in 1848, when in reality it was 1847 (see Fang and Tu, p. 178).

8 Chang Chung-li, *The Chinese Gentry: Studies on Their Role in Nineteenth-Century Chinese Society* (Seattle: Univ. of Washington Press, 1955), p. 21.

9 In Li Hung-chang, *Li Hung-chang chia-shu* (The Family Letters of Li Hung-chang) (Shanghai: Chung-yang shu-tien, 1934), p. 13, there is a letter in which Li told his mother how he became Tseng's student. This letter is not dated, but internal evidence points to the year 1843. However, the authenticity of this volume is suspect and, therefore, cannot be relied upon.

10 Hsüeh Fu-ch'eng, "Li Fu-hsiang ju Tseng Wen-cheng-kung mu-fu" (Li Hung-chang Enters Tseng Kuo-fan's *Mu-fu*), in Tso Shun-sheng, comp., *Chung-kuo chin-pai-nien shih tzu-liao ch'u-pien* (Taipei, Taiwan: Chung-hua shu-chü, 1958), p. 160.

11 *Ibid.*

12 *Ibid.*; Huang Yün-hsiu, *chüan* 96, p. 2a.

13 Stanley Spector, "Li Hung-chang and the Huai-chün" (unpublished Ph.D. Dissertation, University of Washington, 1953), p. 11. Cited from *Tseng Wen-cheng-kung shu-cha* (1945 edition), *chüan* 4, pp. 20a–b; Wu Ju-lun, "Li Wen-

time Tseng informed Li's elder brother, Han-chang, of this recommendation and said that he considered Li Hung-chang as "one of the four talented men of the *ting-wei* year [1847]," and, of those four, "the only one who had had an opportunity to demonstrate his ability." [14]

Tseng Kuo-fan's ties with the Li family of Ho-fei were not severed by his separation from Li Hung-chang. The close connection was resumed in 1853 when Li Han-chang, the eldest of the Li brothers, entered Tseng's *mu-fu* and was put in charge of supplies for the *Hsiang-chün*.[15] In the 29th year of Tao-kuang (1849), Li Han-chang had been selected as a senior licentiate of the first degree (*pa-kung-sheng*) at one of the special examinations given every twelve years, and for the next four years he had served as a Magistrate in various districts in Hunan.[16] When the Taiping rebels attacked Ch'ang-sha in 1853, Han-chang had commanded troops in the defense of the city under the direction of the Governor, Lo Ping-chang, and was rewarded with the 7th official rank. It was shortly after this that Tseng Kuo-fan summoned him to join his *mu-fu*.[17]

For the next nine years, Li Han-chang served in various supply capacities with the *Hsiang-chün*. When the army left Hunan in 1854 to campaign in Hupeh, he was in charge of the commissariat.[18] During the Kiangsi campaign in 1855, he and Kan Chin were in charge of the supply station.[19] In the 5th month of the 5th year of Hsien-feng (June 14–July 13, 1855), when Han-chang's father died, Tseng Kuo-fan memorialized to retain him with the army rather than permit him to go into mourning, and it was granted.[20] In 1858, when Tseng established the supply bureau in Hu-k'ou (see Chapter III),

chung-kung shen-tao-pei," *in Li Wen-chung-kung ch'üan-chi*, chüan-shou, p. 62a.

[14] Spector, p. 11. Cited from *Tseng Wen-cheng-kung shu-cha* (1945 ed.), *chüan* 4, pp. 35b–36a. *Ting-wei* was the year Li received his *chin-shih* degree.

[15] *Ch'ing-shih lieh-chuan* (Taipei, Taiwan: Chung-hua shu-chü, 1962), *chüan* 59, p. 23b.

[16] *Ibid.*; Chang Chung-li, pp. 27–28.

[17] *Ch'ing-shih lieh-chuan*, *chüan* 59, p. 23b; Chang Chung-li, pp. 27–28.

[18] Yü Yü-ti "Tseng Kuo-fan mu-fu pin-liao nien-p'u" (A Chronological Record of Tseng Kuo-fan's *Mu-fu* and Its Members) (unpublished Bachelor's Thesis, National Taiwan University, Taipei, Taiwan, 1960), p. 16. Cited from *Ching-shih lieh-chuan*, *chüan* 59.

[19] Yü, p. 56. Cited from *Tseng Kuo-fan nien-p'u* and *Ch'ing-shih lieh-chuan*, *chüan* 59.

[20] *Ch'ing-shih lieh-chuan*, *chüan* 59, p. 23b.

Li Han-chang was placed in charge,[21] and in 1860 Tseng recommended that he manage the *likin* affairs for Kiangsi, which he did.[22]

Between 1853 and 1859 while Li Han-chang was serving in Tseng's *mu-fu*, his younger brother, Li Hung-chang, was in Anhwei engaged in campaigning with militia against the Taiping rebels. Although Li Hung-chang had achieved a certain degree of success and had acquired considerable military experience, his overwhelming confidence in his own abilities made serving in what he considered petty positions and under incompetent superiors, who failed to recognize his true worth, very galling. He sought to rejoin Tseng whom he respected and whom he knew would appreciate his talents. "In the 8th year of Hsien-feng, the 12th month [January 4–February 2, 1859], I again began to follow the teacher [Tseng Kuo-fan] in Kiangsi." So wrote Li Hung-chang after Tseng's death.[23] The events surrounding this reunion, as described by Hsüeh Fu-ch'eng, throw additional light on the relationship between the two men.

Li Hung-chang had been serving in a military capacity in the *mu-fu* of Fu-chi, the Governor of Anhwei, but was discontent with his policies. Thus, late in 1858, he resigned and set out to join Tseng Kuo-fan.[24] He felt that Tseng would certainly remember an old friend and use him. Arriving at Tseng's headquarters in Kiangsi, however, he met with a cold reception. After waiting a month to see Tseng, he asked his classmate, Ch'en Nai, who had recently joined Tseng's *mu-fu*, to intercede for him. Ch'en and Li were both *ting-wei chin-shih* and former members of the Hanlin Academy. Ch'en went to Tseng and said, "'In former years Shao-ch'üan [Li Hung-chang] was an old friend, and now he wants to serve you in order to benefit from the experience.' Tseng replied, 'It is true that Shao-ch'üan is a Hanlin, and that his ambition is great and his talents are exceptional. However, this place is narrowly confined. I fear that such a large warship could not be contained by such shallow waters. Why doesn't he return to the capital and resume his duties?' Ch'en Nai said, 'Shao-ch'üan has experienced many ordeals. His present attitude cannot be compared with that of former years. Why not be lenient and try him?' Tseng promised he

21 William James Hail, *Tseng Kuo-fan and the Taiping Rebellion* (New Haven: Yale Univ. Press, 1927), pp. 208–209.

22 Yü, p. 76. Cited from *Ch'ing-shih lieh-chuan, chüan* 59.

23 *LWCK-PL, chüan* 12, p. 6b.

24 Hummel, I, 464.

would do so, and Li came to live in the *mu-fu*."[25] Tseng had purposely let Li "cool his heels" in order to chasten him and make him control his arrogance.[26]

On entering Tseng's *mu-fu*, Li at first was put in charge of the clerks. Later he rose to the position of correcting drafts and drafting memorials. Several months after this, Tseng is reported to have said to him: "Shao-ch'üan, you have a special talent for writing public documents. Your memorials, despatches, letters, and criticisms are far better than those of other men. In the future your fate will not be common. Perhaps you have already surpassed your master; however we still cannot tell."[27]

It was the custom in Tseng's *mu-fu* for all the members to join with him at dawn to eat breakfast. However, the customs of the Chiang-nan-pei region, where Li came from, and those of Hunan were different, and Li was not used to eating so early and did not like to do so. One day, rather than get up for breakfast, he made the excuse of having a headache. However, after a short time, Tseng sent a guard to tell him to come. After a further wait, another servant came and said to Li that all the *mu-liao* must be present before they could start eating. Li threw on some clothes in a hurry and went to join them. "Tseng did not say a word all through the meal, but when he had finished eating, he set aside his chopsticks, composed himself, and then said to Li, 'Shao-ch'üan, ever since you entered my *mu-fu*, I have sought to instruct you. In this place, the one word which we esteem is "honesty," and that is all.' There was nothing more to be said, and they dispersed. Li was surprised, somewhat afraid, and angry."[28]

Li's duties in Tseng's *mu-fu* were not solely confined to writing memorials. In the 5th month of the 9th year of Hsien-feng (June 1–29, 1859), he accompanied Tseng's brother, Tseng Kuo-ch'üan, as a military adviser in the attack and capture of Ching-te-chen.[29] When Tseng was made the Liangkiang Governor-General in 1860 and shifted his headquarters to Ch'i-men, Anhwei, Li disputed the move with him on the basis of military strategy. He said that the geogra-

[25] Hsüeh, "Li Fu-hsiang ju Tseng Wen-cheng-kung mu-fu," pp. 160–161.
[26] Yü, p. 69. Cited fom *Tseng Kuo-fan nien-p'u.*
[27] Hsüeh, "Li Fu-hsiang ju Tseng Wen-cheng-kung mu-fu," p. 161.
[28] *Ibid.*
[29] Li Shu-ch'un, p. 103; Yü, p. 71 (cited from *Tseng Kuo-fan nien-p'u*); Hail, p. 213.

phy of the area made it strategically dangerous as it was like being at the "bottom of a cauldron," with no chance of advancing or retreating. When Tseng did not heed his advice, he continued to argue the point. Tseng finally said that if he was afraid, he could resign.[30] However, in the next month (7th month, August 17–September 14), when Tseng proposed to establish a naval force in the Huai-yang area in order to support the land forces and, at the same time, to protect the rice and salt-producing area north of the Yangtze, he recommended that Li be given command of the force with the official position of Liang-huai Salt Commissioner (*Liang-huai yen-yün-shih*). The fact that Li was from the Huai area was, no doubt, a major factor in Tseng's recommending him for the position. In his recommendation he also said, "Li, having great talent and a careful sense of responsibility, is qualified to be entrusted with the duties of a governorship." The proposal, however, came to nought.[31]

By 1861, Li had been serving in Tseng's *mu-fu* for almost two years, and during this time there seems to have been almost constant tension between the two men. Although Li was the disciple and Tseng the master, Li seemed to rebel against his inferior position. He was a Hanlin, as was Tseng, had had a good deal of military experience, was talented, and, above all, was arrogant and ambitious. He continually disputed Tseng's decisions and acted as though he was Tseng's equal rather than his subordinate. Tseng's disciplinary measures and attempts to mold him into a more stable personality, no doubt, also rankled Li. The situation came to a head over the defeat of Li Yüan-tu at Hui-chou, Anhwei, in the 12th month of the 10th year of Hsien-feng (January 11–February 9, 1861).

Li Yüan-tu, a *chü-jen* of 1843 from Chekiang, was serving as a District Director of Schools (*chiao-yü*) in Hunan when Tseng began to establish the *Hsiang-chün* in 1853. He was invited to join Tseng's *mu-fu* and was put in charge of planning military affairs.[32] When Tseng suffered defeats in 1855, it was Yüan-tu who, according to some accounts, dissuaded him from committing suicide.[33] Early in 1861, he was in charge of the defense of Hui-chou and had

30 Hsüeh, "Li Fu-hsiang ju Tseng Wen-cheng-kung mu-fu," p. 161.

31 Wu Wei-p'ing, "The Rise of the Anhwei Army," Harvard University, Center for East Asian Studies, *Papers on China*, Vol. 14, pp. 32–33, cited from *Tseng Wen-cheng-kung tsou-kao* 14:25; Li Shu-ch'un, p. 103.

32 Yü, p. 10. Cited from *Ch'ing-shih lieh-chüan* and *Hsü-pei chuan-chi, chüan* 39.

33 Yü, p. 55.

been ordered by Tseng not to leave the city to attack the rebels. In defiance of these orders, he left the city, was defeated, and Hui-chou fell into the hands of the enemy. For awhile no one knew whether Yüan-tu was dead or alive, but when he finally appeared at Tseng's camp and then left before an investigation could be held, Tseng, the Confucian moralist and disciplinarian, intended to impeach him. Li Hung-chang went to Tseng, when he heard of Tseng's intentions, and tried to dissuade him. He pointed out Tseng's long and close association with Li Yüan-tu, the hardships they had suffered together, how Yüan-tu had stood beside him in times of adversity, and ended by saying, "'If you really must impeach him, I do not dare draw up the draft.' Tseng said, 'I myself will undertake the draft.' Li said, 'If this is the case, then I also will take my leave, and am not able to stay and serve you.' Tseng said, 'I await your convenience.'" Thereupon Li Hung-chang resigned from the *mu-fu* and went to Kiangsi.[34]

What Li Hung-chang did in Kiangsi remains a mystery, but about eight months later, when Li heard that Tseng's forces had recaptured An-ch'ing (September 5, 1861), he wrote to Tseng to congratulate him on the victory. Tseng wrote him, in reply, that if there was nothing to keep him in Kiangsi, then he could come to An-ch'ing, where Tseng had set up his headquarters. Li thereupon packed up and left Kiangsi. On his arrival at Tseng's headquarters he was invited to rejoin the *mu-fu*. It was a chastened Li that went to work for Tseng, and from then on there was a greater intimacy and feeling of respect between the two men.[35]

On November 18, 1861, Tseng Kuo-fan received a delegation in An-ch'ing from the beleaguered merchants and Soochow gentry in Shanghai begging for military aid. Feng Kuei-fen, a noted Soochow scholar, had written a letter, which the delegation presented to Tseng, outlining the strategic advantages of Kiangsu as a major base of operations against the Taiping rebels. Taking this recommendation into consideration, Tseng decided not only to send Tso Tsung-t'ang with an army to Chekiang to be the southern flank but also to establish another army for the recovery of Kiangsu. The new army was entrusted to Li Hung-chang, who was at that time in charge of a section of the naval forces on the Yangtze. Tseng asked Li to return

34 Hsüeh, "Li Fu-hsiang ju Tseng Wen-cheng-kung mu-fu," pp. 161–162.
35 *Ibid.*, p. 162.

to his native area, the Huai-nan region of Anhwei, to recruit the new army, which eventually came to be known as the *Huai-chün*.[36]

While the above matter was under consideration, Tseng had received an order from the court on December 15, 1861 to investigate the capabilities of the governors of Kiangsu and Chekiang Provinces. In his reply, which was dated December 26, 1861, Tseng said that neither of the two men was qualified and, in an appended note, guaranteed and recommended Li Hung-chang for the post of Kiangsu Governor; he pointed out that Li had "great talent and a careful mind," as well as "a strong spirit," and was "internally composed."[37] Tseng had originally intended to recommend Shen Pao-chen, a classmate of Li's for the post, but his lack of military experience caused Tseng to suggest Li instead.[38] The exigencies of the times made it almost imperative that the real command of the provincial military forces and the supreme provincial civil authority reside in one person. As commander of the *Huai-chün*, which would be operating in Kiangsu, Li would not have to contend with the problems of conflicting authority and clashing personalities if he also was the Governor of Kiangsu. Wherever possible, Tseng seems to have tried to unify authority in order to forestall the divisiveness experienced by the Green Standard.

When Li Hung-chang returned to An-ch'ing on February 22, 1862 with his newly recruited Anhwei army, he set to work to train and organize his troops along the lines of the *Hsiang-chün*,[39] and several battalions of the Hunan army were detailed by Tseng to help in the training. Tseng also assigned two of his generals, Ch'eng Hsüeh-ch'i and Kuo Sung-lin, with their armies to Li's command. By the end of March, the main force of the army was ready to head down river to Shanghai. The original plan had been for the *Huai-chün*, accompanied by Tseng Kuo-ch'üan's army, to fight its way to Shanghai, but the need for the army in Shanghai was felt to be so

---

[36] Wu Wei-p'ing, p. 32; *TWCK-NP*, p. 88; *LWCK, chüan shou*, p. 12b.

[37] *TWCK-TK*, pp. 436–437; *TWCK-NP*, p. 89; Hsüeh, "Li Fu-hsiang ju Tseng Wen-cheng-kung mu-fu," p. 162.

[38] Hsüeh Fu-ch'eng, "Shu Ho-fei po-hsiang Li-kung yung Hu p'ing Wu" (How Li Hung-chang Used Shanghai to Pacify Soochow) *in* Tso Shun-sheng, comp., *Chung-kuo chin-pai-nien shih tzu-liao ch'u-pien* (Taipei, Taiwan: Chung-hua shu-chü, 1958), p. 164.

[39] Hail, p. 242; Li Chien-nung, *The Political History of China, 1840–1928*, transl. and ed. by Teng Ssu-yü and J. Ingalls (Princeton: D. Van Nostrand Company, Inc., 1956), p. 77.

urgent that seven foreign steamers were hired by the Shanghai gentry, and the entire army was carried down river in three trips during the month of April. On April 28, 1862, Li Hung-chang received his long-expected formal appointment as the Acting Governor of Kiangsu.[40]

Now that Li had been given an official position, he was no longer considered a member of Tseng's *mu-fu*. However, as the Governor of Kiangsu he was subordinate to Tseng, who, as the Liangkiang Governor-General, had jurisdiction over Anhwei, Kiangsi, and Kiangsu provinces. The student-teacher relationship, nevertheless, continued to exist between the two men, and they operated in close association. In the letters that flowed back and forth between Shanghai and An-ch'ing, they discussed military strategy, financial measures, procurement and advancement of personnel, how to handle the foreigners, and the like. For the most part their relations were extremely amicable, and Li deferred to Tseng as his superior. However, in matters concerning the *Huai-chün*, Li jealously guarded his authority. In 1862 when Tseng detained nine of the newly recruited battalions of the *Huai-chün* to defend Wu-wei and Lu-chiang in Anhwei, Li repeatedly insisted that they be released and sent to Shanghai. Tseng continued to detain them because there were no other troops available, and because he felt that the real threat from the Taiping rebels, at that time, was in Anhwei, not in Shanghai. Li still insisted that they be released, and Tseng finally acquiesced. He wrote to Li saying, "Because of my many years in the provinces and having been often humiliated and defeated, therefore I often am overly cautious and lacking in propriety, and am anxious about faulty planning. I hope you will forgive me." [41]

With the establishment of Li Hung-chang in Kiangsu and Tso Tsung-t'ang in Chekiang, Tseng, as the supreme military commander, now had two new armies to work in conjunction with his main force, which was led by his brother, Kuo-ch'üan, and was fighting its way down the Yangtze. The Taipings were caught in a three-way pincer, and the fortunes of the Ch'ing began to improve. Li was the first of the three to accomplish his mission, the recovery of Kiangsu Province. With the aid of the American, Frederick Town-

---

[40] Hail, p. 242; Li Shu-ch'un, pp. 103–104.
[41] Lo Erh-kang, "Ch'ing-chi ping wei chiang-yu ti ch'i-yüan" (The Origin of the Personal Armies at the End of the Ch'ing), *Chung-kuo she-hui ching-chi shih chi-k'an*, V, No. 2 (June, 1937), 248.

send Ward, and his Ever-Victorious Army, which was commanded by Charles George ("Chinese") Gordon after Ward's death, Li finally was able to recapture Soochow, the provincial capital, on December 5, 1863. After securing the rest of the province, Li was ordered to proceed at once to help Tseng Kuo-ch'üan's forces, who were beseiging Nanking, the Taiping capital.

Li had never before evaded an unpleasant task or shirked a responsibility, but this time he delayed in advancing and sent all sorts of excuses. When Li was reprimanded by the court for not showing more alacrity, Tseng recognized the reasons behind his actions and came to his defense. "When it comes to handling affairs, Li Hung-chang is usually the bravest, and in advancing his troops, he is the quickest. However, at this time in joining the attack on Nanking, he moves forward slowly and stops. Now he has no intention of avoiding the fight, but merely intends not to steal the glory." [42] Tseng Kuo-ch'üan had been besieging Nanking without any outside help, and, now that it was apparent that the city would soon fall, Li did not want to detract from Kuo-ch'üan's glory by joining him at the last minute. Tseng, as Commander-in-Chief, found himself in an awkward position: he was duty bound to order Li to Nanking in order to hasten its fall, but, by doing so, he would, in effect, be robbing his brother of part of his well-earned rewards. By his delicacy of feeling and perception of the factors involved, Li was able to provide Tseng with a means of "saving face." The fact that Tseng was not displeased by his actions, but came to his defense, attested to Li's correct interpretation of the situation. [43] Li's conduct in this instance was in sharp contrast to that of Tso Tsung-t'ang in regard to the escape of Hung Fu, the boy Emperor of the Taiping rebels.

When Nanking fell, it was reported that the boy Emperor, successor of the original Taiping Emperor, had been killed in the subsequent slaughter. Tseng believed the report and in a memorial conveyed the information to the throne. A few days later, Tso Tsung-t'ang's spies informed Tso that the boy was alive and had been seen entering Huchow. Tso reported this to the throne, and his memorial was referred to Tseng for comment. Thinking that Tso was trying to discredit him in order to increase his own prestige, Tseng became

---

[42] Li Shao-ling, *Tseng Kuo-fan* (Kao-hsiung, Taiwan: Ta-yeh shu-tien, 1955), p. 81.
[43] Hail, pp. 288–289.

thoroughly indignant and wrote a memorial denouncing Tso and insisting that the boy Emperor, Hung Fu, was dead. Tseng's memorial was referred to Tso for comment. Tso became enraged at Tseng's criticisms and replied with a very intemperate memorial in which he aired every grudge he had against his master. The emperor referred Tso's memorial to Tseng and tactfully advised both parties to forget the matter. In the meantime Hung Fu was captured and, in deference to Tseng, was executed without any fanfare. In such a situation it seems likely that Li Hung-chang would have quietly executed the boy without bringing it to the attention of the throne, and, would then have discreetly informed Tseng of his error.[44]

With the fall of Nanking on July 19, 1864, the Taiping Rebellion ended. Tseng Kuo-fan began to disband his *Hsiang-chün*; having fought since 1853, Tseng's "braves" were worn out and insisting on going home to Hunan. In addition, the court had become apprehensive of Tseng's power, and he deemed it wise to divest himself of his personal army. In its place he felt that he could rely on the *Huai-chün*, which had only been fighting for a couple of years, was from a more northerly region, and thus would be more amenable to fighting in the north, and was controlled by his disciple.

Although the Taiping Rebellion had been crushed, some of the rebels had escaped to the north and had joined the Nien rebels, who had been fighting against the imperial authority for a number of years in northern Anhwei, Honan, Shantung, and southern Chihli. On May 27, 1865, Tseng Kuo-fan was given the command of the campaign against the Nien rebels; Li Hung-chang replaced him temporarily in Nanking but was only given the rank of Acting Liangkiang Governor-General.[45] This move was in direct violation of the "Laws of Avoidance," since Li's native province was Anhwei, which would be under his jurisdiction. However, the court must have felt that the urgency of the situation demanded concessions and salved its conscience by making Li only "Acting" Governor-General.

In his campaign against the Nien rebels, Tseng was forced to rely on Li's *Huai-chün*. Yet Tseng knew better than anyone else

---

[44] W. L. Bales, *Tso Tsung-t'ang: Soldier and Statesman of Old China* (Shanghai: Kelley and Walsh, Ltd., 1937), pp. 170–173.

[45] Mary C. Wright, *The Last Stand of Chinese Conservatism. The T'ung-Chih Restoration, 1862–1874.* (Stanford: Stanford Univ. Press, 1957), p. 103.

that, although he commanded it, his chances of success were limited because he was not a Huai man himself. He had no ties with the troops based on regional affinities, the very relationship that he had insisted upon in his own military organization. Tseng succinctly stated the situation when he said, "although your Huai armies belong to my family, I wonder whether, if they leave Kiangsu and go to Shantung, they will be harmonious with me in heart and character."[46] However, he felt that if Li's younger brothers, Ho-chang and Chao-ch'ing, accompanied him, he would have a more direct and personal control over the army. Consequently, he urged Li to persuade his brothers to assist him. Tseng felt that the Li brothers would have the support of the various *Huai-chün* commanders, and he hoped that, because of his past connections with their elder brothers and their father, they would be amenable to his authority.[47] Moreover, Li Ho-chang had served in Tseng's *mu-fu* in a military capacity from 1859 until 1862, when he followed his brother to Shanghai in the *Huai-chün*. Li informed Tseng that they would go with him in a letter dated June 11, 1865: "My third [Ho-chang] and sixth [Chao-ch'ing] younger brothers are indebted to you for your letter to transfer them. I fear they will not be able to suffer the hardships and will be ungrateful for your kindness."[48] As it turned out, though, only the youngest brother, Chao-ch'ing, ended up serving under Tseng during the Nien campaign.

Tseng had his own plans and strategy on how to use the *Huai-chün* against the Nien rebels and did not want any interference from Li, who was the real master of the army. Li, however, felt that he had a right to express an opinion on crucial decisions and could not help from intervening in routine matters as well. Finally, in 1866, Tseng wote to Li in a very direct manner: "At the present time, since the command of the Huai Army is shifted to me, you should keep yourself completely aloof, so that the generals can have a unified guidance and, meanwhile, I may direct them smoothly."[49] Nevertheless, after a year's experience Tseng became convinced that the *Huai-chün* could suppress the Nien rebels only if members of

[46] Spector, p. 245. Cited from *Tseng Wen-cheng-kung shu-cha* (1945 ed.), *chüan* 24, p. 30b.

[47] Spector, p. 245.

[48] *LWCK-PL, chüan* 6, p. 23b.

[49] Chiang Siang-tseh, *The Nien Rebellion* (Seattle: Univ. of Washington Press, 1954), p. 115. Cited from *Tseng Wen-cheng-kung shu-cha, chüan* 25, p. 33.

the Li family commanded it. The degree of control which Li had forged between himself and his subordinate commanders was something that Tseng had never attempted with the *Hsiang-chün* commanders. In Tseng's opinion, "the Huai commanders were always beneath the heels" of Li.[50] He had promised Li, early in 1866, that if there was no sign of progress in the campaign by the summer, he would resign and recommend Li as his successor. The various *Huai-chün* units did not disobey Tseng's orders, but neither did they bring a zest to their campaigning. Tseng frankly admitted, "Whereas I am not able to ride and conduct battles in the field, you [Li] can gallop at the head of the army. After your personal attendance in the battle but once or twice, the combatants' morale will mount a hundred times higher."[51]

On December 12, 1866, the court accepted Tseng's resignation and ordered him to trade places with Li. Tseng returned to Nanking to take charge of supplying the army in the field, as Li had been doing, and Li received the seal of the Imperial Commissioner in charge of the campaign. With Li again in command of the *Huai-chün*, its spirits revived, and the Nien rebels were crushed in 1868.

With the Nien Rebellion out of the way, it might have been expected that the *Huai-chün* would be disbanded. However, such was not the case.[52] The Moslems were rebelling in Kansu, there was always the threat of other rebellions breaking out, and the court was apprehensive with regard to the intentions of the Western powers. The *Huai-chün* was the best army in China, and it was proposed by Ying-han, the Governor of Anhwei, that the Huai "braves" be substituted for the Chihli *lien-chün* — an imperial force trained along Western lines — to defend the imperial capital.[53] Tso Tsung-t'ang, who was not on especially friendly terms with Li, and Mao Ch'ang-hsi, the President of the Censorate, recommended that Liu Ming-ch'uan, the most outstanding of the *Huai-chün* commanders, be appointed to the vacant post of Chihli Provincial Commander-in-Chief. None of these men had any personal interest in preserving the *Huai-chün*, but the Chihli *lien-chün* had shown its weakness during the Nien campaigns and a strong army was needed to replace it.[54] At first Li rejected this offer on the grounds that Liu

[50] Chiang Siang-tseh, p. 115.
[51] *Ibid.*
[52] *Ibid.*, p. 137.
[53] *Ibid.*
[54] *Ibid.*; LWCK-PL, *chüan* 8, p. 52a.

Ming-ch'uan's temperament did not make him suitable to serve under the nobles and high officials of the capital.[55] Actually Li did not want to lose direct control of any of the units of the *Huai-chün*. However, in September, 1868, when he heard that Tseng Kuo-fan was being transferred to the post of Chihli Governor-General, he changed his mind and permitted the *Ming-chün*, the division under Liu Ming-ch'uan and the strongest in the Huai army, to come under Tseng's command. On September 13, 1868 he wrote to Tseng, saying: "Yesterday I learned that you are coming north. I have ordered Liu Tzu-wu [Sheng-tsao], Ting Le-shan [Shou-ch'ang], and others to keep the *Ming-chün* temporarily at Chang-ch'iu while we wait for you. Once you arrive we can take our time in discussing and settling the matter, so that you will not be isolated and have nothing prepared for contingencies."[56] Earlier, when Tseng had assumed command of the Nien campaign, Li had expressed the view that in emergencies the two of them could only rely on their own generals,[57] and now that Tseng was going to a new post in a strange province, he wanted to be sure that his master had a military force on which he could rely.

The *Ming-chün* stayed in Chihli under Tseng's command to defend the imperial domain; meanwhile, on March 1, 1869, Li went to Hupeh to take up his post as the Hu-kuang Governor-General. The separation of this unit of the *Huai-chün* from the main force lasted only a little over a year. In the summer of 1870, Li was ordered north from Wuchang to assist in the suppression of the Moslem uprising. Upon reaching Sian in July, however, he received further orders to proceed to Chihli with his army in order to assist Tseng in the settlement of the Tientsin Massacre and to defend the capital area if a war with France ensued. While enroute to Tientsin, he was appointed Governor-General of Chihli, to replace Tseng, who had fallen from favor because of his handling of the settlement. Tseng returned again to Nanking as the Liangkiang Governor-General, and Li concluded the treaty with the French, which Tseng had virtually settled before he left Tientsin.[58] Once again the disciple had replaced the master and assumed the leadership, only this time the change in positions was permanent. It was while in Chihli in 1872 that Li received the news of Tseng's death in Nanking.

55 *LWCK-PL, chüan* 8, p. 52a.          56 *Ibid.*; Chiang Siang-tseh, p. 138.
57 *LWCK-PL, chüan* 6, p. 22a.
58 Hail, pp. 320–321; *LWCK-IC, chüan* 4, p. 9a.

Without Tseng Kuo-fan there probably would never have been a Li Hung-chang. Tseng trained him and then gave him the opportunity to prove himself by recommending him for high provincial office. Once having achieved recognition, Li still was under the supervision and guidance of his master, and it was only in Tseng's declining years that his student forged ahead. During the entire period of their association, Li acknowledged Tseng as his teacher and was well aware of the tremendous debt he owed him. Writing to Wu T'ang (Chung-hsien) in 1863, Li referred to himself as "a fly on the tail of a famous horse"[59]

It was in Tseng's *mu-fu* that Li further developed his military techniques, learned about Western weapons of war, and was introduced to the problems of self-strengthening. Up to the time that Li arrived in Shanghai in 1862, he had never been in the coastal provinces and probably had had little or no association with Westerners. The earliest record of his actual contact with a Western steamship was on February 19, 1862 in An-ch'ing, when he accompanied Tseng to inspect the first foreign steamship purchased by his master.[60] While temporarily residing in Shanghai, as the Governor of Kiangsu, Li came into frequent contact with Westerners and had a chance to see for himself the efficacy of their weapons and training, and to learn about other features of Western civilization. His thinking, however, was still guided by Tseng, even though he was no longer a member of Tseng's *mu-fu*. In his approach to self-strengthening and problems arising out of the necessity of dealing with foreigners, Tseng's primary concern seems to have been with the moral issues involved; Li also was concerned with morality, but he placed more emphasis on the practical aspects. In the exchange of letters between the two men in 1862 and 1863, Tseng stated his basic principle that in warfare men were more important than weapons and that, in dealing with the foreigners, Li should be guided by four words: loyalty (*chung*), trust (*hsin*), honesty (*tu*) and respect (*ching*).[61] In addition, he admonished Li to see that his troops were humble (*ch'ien*) and restrained (*i*) in their conduct.[62] Li obediently acknowledged his teacher's moral leader-

[59] *LWCK-PL, chüan* 3, p. 21a.
[60] Gideon Chen, *Tseng Kuo-fan, Pioneer Promotor of the Steamship in China* (Peiping: Yenching University, 1935), p. 38.
[61] *LWCK-PL, chüan* 1, p. 25b; *chüan* 2, p. 46b.
[62] *Ibid., chüan* 1, p. 36b.

ship, and the exemplary conduct of his troops in the Shanghai area astonished the local populace.[63] Li, however, while not neglecting morality, was more concerned with explosive shells, rifles and artillery, pontoon bridges, and other munitions and equipments of war which the foreigners had, but which China lacked. Li's attitude reflected his personal observations in the Shanghai area and his visits on board English and French naval vessels.[64] Yet, despite their divergent approaches to the problem, both men were firmly convinced that Chinese, as men, were superior to Westerners, and that once China's armies were equipped with the superior weapons of the West, she would be able to control the foreign invaders and to assert her natural superiority.[65] In keeping with his practical approach, Li urged Tseng to be more than just a moral leader and to take over the effective leadership of self-strengthening and foreign affairs. Li argued that, because of his power and prestige, Tseng was the only one who could effectively deal with the problems, and that such a task would be extremely difficult for officials like himself who were of a junior generation.[66] Tseng was the respected teacher, and Li was the obedient but prodding student.

Not only did Li Hung-chang owe a debt to Tseng, but so did his brothers. Both his elder brother, Han-chang, and his younger brother, Ho-chang, had served in Tseng's *mu-fu*, from which the elder rose to be a governor-general. The youngest brother, Chao-ch'ing, had served under Tseng during the suppression of the Nien Rebellion. When Tseng died, the Li brothers, in respect for Tseng as their master, undertook the publication of his collected works as part of their duty as his pupils.[67]

Liang Ch'i-ch'ao, in speaking of the relationship between Tseng and Li, said it "was like Kuan Chung's relation to Pao Shu [i.e., David and Jonathan], like Han Hsin's relation to Hsiao Ho."[68] That such a close relationship could develop between two men of such divergent characters attests to the depth of their feelings and to the efficacy of the Confucian relationships. Li was physically active and powerful, energetic, full of self-confidence, alert, ambitious, and

---

[63] *Ibid., chüan* 1, p. 12a.
[64] *Ibid., chüan* 1, p. 20b; *chüan* 2, p. 46b; *chüan* 3, p. 17a.
[65] *Ibid., chüan* 1, pp. 32a, 33a; *chüan* 2, pp. 46b, 47a; *chüan* 3, p. 17a.
[66] *Ibid., chüan* 1, p. 20a; *chüan* 2, p. 43a.
[67] Chiang Siang-tseh, p. 147.
[68] Li Shao-ling, p. 80; Liang Ch'i-ch'ao, *Lun Li Hung-chang* (On Li Hung-chang) (Taipei, Taiwan: Chung-hua shu-chü, 1958), p. 81.

practical. Tseng was of middle height and rather dumpy. He tended to be cautious and anxious, and often desired to withdraw from official life. Yet he was morally upright and, in the eyes of most Chinese, epitomizes the true Confucian gentleman.[69] In an association of this nature, there was bound to be some conflict. Li criticized Tseng's slowness and indecision[70] and, during his early years in Tseng's mu-fu, was impatient and rebellious. However, as Li grew older, Tseng's teachings began to bear fruit, and their influence can be seen in Li's career after Tseng's death.

Despite Li's great debt to Tseng, he owed a far greater debt to the mu-fu system. Tseng Kuo-fan would probably have made a name for himself even if there had been no Taiping Rebellion and the resultant need for an expanded mu-fu system. He was already well established in the government circles in Peking, and his character was more in keeping with the orthodox patterns. However, for Li Hung-chang, the rebellion, the mu-fu system, and the subsequent demands of self-strengthening were his salvation. His character was such that even if he had started in the orthodox fashion, the restrictions of orthodoxy would have stifled him.

The Legalist aspects of the mu-fu system — its adherence to the principles of professionalism and the ability to change to meet new situations — made it possible for China to call on her best talents in times of internal rebellion or foreign invasion, talents which were often outside the accepted patterns of the orthodoxy and which in times of peace and stability were considered below the dignity of the orthodox scholar-officials. Yet, despite its functional attributes, this system was a product of the orthodox society, was imbued with its values and mores, and, as a result, was unable to fulfill its potential and successfully shore up the particularistic Chinese world. The mu-fu system was organized on the basis of personal relations, which overshadowed all else in the eyes of society, and yet it was called upon to do a job in the nineteenth century which required a total and impartial devotion to the state. It raised the unorthodox to positions of importance and leadership, but could not break them out of

---

[69] Hosea Ballou Morse, In the Days of the Taipings (Salem, Mass.: The Essex Institute, 1927), p. 415. Although this book is a novel, the author spent many years in China and at one time worked for Li Hung-chang.

[70] Hsiao I-shan, Tseng Kuo-fan chuan (A Biography of Tseng Kuo-fan) (Taipei, Taiwan: Chung-hua wen-hua ch'u-pan shih-yeh wei-yüan-hui ch'u-pan, 1955), p. 194.

their orthodox cocoon. The demands of the late nineteenth century and the flexibility of the *mu-fu* system provided Li with the opportunity to develop his more unorthodox talents and achieve his goals of wealth, power, and fame, but the orthodox context foredoomed his efforts to protect the world he knew. Li Hung-chang can truly be called the greatest product of the *mu-fu* system, its most skillful manipulator, and its last great practitioner.

# V. The Three Legs of Li Hung-chang's Mu-fu

The *mu-fu* system was completely dependent on the official bureaucratic structure for its existence. The inherent weaknesses of the bureaucracy provided its *raison d'être*, and the rank, wealth, and character of the officials were the three legs on which it rested. Without provincial rank there could be no *mu-fu*, as the term itself implies. If a host was not a provincial official, his followers and friends could not be considered *mu-yu*. In addition, the size of the *mu-fu* was almost directly proportional to the official's rank and the scope of his responsibilities. Only a provincial official with personal wealth could afford to hire *mu-yu*, and his fortune was usually the result of his being an official. The last of the three legs was the character of the official. Whether a *mu-fu* operated efficiently and whether for good or evil depended on the character of the host official. A bad official could destroy himself and his *mu-fu*, while a good one could enhance his own position and, in the process, that of his *mu-yu*. Li Hung-chang had high provincial office, great wealth, and a strong character, but he was also endowed with those character traits which defy description but which are so essential to greatness. Because of this and a fortunate combination of circumstances, he soared to that empyreal realm of the truly great, and the scope and importance of his *mu-fu* expanded beyond its traditional confines and impinged on the sacrosanctity of the bureaucracy itself.

Li Hung-chang's long career as an official and his rise to greatness began propitiously in 1843 when, at the age of twenty, he passed the first of the official examinations and was made a senior licentiate (*yu-kung*). Shortly thereafter he set out from his home in Tung-hsiang, Ho-fei *hsien*, Anhwei, to make a name for himself in Peking.[1]

---

[1] Li Hung-chang, *Li Wen-chung-kung i-chi* (Posthumous Collection of the Writings of Li Hung-chang) *in* Li Kuo-chieh, ed., *Ho-fei Li shih san shih i-chi*

In rapid succession he became a *chü-jen* (1844) and then a *chin-shih* (1847). Having passed the highest of the official examinations, he was furthered honored by being selected as a Bachelor (*shu-chi-shih*) of the Hanlin Academy and three years later, in 1850, was promoted to Second Class Compiler (*pien-hsiu*).[2] His achievements placed him among the comparatively select few of the empire, and to have accomplished so much at such an early age (twenty-seven) was an even more remarkable feat. He could look forward to a promising career as a scholar among the officials of the capital. However, this auspicious beginning as a scholar-official was abruptly cut short in his thirtieth year, when the exigencies of dynastic survival switched him onto a new and different track.

On March 4, 1853, Lü Hsien-chi, a Vice-President of the Board of Works (*kung-pu shih-lang*) and a native of Anhwei, received an imperial command to return to his native province to take charge of the local militia affairs. Lü memorialized to take Li Hung-chang and the Junior Metropolitan Censor (*chi-shih-chung*), Yüan Chia-san, with him, and it was granted.[3] "When I was twenty I had the ambition of being a scholar, but I found myself in a very chaotic age and was led by Lü Wen-chieh [Hsien-chi] to join the army."[4] Thus Li began his military career as a *mu-yu*, and through it, rather than through the orthodox bureaucratic channels, he was to achieve high provincial office and fulfill his own expectations of greatness.

Between 1853, when he returned to Anhwei as a *mu-yu* of Lü Hsien-chi, and 1859, when he joined Tseng Kuo-fan's *mu-fu*, Li served in the *mu-fu* of the successive governors of Anhwei and commanded militia units against the Taipings and the rising Nien rebels. For his military exploits he was awarded various official ranks and honors and made a name for himself as a military commander.[5]

([no place]: The Li Family of Ho-fei, 1904), *chüan* 6, p. 1b (hereafter cited as *LWCK-IC*); Huang Yün-hsiu, *Hsü-hsiu Lu-chou fu-chih* (Revised edition of the Lu-chou Prefecture Gazetteer) (1885), *chüan* 31, p. 10a.

    2 *Ch'ing shih-kao* (Draft History of the Ch'ing Dynasty), ed. by Chao Erh-hsün, *et al.* (Hong Kong: Hsiang-kang wen-hsüeh yen-chiu she, [1960?]), lieh-chuan 198, *hsia*, p. 1333; Li Hung-chang, *Li Wen-chung-kung ch'üan-chi* (The Complete Works of Li Hung-chang), ed. by Wu Ju-lun (Nanking, 1908), Kuo-shih pen-chuan, chüan-shou, p. 12a (hereafter cited as *LWCK-KSPC*).

    3 Huang Yün-hsiu, *Hsü-hsiu Lu-chou fu-chih*, *chüan* 22, p. 2b.

    4 *Li Wen-chung-kung ch'üan-chi*, P'eng-liao han-kao (Letters to Friends and Colleagues), *chüan* 4, p. 21b (hereafter cited as LWCK-PL).

    5 Li Shu-ch'un, "Li Wen-chung-kung Hung-chang nien-p'u" (A Chronological Biography of Li Hung-chang), *Shih-hsüeh nien-pao*, No. 1 (July, 1929), pp. 101–102; *LWCK-KSPC*, chüan-shou, pp. 12a–b; Hu Pin, *Mai-kuo-tse Li Hung-*

Late in 1858, after the disastrous defeat of the imperial troops in the defense of Ho-fei, Li resigned in anger from the *mu-fu* of Fu-chi, the Governor of Anhwei, who had been one of Li's examiners for the *chin-shih* degree and whom Li had served since 1854, and went to join Tseng Kuo-fan in Kiangsi.[6] His disagreements with his former examiner centered around military strategy. Fu-chi had not had any previous military experience before becoming the Anhwei Governor in 1854, was not a very good administrator, and tended to be rather conservative.[7] Li, on the other hand, was young, energetic, and demanded bold measures. Because the imperial troops habitually retreated in the face of the enemy, Li became disgusted with them and clashed with their commander.[8] Li was also disgruntled over having to serve in what he considered a backwash area where there was little opportunity for his abilities to be recognized. The years had served him well though, for he had acquired combat experience, had achieved honors and a degree of fame, and had unknowingly established the bonds of friendship which would eventually be the basis of his own army.

During his more than two years of service in Tseng Kuo-fan's *mu-fu* (1859–1862), Li acquired further experience in military strategy and participated in a much larger operation. From this he was able to learn about the multiplicity of problems involved in governing a large area and in commanding a complex military establishment. His nine-year period of tutelage drew to an end in 1861, when he was ordered by Tseng to return to Anhwei to recruit an army of "braves." Early in 1862, after he had returned to Tseng's headquarters in An-ch'ing with his new army, Li was at first made the Acting Governor of Kiangsu, and shortly thereafter the substantive Governor, on Tseng's recommendation. He had thus achieved high office as a *mu-yu* in the provinces, rather than as a scholar-

*chang* (The Traitor Li Hung-chang) (Shanghai: Hsin chih-shih ch'u-pan she, 1955), p. 8.

[6] Li Shu-ch'un, pp. 101–102; *Ta-Ch'ing li ch'ao shih-lu* (Veritable Records of the Successive Reigns of the Ch'ing Dynasty) (Tokyo, 1937–1938) Tao-kuang, *chüan* 440, pp. 4a–b; U.S. Library of Congress, Asiatic Division, *Eminent Chinese of the Ch'ing Period (1644–1912)*, ed. by Arthur W. Hummel (Washington, D.C.: U.S. Gov't. Printing Office, 1943), I, 464 (herafter cited as Hummel); Hsüeh Fu-ch'eng, "Li Fu-hsiang ju Tseng Wen-cheng-kung mu-fu" (Li Hung-chang Enters Tseng Kuo-fan's *mu-fu*), *in* Tso Shun-sheng, comp., *Chung-kuo chin-pai-nien shih tzu-liao ch'u-pien* (Taipei, Taiwan: Chung-hua shu-chü, 1958), p. 160.

[7] Hsüeh, "Li Fu-hsiang ju Tseng Wen-cheng-kung mu-fu," p. 160.

[8] *Ibid.*, p. 160.

official in Peking, and the lessons he had learned as a *mu-yu* would hold him in good stead as a governor, and later as governor-general, with his own *mu-fu*.

Li's position as Governor of Kiangsu was the first substantive civil office he had held since leaving Peking nine years earlier. He had been appointed a Prefect in 1854,[9] an Expectant Taotai in 1855,[10] a Provincial Judge in 1856,[11] and a Taotai in 1859;[12] but either these titles were empty ones, or Li had remained with the army and not taken up the posts. Even though Li was now a high civil official, his career for the next eight years would be primarily that of a military leader, and his *mu-yu* would be basically military men. In 1865, after the victorious conclusion of the Taiping Rebellion, he was transferred to the post of Acting Governor-General of Liangkiang to support Tseng Kuo-fan's operations against the Nien rebels; however, in the next year the two men switched positions, and Li took command of the campaign. In 1867 he was made the Hu-kuang (Hupeh and Hunan) Governor-General but did not take up the post until 1869, after the successful suppression of the Nien revolt. Between 1869 and 1870, when he replaced Tseng Kuo-fan as the Chihli Governor-General, Li was engaged in investigating the anti-Christian riots in Szechwan and Kweichow, in negotiating their settlement with the French Minister, and in preparing for campaigns, first against the Miao in the southwest and later against the Moslems in the northwest.[13] Li had been given his various posts on the strength of his army, the *Huai-chün*, and it was because his army was the only one worthy of the name that he was assigned the most important provincial post in the empire, the Chihli Governor-Generalship, which entailed the defense of the capital and the imperial domain.

All the honors that Li received prior to 1870 were the result of his military exploits. In 1853 he was awarded the Blue Plume (*lan-ling*) for warding off the rebels at Ho-chou, Anhwei,[14] and in 1854 he was awarded the Single-Eyed Peacock Feather (*hua-ling*) for his efforts in the recovery of Han-shan.[15] When his army recaptured Soochow from the Taipings in 1863, he was made Grand Guardian

[9] Li Shu-ch'un, p. 102.                    [11] *Ibid.*
[10] *LWCK-KSPC*, chüan-shou, p. 12b.    [12] *Ibid.*
[13] *Ch'ing shih-kao*, lieh-chuan 198, *hsia*, p. 1333; Hummel, I, 465–466.
[14] Li Shu-ch'un, p. 101; *LWCK-KSPC*, chüan-shou, p. 12a; Hu Pin, p. 8.
[15] Li Shu-ch'un, p. 102.

of the Heir Apparent (*t'ai-tzu t'ai-pao*) and became entitled to wear the Yellow Riding Jacket (*huang-ma-kua*), the highest military award. After the fall of Nanking in 1864, which ended the Taiping Rebellion, the emperor bestowed on him the hereditary title of First Rank Earl (*i-teng su-i po*) and the Double-Eyed Peacock Feather (*shuang-yen hua-ling*).[16] At the successful conclusion of the Nien campaign in 1868, his honors, which had been stripped from him during the campaign because the rebels had succeeded in breaking out of his encirclement and had threatened the capital, were restored to him, and he was made an Assistant Grand Secretary (*hsieh-pan ta-hsüeh-shih*).[17]

By 1870 Li had reached the pinnacle of provincial office, but not the pinnacle of his career. During the next twenty-five years he became the mainstay of the dynasty as China's virtual Foreign Secretary; as the supreme commander, in effect, of all military and naval forces and establishments in the north of China; as the leading entrepreneur for industrial and commercial development in the empire, with a practical monopoly of all such enterprises in the north; and as a trusted adviser of the Empress-Dowager. Few statesmen, whether in Asia, Europe, or America, have held so much responsibility, and he has justifiably been compared with Bismarck, Gladstone, and Itō Hirobumi.

This third stage of Li's career began in 1870 when he was made the Imperial Commissioner of Trade for the Northern Ports (*pei-yang t'ung-shang shih-wu ta-ch'en*), an office he held concurrently with his governor-generalship, and which placed him in charge of all foreign commercial affairs in the treaty ports north of Shanghai.[18] It was through this post that he became enmeshed in China's foreign affairs. In 1871 he negotiated China's first modern treaty with Japan and was also China's principal representative in the discussions with Japan between 1871 and 1880 over the question of the possession of the Liu-ch'iu Islands. He also was involved in China's defense of Formosa when Japan sent a punitive expedition against the Formosans in 1874. During the 1870's, he negotiated the final settlement of the Margary case with the British at Chefoo (1876), and concurrently advised Korea in negotiations with Japan (1876), the United States (1882), and the European countries over commer-

---

[16] *Ch'ing shih-kao*, lieh-chuan 198, *hsia*, p. 1333.
[17] *Ibid.*                    [18] *Ibid.*

cial treaties. In the 1880's, Li was embroiled in both the diplomatic and military phases of the Sino-French conflict, which led to war in 1885; during the same decade he attempted, rather successfully, to restore China's position in and control over Korea, and in 1882 he warded off Japan's aggressive designs on Korea with the Li-Itō Convention. When the British occupied Port Hamilton in 1885, Li was able to play on their fears of Russian expansion and persuade them to evacuate that port. In 1886 he proposed to establish direct relations with the Vatican, as a more effective means of handling Christian affairs in China, but was defeated by French intervention. When the Korean situation became critical in 1893, it was Li Hung-chang who tried to keep the "war party" in check and negotiate with Japan; when this failed and war broke out in 1894, it was his army and navy that fought the Japanese and were defeated, and it was Li who suffered the disgrace.[19]

In addition to maintaining the *Huai-chün* as the most effective fighting force in China, Li also created his own navy, and in 1885 he was made Co-Director of the newly established Board of the Admiralty, an office which gave him national power. To staff and supply his army and navy he established naval (1880) and military (1885) academies, shipyards, arsenals, technical training schools, and a series of defensive forts from Port Arthur to Shantung. He also sponsored various commercial and industrial enterprises for the purpose of recovering China's economic rights. In 1872 he established China's first steamship company, which he followed up with China's first modern coal mine (1877), first railway (1880), first telegraph line (1881), first cotton spinning mill (1882), and first modern gold mine (1887).[20] As a reward for his labors on China's behalf, Li was awarded the post of Grand Secretary (*ta-hsüeh-shih*) (1873), an honor which was shared by only two Manchus and two Chinese throughout the empire,[21] Grand Tutor to the Heir Apparent (*t'ai-tzu t'ai-fu*) (1879),[22] and the Triple-Eyed Peacock Feather (*san-yen hua-ling*) (1894), an honor heretofore reserved exclusively for

[19] Hummel, I, 466–469.

[20] John Lang Rawlinson, "The Chinese Navy, 1839–1895" (unpublished Ph.D. Dissertation, Harvard University, 1959), pp. 636, 637–639, 639–640, 644, 645, 681–682, 687, cited with the author's permission; Hummel, I, 467.

[21] *Ch'ing shih-kao*, lieh-chuan 198, *hsia*, p. 1333; H. S. Brunnert and V. V. Hagelstrom, *Present Day Political Organization of China*, transl. by A. Beltchenko and E. E. Moran (Taiwan reprint, 1961), No. 131, p. 43.

[22] *Ch'ing shih-kao*, lieh-chuan 198, *hsia*, p. 1333.

Manchu princes.[23] Before his fall from power in 1895, Li had attained a provincial and national position which few, if any, other Chinese had ever achieved under the Manchus.

Commensurate with his official position, and dependent upon it, was Li Hung-chang's financial position. Wealth in China was derived primarily from official rank, and in keeping with Chinese mores Li took advantage of his high offices and power to amass a large fortune. Rumors abounded as to the immensity of his wealth, and his fortune at his death was reported at anywhere from Tls. 40,000,000 to Tls. 500,000,000 — equivalent to from about forty-two to five hundred thirty-five million dollars.[24] However, no one really knew just how large it was, and the only concrete evidence available on this subject is the "Agreement" drawn up between Li's surviving sons and grandson on April 4, 1904, which divided up his real estate. This document served in lieu of a will and could not be written until after the period of mourning was completed. The property was divided between Li Ching-fang (the eldest son), Li Kuo-chieh (the eldest son of Li's second son, deceased), and Li Ching-mai (the fourth son). The provisions of this agreement were as follows:

1. Twelve farms, a graveyard, a dike, and four pieces of city property, all within T'ung-ch'eng hsien, Anhwei, plus fourteen items consisting of houses and lands in the provincial city of An-ch'ing were set aside to support the sacrificial temple of Li's first wife, née Chou, and were turned over to Ching-fang to administer.

2. One farm near the Ts'o village in Ho-fei hsien was set aside to support sacrifices to two of Li's concubines and Ching-fang's first wife, all of whom were buried there. The administration of this farm was turned over to Ching-fang.

3. Two farms in Ho-fei hsien were set aside as sacrificial fields for Ching-shu (Li's second son), who was buried on one of them, and the administration was turned over to his son, Kuo-chieh.

---

[23] Ibid., lieh-chuan 198, hsia, p. 1334; U.S. Department of State, Despatches from United States Consuls in Tientsin, 1868–1906 (Washington, D.C.: The National Archives, 1947), Vol. 4, Read to Uhl, February 16, 1894.

[24] Yung Wing, My Life in China and America (New York: Henry Holt and Co., 1909), p. 142; Liang Ssu-kuang, Li Hung-chang mai-kuo shih (A History of the Traitor Li Hung-chang) (Tientsin: Chih-shih shu-tien, 1951), p. 5; Pierre Leroy-Beaulieu, La Rénovation de l'Asie, troisième édition (Paris: Armand Colin et Cie., 1900), p. 372; W. A. P. Martin, A Cycle of Cathay (London: Oliphant Anderson and Ferrier, 1896), p. 348; Robert K. Douglas, "Some Peking Politicians," The Nineteenth Century, XL (Dec., 1896), 896.

4. Two fields, three farms, and a cemetery in Ho-fei *hsien* were designated as the sacrificial fields and cemetery for Ching-mai and were entrusted to his care.

5. The balance of Li's fields in Ho-fei *hsien*, Ch'ao *hsien*, Liu-an *chou*, and Huo-shan *hsien*, plus his house lots in Lu-chou *fu*, Ch'ao *hsien*, Che-kao village, Liu-an *chou* city, and Huo-shan *hsien* city were all to be considered as composing his sacrificial fields and estate. This property was never to be divided, mortgaged, or sold, and the revenue from it was to be used to acquire more property, after the expenses for sacrifices and the maintenance of the temple in Lu-chou *fu* city had been taken care of. Kuo-chieh was to administer it.

6. After ten years from the date of this agreement, if the revenue from Li's sacrificial fields and estate had exceeded the sum of 20,000 piculs, after expenses, all amounts in excess of that figure were to be equally divided among the households of the three heirs, and this provision was never to be changed.

7. Li's father's graveyard and lands in Tung-hsiang, Ho-fei *hsien*, were to be maintained and not to be divided, mortgaged, or sold.

8. A combined foreign- and Chinese-style house in Shanghai, worth Tls. 45,000, was to be sold, and Tls. 20,000 of the proceeds were to pay for the postmortem expenses at Li's memorial temple in Shanghai. The balance of Tls. 25,000 was to be used to buy land and build a house in the foreign settlement in Shanghai, which was to be considered the public residence of all three households and was to be jointly owned and managed.

9. The proceeds from a pawnshop in Yang-chou *fu*, Kiangsu, were to be used for the postmortem expenses of Li's memorial temple in Chiang-ning (Nanking) provincial city.

10. The proceeds from the sale of two houses, one in Chiang-ning (Nanking) and the other in Yang-chou, were to be used to enlarge the joint-family residence in Shanghai.

11. The Li family examination hall in Chiang-ning (Nanking) was to be turned over to Kuo-chieh as his family residence, and a house in Yang-chou was to be assigned to Ching-mai as his family residence, in accordance with Li's former instructions.[25]

The "Agreement," unfortunately, does not give specific details as to the size, location, or value of the various farms and city real estate so that their total worth could be determined, nor does it

[25] Chang Tsung-i, "Ho-t'ung" (An Agreement [between the surviving sons and grandson as to the division of Li Hung-chang's property after his death]). MS, April 4, 1904, plus a codicil dated May 10, 1918. Photocopy of the original is in the author's possession. The original was in the possession of the late Li Kuo-ch'ao, San Francisco, California.

mention any cash, jewels, furs, or other valuables. Li's late grandson, Li Kuo-ch'ao (the only son of Li Ching-mai), was unable to shed any light on the disposition of Li's movable wealth when questioned by the author. In all probability it was divided up prior to Li's death, or shortly thereafter.[26] This document does show the extent of Li's landholdings and that they were all in either Anhwei or Kiangsu, since there is no mention of any real estate in Tientsin or Peking, despite his long years of service in the north. Also, despite rumors that Li owned pawnshops all over China, only one is mentioned. Whether Li was the wealthiest man in China, as was stated by some people, is open to question, but even his late grandson admitted that he was a fairly wealthy man.[27]

The Chinese regarded the acquisition of wealth as a natural desire, and no man was considered great, even though he may have had sons and lived a long time, unless he was wealthy.[28] Men sought official position, either by merit or purchase, as a means of enriching themselves. When Li met General Grant's son in New York in 1896, one of the first questions he asked him was whether or not he was rich. When Grant answered to the contrary, Li replied, "Do you mean to tell me that your father was a General during a rebellion that lasted five years, and brought it to a successful conclusion, and that he was then afterwards twice elected President of the United States, and that yet you his son are poor! Well, I do *not* understand how that could possibly be!"[29] Even if the official was prone to be scrupulously honest, he was still committed to the support of his family and relatives in a comfortable, if not luxurious, manner. Social pressure, in the end, usually outweighed moral considerations.[30] The justification for wealth could also be found in the *Classics*; as Confucius said, "'When a country is well governed, poverty and a mean condition are things to be ashamed of.' The

[26] Interview with Li Kuo-ch'ao, San Francisco, California, June 13, 1963. Mr. Li was the grandson of Li Hung-chang and the only son of Li Ching-mai.

[27] James Martin Miller, *China: Ancient and Modern* (Chicago: J. M. Miller, 1900), p. 321; interview with Li Kuo-ch'ao, San Francisco, California, June 13, 1963; Li Chia-huang, correspondence, Hong Kong, February 28, 1962.

[28] Lewis Charles Arlington, *Through the Dragon's Eyes* (London: Constable & Co., Ltd., 1931), p. 24; J. O. P. Bland, *Li Hung-chang* (New York: Henry Holt & Co., 1917), p. 22.

[29] Mrs. Archibald Little, *Li Hung-Chang. His Life and Time* (London: Cassell and Company, Ltd., 1903), pp. 262–263.

[30] Chang Ch'un-ming, "The Chinese Standards of Good Government," *Nankai Social & Economic Quarterly*, VIII, No. 2 (July, 1935), 226.

virtuous should be wealthy and honored, and the unworthy should be poor and humble."[31] An official was, in theory, a virtuous man, and therefore he should be wealthy.

An official's salary, however, was only nominal—for a *hsien* magistrate from Tls. 100 to Tls. 300 a year—and he was expected to pay his official and personal expenses out of his own pocket.[32] To alleviate this condition, in 1728 the Yung-cheng Emperor authorized the payment of a supplementary salary, known as *yang-lien yin* ("money to nourish honesty"), which was several times greater than the basic salaries.[33] The amount varied from place to place and from official to official, but in 1871 the *yang-lien yin* for the Governor-General of Chihli was Tls. 15,000.[34] Even with this increase in salary, the officials could not hope to cover all their official expenses and pay their *mu-yu*. As a result, they were forced to syphon off a percentage of the imperial revenue that passed through their hands and also to charge the public all the traffic would bear for their services. There were no fixed fees for official services, and custom served as the only check.[35] The court was well aware of this situation, and in 1709 the K'ang-hsi Emperor wrote to the Governor of Hunan, "It is impossible for any magistrate to support his family and to pay for the services rendered by his secretaries and servants without charging a single cash in excess. A magistrate charging ten percent in excess of the regular taxes may be considered a good official."[36]

Li Hung-chang, as a high provincial official, was responsible for literally millions of taels of government revenue in the form of military and naval funds, provincial tax revenues, remittances from other provinces, and so forth. It would be impossible to determine

---

[31] Ch'ü T'ung-tsu, "Chinese Class Structure and Its Ideology," in *Chinese Thought and Institutions*, ed. by John K. Fairbank (Chicago: Univ. of Chicago Press, 1957), p. 238.

[32] Hosea Ballou Morse, *The International Relations of the Chinese Empire* (Taiwan reprint), I, 17; Ch'ü T'ung-tsu, *Local Government in China Under the Ch'ing* (Cambridge: Harvard Univ. Press, 1962), p. xiii.

[33] Ch'ü, *Local Government in China Under the Ch'ing*, pp. 22 and 215, note 36.

[34] *Ta-Ch'ing chin-shen ch'üan-shu* (The Complete Record of the Officials of the Ch'ing), T'ung-chih 10 (1871), Vol. 2, p. 6b.

[35] Justus Doolittle, *Social Life of the Chinese* (New York: Harper & Brothers, 1865), I, 304.

[36] Sybille van der Sprenkel, *Legal Institutions in Manchu China* (London: The Athlone Press, 1962), p. 43.

how much he syphoned off, but even if it were only ten per cent, it would have been a considerable amount. In addition, Li received an undetermined income from the commercial and industrial enterprises he sponsored in the form of dividends from shares which he had either purchased or was given.[37] These companies also provided him with special services, such as the free transport of merchandise, which, when combined with the other advantages of his position, permitted him to engage in duty-free trade.[38] He received numerous gifts from those seeking favors, and on the occasion of his birthday his junior officials were expected to send tokens of their respect. It was also reported that he controlled the rice trade from Anhwei and grew opium poppies on his family estate.[39] The veracity of these reports is questionable, but there is no question that Li used his official position to acquire wealth in both the native and foreign sectors of the Chinese economy. His desire for wealth, however, was not just for its own sake but, more importantly, as a means to power.

Money was a necessary adjunct to high position and power in China. It opened doors, provided protection, welded alliances, and was the lubricant of human intercourse. Any high provincial official who did not fortify his position in the capital through sizable gifts of money would soon lose his backing and position. In the novel, *In the Days of the Taipings*, there is an incident in which the hero, a Chinese scholar serving in the Ever-Victorious Army, describes to some Englishmen how much it cost his great-grandfather, a Grand Secretary, to retire from office:

"A day was fixed for his farewell audience, and he then had to pay his way to secure access to the presence of the Emperor. As Grand Secretary he was already inside the walls of Peking, and so was not required to

---

[37] Albert Feuerwerker, *China's Early Industrialization: Sheng Hsuan-huai (1844–1916) and Mandarin Enterprises* (Cambridge: Harvard Univ. Press, 1958), pp. 22, 99, 177–178, 179, 180, 182, 206, 250; Demetrius C. Boulger, *The Life of Sir Halliday Macartney* (London and New York: J. Lane, 1908), p. 125; interview with Li Kuo-ch'ao, San Francisco, California, June 13, 1963; Ellsworth C. Carlson, *The Kaiping Mines (1877–1912)* (Cambridge: Harvard Univ. Press, 1957), p. 34; Stanley Spector, "Li Hung-chang and the Huai-chün" (unpublished Ph.D. Dissertation, University of Washington, 1953), p. 558; Li Chia-huang, correspondence Hong Kong, February 28, 1962.

[38] Stanley F. Wright, *Hart and the Chinese Customs* (Belfast: Wm. Mullan and Sons, Ltd., 1950), p. 603; Spector, p. 546.

[39] Bland, *Li Hung-chang*, pp. 120–121; Morse, *The International Relations of the Chinese Empire*, II, 376.

pay fees for entrance to the city; but he had to fee heavily, first the keepers
of the gates of the Imperial City, then the keepers of the gates of the
Forbidden City, then the guardians of the throne hall, and after that
he had to pay the Imperial Chamberlain, the Master of the Household,
the Master of Ceremonies, the Introducer of Personnages, the Chief
Eunuch, and some others, before he could reach the foot of the throne."

"What would have happened, if he refused to pay?" asked Mr. Burgess.

"He would have been accused of contumacy and disloyalty for failure
to present himself at the audience; would have been tried and sentenced,
probably, to banishment to the frontier, which is a living death; and his
estates would have been entirely confiscated.

"It cost my great-grandfather over twenty-five myriad [250,000] taels
to get access to the Emperor. . . . and his presents to the Emperor and
the Empress Consort amounted to as much more."[40]

There is a report that when Li was deprived of his Governor-
Generalship and ordered to Peking in 1895, he was forced to dis-
tribute among the court officials and others a sum of eight million
taels — equivalent to about eight and one-half million dollars — to
protect himself from his political enemies.[41] It is highly possible
that one of the reasons why Li was able to maintain his position
in Chihli for twenty-five years was because he regularly sent gen-
erous gifts to the Empress Dowager and other members of the
court.[42] The phenomenon of giving gifts was so common and such
an accepted part of the course of official business that it was seldom,
if ever, mentioned in the official records. However, it can readily
be surmised from Li's character, his acquisition and retention of rank
and power, and his political acumen that he used his wealth to
great political advantage, and that he regarded it as an essential
tool in his struggle for power.

Westerners who knew him described Li's private life as being
plain and unostentatious. His meals were simple, and his habits
were temperate.[43] In a typically Confucian way, he stressed the
concept of frugality in the epitaphs he wrote for his father and

[40] Hosea Ballou Morse, *In the Days of the Taipings* (Salem, Mass.: The Essex
Institute, 1927), p. 54. Although this is a novel, Mr. Morse served under Li
Hung-chang and was well acquainted with the official mores of the period.

[41] Robert K. Douglas, "Some Peking Politicians," p. 896.

[42] Teng Ssu-yü and John K. Fairbank, *China's Response to the West* (Cambridge: Harvard Univ. Press, 1954), p. 89.

[43] Juliet Bredon, *Sir Robert Hart, The Romance of a Great Career* (London:
Hutchinson and Co., 1909), p. 143; Little, p. 332.

friends, and was notorious among Westerners for being avaricious and stingy.[44] Although Li took exception to the charge of stinginess,[45] he was apparently loath to part with his money unless it served a useful purpose.

Money was power, and for this reason Li sought to acquire it. For the same reason, he used it judiciously, but also lavishly whenever the occasion demanded it. Money kept the channels of communciation with the court open and provided him with the means to hire capable *mu-yu*. He believed that the prospect of honor and profit had a universal appeal and that this was the best incentive for getting men to devote their energies to a particular end.[46] How much he paid his *mu-yu* is not known, but in his service many of them acquired considerable wealth. Li Hung-chang's high position, his large fortune, and his *mu-fu* were, nevertheless, dependent upon that third and final ingredient, his physical and mental make-up.

Among the many facets of Li Hung-chang's character, the one which stood out from the rest was his intense desire to be an official and to achieve fame and fortune. This desire was common to most men in China, but with Li the life of an official became almost an end in itself.

At the age of twenty, when Li Hung-chang went up to Peking, he expressed his ambition and, at the same time, predicted his future career in the following poem:

> The man grasps in his single hand a precious sword.
> His ambition is higher than a hundred-foot tower.
> In the past ten thousand years, who has written any
>     history?
> And three thousand *li* away, I desire to seek a
>     marquisate.
> I certainly must nimbly follow the footprints of the
>     thoroughbred horses.
> How can I have the leisure to pursue wild seagulls?
> Smilingly, I point my finger at the road beside the
>     Lu-kou-ch'iao.

---

[44] *LWCK-IC, chüan* 3, pp. 3b, 17b, *chüan* 4, pp. 3a, 9a; Morse, *In the Days of the Taipings*, p. 286; Little, p. 194; Boulger, *The Life of Sir Halliday Macartney*, p. 80; J. J. Matignon, "La grande figure de la vieille Chine: Li-Houng-Tchang," *La Nouvelle Revue* (1 sept. 1925), p. 26.

[45] *LWCK-PL, chüan* 13, p. 8b.          [46] Teng and Fairbank, p. 71.

Someone has followed this way and reached the Isle of
Immortality.[47]

In the first line of this poem, Li indicates that, having reached the
age of twenty, he is a man and is setting out to seek his fortune; in
pre-Ch'ing times it was common to carry a sword when setting out
on a journey. In the third line, he is implying that he will become
a great scholar and surpass all others in writing history. The references to the "marquisate" in the fourth line infers that he hopes to
emulate such great military leaders as Pan Ch'ao of the Han
Dynasty, who became a marquis (*hou*) by fighting the barbarians
on the frontier, "three-thousand *li* away." A distinguished scholar
or statesman was commonly referred to as a "thoroughbred horse,"
and Li proposed to follow their examples. The Lu-kou-ch'iao was
the famous Marco Polo Bridge outside Peking over which many
famous men had passed on their way to the capital; here they
achieved everlasting fame, which was Li's ambition.[48]

In other poems, also written on the occasion of his going up to
Peking, Li further expressed his great ambition. He regretted that
he had wasted the first twenty years of his life in doing nothing
and said that in order to achieve anything, he must leave his native
place and go to the capital where there were famous scholars from
whom he could learn.[49] He took the two characters "merit" (*kung*)
and "fame" (*ming*) as his lode stars [50] and vowed to work hard when
young in order to become a noble.[51] A review of his actual career
shows that he achieved almost all of the desires expressed in these
poems, with the exception of becoming a famous scholar.

Tseng Kuo-fan said of Li Hung-chang that he "disregards life to
be an official" (*p'in-ming tso-kuan*).[52] This expression is an apt description of Li: from the time he became Governor of Kiangsu in
1862 until his death in 1901, almost 40 years, he was never out of
office, except for a few months in 1882 when he was allowed to go
into mourning for his mother. Even during his period of eclipse,

[47] *LWCK-IC, chüan* 6, p. 1b. I am indebted to Mr. Fang Chao-ying for
pointing out this poem to me.
[48] I wish to thank Professor Ch'en Shih-hsiang of the University of California
for checking my translation of this poem and for elucidating the meaning.
[49] *LWCK-IC, chüan* 6, pp. 1b–2a.
[50] *Ibid., chüan* 6, p. 2a.
[51] *Ibid., chüan* 6, p. 2b.
[52] Li Shao-ling, *Tseng Kuo-fan* (Kao-hsiung, Taiwan: Ta-yeh shu-tien, 1955),
p. 82.

from 1895 to 1900, he still held some office and looked forward to the time when he could regain his former high position. Whereas most Chinese officials evaded responsibility, Li seemed to reach out for it; he never shirked an unpleasant task and could always be counted on to take the initiative.[53] He was an admirer of Han Yü (768–824)[54] and seems to have followed his injunction not to retire from the struggle in the face of political or public opposition. Han Yü, however, was struggling for the preservation of Confucianism and never would have subscribed to Li's almost blind devotion to official position.[55]

Throughout his life, Li Hung-chang displayed an inordinate amount of physical energy and courage. Whereas morality was associated with Tseng Kuo-fan, physical vigor was associated with Li Hung-chang.[56] He was at least six feet tall and stood head and shoulders above most of his countrymen. His frame complimented his height, and his general appearance was one of rugged physical power.[57] In his bearing he was stately and dignified and impressed people as being intelligent, alert, and decisive.[58] While in England in 1896, during his trip around the world, his majestic appearance, even at the age of 73, elicited the following description:

As I was making my way out of the House [of Commons] I was suddenly brought face to face with Li Hung-chang, who was being ushered in to hear a debate. A wondrously tall, beneficent-looking stranger from another

[53] Alexander Michie, *The Englishman in China* (Edinburgh: W. Blackwood and Sons, 1900), II, 328.

[54] *LWCK-IC, chüan* 1, p. 8a.

[55] William T. DeBary, "A Reappraisal of Neo-Confucianism," *in* Arthur F. Wright, ed., *Studies in Chinese Thought* (Chicago: Univ. of Chicago Press, 1953), p. 86.

[56] Mary C. Wright, *The Last Stand of Chinese Conservatism. The T'ung-Chih Restoration, 1862–1874* (Stanford: Stanford Univ. Press, 1957), p. 75. Cited from *The North China Herald*, 1865 and 1868.

[57] Matagnon (1 Sept. 1925), pp. 18, 20; Arlington, p. 23; Bland, *Li Hung-chang*, p. 3; Little, pp. 1, 6; Robert K. Douglas, *Li Hungchang* (London: Bliss, Sands and Foster, 1895), p. 24; Henry Norman, *The Peoples and Politics of the Far East* (London: T. Fisher Unwin, 1900), p. 251; Timothy Richard, *Forty-five Years in China* (New York: Frederick A. Stokes Co., 1916), p. 298; Macgowan, "His Excellency Li Hung-chang," *The Far East*, Series 2, I, No. 3 (July, 1876), 74; John Watson Foster, "The Great Chinese Viceroy and Diplomat," *International Monthly*, II (November, 1900), 587; Martin, *A Cycle of Cathay*, p. 349; John Russell Young, *Around the World With General Grant* (New York: The American News Co., 1879), II, 373; Morse, *In the Days of the Taipings*, p. 284.

[58] Morse, *In the Days of the Taipings*, p. 415.

world he seemed — glorious in his blue robes, dignified in his gait and
bearing, and beaming with courtly smiles of appreciation at all he saw.
For distinction of appearance it would be hard to think of any man of
this or the last generation to approach Li Hung-chang. It was not that
he gave you the impression of great achievement or personal power, but
his mien conveyed a sense of personal dignity as of some demi-god, self-
sufficient and detached, yet suave and condescending to struggling
mortals.[59]

Li Hung-chang's unorthodox display of physical energy and his
uncommon physique were matched by an equally unorthodox display of physical and mental courage and a concern for a sound
body and mind. During the Taiping and Nien rebellions he was
noted for leading his troops into battle and for braving the elements
in the conduct of the campaigns.[60] In his later years, when his policy
of negotiate rather than fight seemed to turn the whole nation against
him, he never flinched in what he felt was right nor stooped to petty
recriminations.[61] Despite his wealth and high position, he did not
indulge in riotous living, but led an orderly and fairly austere existence.[62] His concern for his own physical well-being did not come to
him, however, until his later years when the maturity acquired
through age and experience brought home to him the importance of
such matters. In a letter to the Governor of Hupeh, Kuo Po-yin
(Yüan-t'ang), written in 1873, Li said, "In recent years I have made

    [59] Bland, *Li Hung-chang,* p. v (Preface by Basil Williams, ed.).
    [60] Little, p. 44; interview with Li Kuo-ch'ao, San Francisco, California,
April 4, 1962; Morse, *The International Relations of the Chinese Empire,* II, 84;
Wu Ju-lun, "Li Wen-chung-kung shen-tao-pei" (The Stone Tablet Before Li
Hung-chang's Grave) *in Li Wen-chung-kuang ch'üan-chi,* chüan shou, p. 62b;
*LWCK-PL,* chüan 1, p. 33a; Wu Wei-p'ing, "The Rise of the Anhwei Army,"
Harvard University, Center for East Asian Studies, *Papers on China,* Vol. 14,
p. 33; Andrew Wilson, *The "Ever-Victorious Army"* (Edinburgh and London:
W. Blackwood and Sons, 1868), p. 296; Chiang Shih-yung, ed., *Nien-chün shih-
liao ts'ung-k'an* (A Collection of Historical Materials on the Nien Army) (Shang-
hai: Shang-wu yin-shu-kuan, 1957), II, 42.
    [61] Little, pp. 195, 331; Alexander Michie, "Li Hung-chang," *Blackwood's
Edinburgh Magazine,* CLXX, No. 1034 (Dec., 1901), 849, 840; Martin, *A Cycle
of Cathay,* p. 355; E. V. G. Kiernan, *British Diplomacy in China 1880 to 1885*
(Cambridge: Cambridge Univ. Press, 1939), p. 245; Michie, *The Englishman in
China,* II, 190; Paul King, *In the Chinese Customs Service* (London: T. Fisher
Unwin, Ltd., 1924), p. 156; Wu Ju-lun, "Li Wen-chung-kung mu-chih-ming"
(Li Hung-chang's Tomb Inscription), *in Li Wen-chung-kung ch'üan-chi,* chüan
shou, p. 66a.
    [62] Yuan Tao-feng, "Li Huang-chang and the Sino-Japanese War," *T'ien Hsia
Monthly,* III, No. 1 (1936), 10; Bredon, p. 143; Little, p. 332.

a resolution. At 11:00 P.M. I go to bed. As a strong, young man I went to bed late and have become accustomed to this old habit. Frequently I lie on the pillow until 1:00 or 2:00 A.M., and then I can fall soundly asleep. But I close my eyes and rest, and my vitality prospers. The strength I acquire from this resolution is great." [63] Li also preached against the evils of opium smoking and tried to discourage the practice among his fellow officials.[64] His formula for mental health was to read the writings of the ancients and to quietly meditate on world affairs. He advised his friends and colleagues to follow this practice in order to achieve the calmness of spirit and the resolution required for the conduct of official business.[65]

His abounding physical energy was an important asset in Li's conduct of official business. He was extremely practical and efficient, with his feet on the ground and his thoughts attuned to the realities of his time. As a man of fact, he did not indulge in speculations or propound theories.[66] In any discussion he was prone to set aside ceremony, rather than let it stand in the way of an amicable agreement, and was able to penetrate to the heart of any matter with amazing clarity of mind.[67] He energetically attacked his tremendous work load and saw to it that all dispatches and other official documents were taken care of expeditiously. When necessary, he would even sit down and write a forceful dispatch himself, rather than wait for one of his secretaries to attend to it.[68] His presence on any commission dealing with the foreigners meant that the work would be carried to completion with a speed that was almost un-Chinese.[69] He was not a moralist or a crusader but attempted to deal with the facts as he saw them and to work within the limitations of the society around him. There is a passage in *The Dream of the Red Chamber* which aptly describes Li's practical attitude. A young and idealistic official was being advised to tread cautiously in bringing down justice on the heads of the well-to-do and powerful. When

[63] *LWCK-PL, chüan* 13, p. 10a.

[64] *Ibid., chüan* 1, p. 15b; Chiang *Shih-yung,* II, 149; Morse, *The International Relations of the Chinese Empire,* II, 376.

[65] *LWCK-PL, chüan* 9, p. 17b; *chüan* 5, p. 12a.

[66] Michie, *The Englishman in China,* II, 381–382.

[67] Little, p. 206; Count Witte, *The Memoirs of Count Witte* (London: William Heinemann, 1921), pp. 88–89.

[68] Little, pp. 140, 207.

[69] P. W. Sergeant, *The Great Empress Dowager of China* (London: Hutchinson and Co., 1910), p. 72.

he objected on the grounds that it would be defeating the ends of justice, his adviser said:

"You are right in theory. But in practice, unfortunately, we cannot always heed such moral considerations nowadays. 'The wise man adapts himself to circumstances,' says the old maxim. 'The wise man strives for a friendly settlement and avoids wicked conflict,' runs another trustworthy rule. If you were to act strictly according to theory, you would soon lose your position and consequently no longer be able to justify the confidence of the Son of Heaven; indeed, you would actually risk losing your head."

Yu Tsun was thoughtful for a moment.

"Good. What, then, in your opinion, should be done?"[70]

In Li's opinion it did no good to tilt at windmills. One could only do what one was capable of doing. "I can only measure my strength and tread on reality."[71]

In the area under his jurisdiction, Li knew the full measure of his strength and prided himself on his stern rule. He effectively maintained the natural harmony which was so important for those who governed, and never permitted any outrages against the foreigners, nor would he brook any competing authority.[72] As the Governor-General of Chihli, he once said that, although there might be troubles in other parts of the country, there would never be a rebellion in his province,[73] and when his troops threatened mutiny in 1874, he suppressed it promptly and decisively, and lopped off a few heads in the process.[74] During his short stay in Canton as the Governor-General in 1900, he succeeded in suppressing the river pirates and in bringing order to the area, something no previous governor-general had been able to do. When he was transferred to Tientsin to negotiate the Boxer Settlement, the Cantonese begged him to remain, as they considered him the best governor-general they had ever had and feared that the lawlessness would break out again as soon as he had departed.[75]

[70] Tsao Hsüeh-chin and Kao Ngoh, *The Dream of the Red Chamber*, transl. by Florence and Isabel McHugh from the German transl. by Franz Kuhn (Taiwan reprint), p. 39.

[71] *LWCK-PL, chüan* 12, p. 14b.

[72] van der Sprenkel, pp. 28–29; Little, p. 67.

[73] *LWCK-PL, chüan* 12, p. 14b.

[74] Morse, *The International Relations of the Chinese Empire*, II, 278.

[75] China, Inspectorate General of Customs, *Decennial Reports on the Trade, Navigation, Industries, Etc., of the Ports Open to Foreign Commerce in China and Corea*, 2nd Issue (1892–1901) (Shanghai: Inspectorate General of Customs, 1904), p. 199; Miller, pp. 323–324.

Despite his stern rule, Li was deeply concerned about the well-being of the local populace. At the conclusion of both the Taiping and the Nien rebellions he energetically carried out the rehabilitation of the devastated areas. In Kiangsu he encouraged the scattered natives to return to their heavily damaged homes, memorialized for the remission of taxes, cleared waterways, rebuilt the *yamen*, and established a postal system between Soochow and Shanghai for the convenience of the local merchants.[76] In the Nien area he was determined to wipe out all traces of the rebellion, but realized that in order to do so, he must first win over the people. He said, "[It is] . . . most necessary to carefully select magistrates who are strict, wise, and kind in order to establish plans and to diligently teach and nourish the people so that after three or more years the traitors can be purified, and then the rebellious source will automatically be stopped."[77] He recognized the need for using both force and benevolence and often spoke of a "hard and soft policy." Rather than blindly insisting that the taxes be collected in times of stress, taxes which he needed in order to run his government, he took a more constructive approach and tried to insure the people's livelihood so that they would be able to pay the taxes.[78] When the use of Western steamships in certain areas threatened the livelihood of the local boatmen, he resorted to various devices in order to preserve their income. On the journey from Shanghai to Wuchang, when he went to take up his post as the Hu-kuang Governor-General in 1869, he favored going up the Yangtze by steamer because it was faster. However, in deference to the local boatmen, he went by native junk — but he had the junks towed by the steamers.[79]

Li appears to have been very sensitive to the feelings of the masses and at times seemed to cater to them. One has the impression that, despite his high office and gentry background, there was a certain affinity between him and the people. His rule was stern, but he was also practical, humane, and had a rough-and-ready nature — qualities which the common people could understand.

Among his close associates, Li was known for his warm geniality and his great sense of humor. His great-great nephew, Li Chia-huang, drawing on impressions received from his elders, has described him as humorous, jovial, and witty.[80] On the other hand, he

---

[76] Douglas, *Li Hungchang*, p. 86.     [78] *Ibid.*, *chüan* 10, p. 33a.
[77] *LWCK-PL*, *chüan* 8, p. 50a.       [79] Douglas, *Li Hungchang*, p. 94.
[80] Li Chia-huang, correspondence, Hong Kong, February 28, 1962.

was also known for his brusque, if not rude, speech, his temper, and his pride and arrogance. He acknowledged his temper because it was a source of suffering to himself,[81] but he never seemed to want to correct his other faults. His brusque speech was a device he used to overawe his opponents, but when they stood up to him, he became more tractable. His pride and arrogance were rooted in his conviction that he was talented and capable and did not believe in hiding the fact behind a façade of false modesty. He once said, "Never during my whole life have I been a false person."[82] When, at the time of the Boxer uprising, a foreign correspondent told him that it was generally believed he was the only man in China who could cope with the situation, he replied, "I believe that myself."[83]

The "*chung*" in Li's posthumous title, Wen-chung, means "loyal," and this quality was one of the predominant aspects of his character. He was noted for his extreme loyalty to China and the Ch'ing rulers, and he repeatedly expressed this devotion in his letters to his friends and colleagues: "We have received the country's great favor and cannot talk of quitting. We can only do our best in order to support the country and exhaust our minds in serving, and that is all."[84] "My post has very heavy responsibilities. There are times when I am anxious and concerned about failing. Besides, when I turn around and look at our country, I am greatly distressed."[85]

Despite his extreme loyalty to the throne, Li was also extremely loyal to his friends, fellow provincials, old comrades-in-arms, family and relatives, and teachers. From a Western, nationalistic point of view, this would appear paradoxical, especially since personal loyalties were a fundamental cause of the decline of central control, but to the Confucian and culturally oriented Chinese such a discrepancy was either not apparent or else irrelevant. The important thing was human heartedness (*jen*), the concern for human feelings. Li was loyal to the throne because he could be loyal to his friends.

---

81 *LWCK-PL, chüan* 9, pp. 1a–b.

82 *Ibid., chüan* 13, p. 8b.

83 Alfred Cunningham, *The Chinese Soldier* (Hong Kong: The "Daily Press" Office, n.d.), p. 91; Martin, *A Cycle of Cathay*, p. 340; Robert Hart, "Letters to Various Westerners in the Chinese Customs Service," *MS*, typed transcripts: 1865–1910, Houghton Library, Harvard University, Hart to E. B. Drew, Peking, 28 September, 1870; Albert Philip Ludwig, "Li Hung-chang and Chinese Foreign Policy, 1870–1885" (unpublished Ph.D. Dissertation, University of California, 1936), p. 406.

84 *LWCK-PL,chüan* 13, p. 32a.      85 *Ibid., chüan* 13, p. 12b.

*Illustrations*

Plate 1. Li Hung-chang (Tientsin, 1871). Photo from Mrs. Archibald Little, *Li Hung-Chang, His Life and Time* (London: Cassell and Co., Ltd., 1903), p. 72.

Plate 2. Li Hung-chang and family (Peking, 1898). *Back row, left to right*: Kuo-chieh's wife (*née* Chang), Ching-shu's daughter, Ching-p'u (Li's youngest daughter), Ching-mai's wife (*née* Pien), Ching-shu's wife (*née* Chu). *Middle row*: Ching-mai, Ching-shu, Li Hung-chang. *Front row*: Kuo-hsiung, Kuo-hsü, Kuo-yen, Kuo-chieh. Photo courtesy of Li Kuo-ch'ao.

Plate 3. Li Kuo-ch'ao and Li Ching-mai (ca. 1910). Photo courtesy of Li Kuo-ch'ao.

Plate 4. Lo Feng-lu and Li Ching-fang (London, 1896). Photo from *The Illustrated London News, Supplement*, Vol. CIX (August 15, 1896), p. 195. By permission of the publisher.

Plate 5. Li Hung-chang and his *mu-yu* (Hong Kong, 1899). T'ang Shao-i is to the left of Li, wearing glasses. Photo courtesy of Li Kuo-ch'ao.

Plate 6. The Lords of the Admiralty (1886). *From left to right:* Shan-ch'ing, Prince Ch'un, and Li Hung-chang. Photo from Mrs. Archibald Little, *Intimate China* (London: Hutchinson and Co., Ltd., 1899), p. 495.

Plate 7. Li Hung-chang (London, 1896). Photo from Mrs. Archibald Little, *Li Hung-Chang, His Life and Time* (London: Cassell and Co., Ltd., 1903), frontispiece.

A world in which one had to choose between state and family would be unfit for human habitation. The Ch'in state and the Legalists had advocated such a world and had been cast out. When Sun Ch'iang-ming (Ch'ü-t'ien), who had been Li's and Shen Pao-chen's teacher (*fang-shih*) for the *chin-shih* examinations, got into trouble in Chekiang, Li interceded on his behalf and asked Tso Tsung-t'ang, the Governor-General of Chekiang and Fukien, to help in finding some means of support for him.[86] Several months later Li wrote to Shen Pao-chen, the Governor of Kiangsi, to see if he could help find Sun an official position in the West River (*Hsi-chiang*) region (Kwangsi and Kwangtung), as jobs were hard to find in Chekiang and Kiang-su.[87] Old soldiers who fought under Li during the Taiping and Nien rebellions constantly received his support, and for those who died in the service of the country, he memorialized for posthumous honors and tried to make sure that their families were provided for:

The Provincial Commander-in-Chief, Yang Shao-ming (Ting-hsün), commanded the Hsün character battalion at my side, participated in the campaigns and battles in the North and South, and received eminent honors. This summer at the Ts'ang-chou and Chien-ho defense headquarters he became ill and died. I have already earnestly beseeched the Emperor to grant him the posthumous title of Chung-ch'in [Loyal and Diligent] and to establish a temple to his memory. The ceremonies were liberal and sufficient to repay his faithful toil and sooth his loyal soul. But his estate was infinitesimal, and the expenses are already great. He is survived by a seventy-year-old mother, his widow, and his fatherless sons. His two elder brothers, Ting-ch'ing and Ting-nai, cannot be ordered to look after them. I, with all my fellow commanders and generals, Liu Sheng-san [Ming-ch'uan], Kuo Tzu-mei [Sung-lin], and others, again and again have deliberated to try to raise money for their support. *As to those who have been devoted to duty, and who have had merits in the army and have died for the country, if we do not take care of them, how can we face our dead friends in the hereafter?* Therefore, I have ordered Yang Ting-ch'ing and others to look after his mother and to return to Szechwan with Chung-ch'in's coffin. I have ordered the Taotai Kao Ti-chou to go with them as an escort.[88]

Li was proud of his origins and took an interest in Anhwei affairs and the well-being of his fellow-provincials. He supported provincial projects with donations of money,[89] praised worthy Anhweinese,

[86] *Ibid.*, *chüan* 5, p. 37a.
[87] *Ibid.*, *chüan* 6, p. 1b.
[88] *Ibid.*, *chüan* 8, p. 57a. Italics mine.
[89] *Ibid.*, *chüan* 4, p. 8a.

sought to secure them official positions,[90] and spoke with affection about his native place.[91] The revision and publication of the Lu-chou Prefecture gazetteer, *Hsü-hsiu Lu-chou fu-chih*, was initiated by Li's younger brother, and, when he died, Li assumed the initiative and got the other members of his family and his fellow-prefecturals, such as Liu Ming-ch'uan, to cooperate in seeing that the work was carried through.[92]

The loyalty which Li showed throughout his life for his friends has become almost legendary. He once wrote that, although loyalty and sincerity were fundamental to proper conduct, such attributes could not be attained unless one had friends. Friends were for the purpose of pointing out one's faults and, therefore, should be equals and should be chosen with care. The criticism of friends, when combined with a desire to improve oneself, would produce the desired loyalty and sincerity.[93] Having friends also entailed sticking by them in times of adversity and using one's influence to help them. Li believed so strongly in this that he was willing to jeopardize his own position to do so. In the case of Tseng Kuo-fan's impeachment of Li Yüan-tu (see Chapter IV), Li resigned from Tseng's *mu-fu* not so much in support of Yüan-tu but in support of the principle of loyalty to friends. However, this seems to have been the last time that Li took such an unswerving position. During his self-imposed exile he evidently began to realize that an unyielding position served no purpose other than to injure oneself. By presenting his case in a more judicious manner, with a concern for the human feelings involved, he could still support his friends, but lessen the injury to the parties involved. On June 29, 1863, Li wrote to Tseng Kuo-fan regarding the latter's order to transfer Huang I-sheng (Ch'ang-ch'i) to the Huai region. Li was determined to keep Huang, who was an important "water troop" commander, and disputed Tseng's transfer order on the grounds of troop morale, strategy, and, above all, the ties of friendship:

Since I received your letter four years ago ordering me with Ch'ang-ch'i to command this army, our relations have been peaceful and harmonious without any interruptions. Now, everytime Ch'ang-ch'i speaks, he constantly desires to remain in partnership. He does not want to be separated. He is truly a friend of death and life and in adversity. Yesterday Ch'ang-ch'i received a letter transferring him to the Huai area. He was sad and

90 *Ibid., chüan* 9, p. 22b.          92 *Ibid., chüan* 20, pp. 5a–b.
91 *Ibid., chüan* 3, p. 5b.           93 *LWCK-IC, chüan* 8, p. 1a.

fearful and at a loss as to what to do. You know the generals' desires and are in accord with the soldiers' hearts. I know you can really be sympathetic about this. If you must have him go, then perhaps you can memorialize to order me to go with him. . . . I look upward in expectation of your reviewing the case and of your moderation.[94]

On July 14, 1863, Li again wrote to Tseng: "Ch'ang-ch'i certainly fears the hardships of the Huai area. Here [in Shanghai] he is the one person we really cannot do without. Formerly the Wu gentry made a public appeal to keep him. I also beseech you to reflect on this."[95] After several more letters in the same vein, Li finally wrote to Tseng in a much more adamant tone. "Ch'ang-ch'i will not go, and I will not send him. If you further punish Ch'ang-ch'i and me, I am willing even unto death. . . . Suddenly you charge me with the crime of withholding troops for personal defense. When the general is far away, the superior's decree is not adhered to. Haven't you heard this? Your calculations are as wide as the sea and abundantly virtuous. I beg you not to use this small and petty thing to cause injury to heaven's peace. Ch'ang-ch'i and I have been together for years."[96] Even though this last letter sounds like an ultimatum, Li tempered his position by appealing to Tseng's sense of human feelings and upright character to smooth over the situation. By this time Li knew Tseng very intimately, and he also knew just how far he could go before things would come to an impasse.

Li was a leader in the true sense of the word. According to Chester Barnard, author of *The Functions of the Executive*, the most important single contribution of the executive is loyalty to the organization, because he is the one person whose presence is required to make the lines of communication function.[97] Li was loyal to both the state and his *mu-fu* and was always on the job. His energy, self-confidence, practicality, and desire to govern set the tone of his whole operation. His official position provided him with the power to try something new, and his wealth made it possible for him to employ *mu-yu* who could advise him and who were capable of carrying out his plans. The loyalty of subordinates can be purchased or commanded, but such ties are tenuous at best. Because of its

---

[94] *LWCK-PL, chüan* 3, p. 33a.  [95] *Ibid., chüan* 3, p. 36a.
[96] *Ibid., chüan* 4, p. 23a.
[97] Chester I. Barnard, *The Functions of the Executive* (Cambridge: Harvard Univ. Press, 1956), p. 220.

personal nature, a *mu-fu*, in order to operate effectively, must be composed of congenial, like-minded men who are bound to the host official, not just by salaries, but by mutual ties of loyalty and interest and by that undefinable quality of personal magnetism, which is so essential to a great leader. Li Hung-chang was such a leader, and he drew to his side *mu-yu* who, like himself, were a composite of the old and the new in China.

# VI. Li Hung-chang's Mu-yu

The official roster of government personnel for the Ch'ing Empire, which was published as the *Ta-Ch'ing chin-shen ch'üan-shu,* listed for the year 1871 the following officials assigned to the Chihli provincial headquarters in Pao-ting *fu*: (1.) Pao-ting *fu* Provincial Capital: a. Governor-General; b. Adjutant and Colonel in command of the Governor-General's Green Standard Brigade; c. Commander-in-Chief of the Peking area and Provincial Director of Education for the entire province. (2.) Office of the Lieutenant-Governor (Provincial Treasurer): a. Lieutenant-Governor; b. Commissary of Records; c. Law Secretary; d. Keeper of the Treasury. (3.) Office of the Provincial Judge: a. Provincial Judge; b. Commissary of Records; c. Jail Warden; d. River Taotai. [1]

These eleven men were the total complement hired by the central government for the Chihli provincial headquarters. The government did not provide the advisers, secretaries, clerks, and the like, who were necessary in order for the officials to govern effectively. Throughout the rest of the province and in all the other provinces, in every *chou, fu,* and *hsien*, the pattern was the same — the central government provided only the key personnel. As a result, the provincial officials were forced to hire privately the people the government failed to provide. This table of organization was not altered to any great degree until almost the end of the Ch'ing, when a general reorganization of the government was undertaken as a final, desperate attempt to save the dynasty.

China had been forced by the Western Powers to establish a Foreign Office, in the guise of the Tsungli Yamen, in 1860 to handle its foreign relations, which were to be based on the Western prin-

---

[1] *Ta-Ch'ing chin-shen ch'üan-shu* (The Complete Record of the Officials of the Ch'ing), T'ung-chih 10 (1871), Vol. 2, pp. 6b–7a.

ciples of the equality of nations and diplomatic representation. However, it was not until 1875 that the first Chinese diplomatic personnel were sent abroad. The only other change in the structure of the government until after the Boxer Rebellion in 1900 was the establishment of the Board of Admiralty in 1885. During the period from 1860 to 1900, when China was attempting to ward off the incursions of the West through diplomatic maneuvers and self-strengthening enterprises, the central government made no move to lead the way and establish bureaus or boards to handle the development of trade, industry, or communications — the first Ministry of Trade was not established until 1903.[2] During this period (1860–1900), whatever measures were taken to improve and strengthen the country in the face of the West had to be done at the provincial level. The court did not "wash its hands" of the whole affair, but the initiative lay with the provincial officials, and the court either approved or disapproved.

The self-strengthening enterprises of a commercial or industrial nature which developed during the late nineteenth century were known as *chü*, as in *Shang-wu chü* (China Merchants' Steam Navigation Company) and *T'ien-chin chi-ch'i chü* (Tientsin Arsenal). The term *"chü"* means "bureau" or "subdivision,"[3] and seems to have been used in a very loose way to describe almost any subdivision and/or adjunct of government. Li Hung-chang referred to the office of the Tientsin Customs Taotai as a *chü*, but Chou Fu also referred to Li's *mu-fu* as a *chü*.[4] Despite the vagueness of the term, it definitely had connotations of government, and, in a table of organization of the Ch'ing government, many *chü* would appear at the lower levels. Li's self-strengthening enterprises were organized as *chü* and were under the final control of the Ch'ing authority, but so was every other local agency or organization, no matter whether it was sponsored by the government or was of local origin.[5] The Ch'ing rulers had forged a system of control which had a hold not

[2] H. S. Brunnert and V. V. Hagelstrom, *Present Day Political Organization of China* (Taiwan Reprint, 1961), pp. 153, 484–490; Ch'ien Shih-fu, *Ch'ing-chi hsin-she chih-kuan nien-pao* (A Table of the Newly Established Officials at the End of the Ch'ing) (Peking: Chung-hua shu-chü, 1961), p. 44.

[3] *Tz'u-hai* (Taipei, Taiwan: Chung-hua shu-chü, 1959), *shang*, pp. 963–964.

[4] Li Hung-chang, *Li Wen-chung-kung ch'üan-chi* (The Complete Works of Li Hung-chang), ed. by Wu Ju-lun (Nanking, 1908), Tsou-kao, *chüan* 17, p. 14b (hereafter cited as *LWCK-TK*); see also the preface by Chou Fu (1916), *in* Li Hung-chang, *Li Wen-chung-kung ch'ih-tu* (The Letters of Li Hung-chang).

[5] Hsiao Kung-ch'üan, *Rural China* (Seattle: Univ. of Washington Press, 1960), p. 6.

only on the officialdom but also on the general population.[6] Because of this, no agency, and especially those such as the self-strengthening enterprises which affected the revenue and security of the state, were in theory free from governmental authority. Even a *mu-fu*, in the final analysis, was controlled by imperial decrees. Nevertheless, despite the omnipotence of imperial authority, it was an authority which chose to review and approve or disapprove rather than to initiate, especially in the realm of foreign affairs.

With the progressive breakdown of imperial authority in the nineteenth century, with the general imperial intransigence regarding things foreign, and with the near-bankruptcy of the Ch'ing treasury, any steps toward modernization in the form of self-strengthening measures fell, of necessity, to the powerful provincial leaders, such as Li Hung-chang.[7] They had the power, personnel, foresight, and initiative required to handle the job. So, although the self-strengthening enterprises were under government authority, still they functioned under the more direct control of the provincial leaders; and it was in these enterprises that the heretofore distinct spheres of operation of the government and the *mu-fu* system became enmeshed. What has been said regarding the *chü* was also true of the personal armies and navies. The authority came from the center, but the actual control and loyalty was in the provinces. Li Hung-chang, and not the Board of War, selected and recommended his officers; and it was he, and not the Board of Civil Appointments, who selected and recommended the managers of his enterprises.

Because the court was either unable or unwilling to change this system and assume the initiative, and because it provided only a skeleton force of official personnel, the responsible provincial officials were forced to hire *mu-yu* in order to undertake the completely new ventures demanded by the conditions of the times. Tseng Kuo-fan had added the military and self-strengthening elements to the *mu-fu* system, but he died while the latter element was still in its initial stages. Li Hung-chang was the heir to Tseng's ideas and policies, and, as such, he carried on the use of personal armies and

[6] *Ibid.*, p. 5.

[7] Albert Feuerwerker, *China's Early Industrialization: Sheng Hsuan-huai (1844–1916) and Mandarin Enterprise* (Cambridge: Harvard Univ. Press, 1958), p. 13.

expanded and developed self-strengthening ideas to an unforeseen dimension.

In keeping with the criteria for *mu-yu* set forth in Chapter II of this study, all of the people that Li relied on to carry out his numerous self-strengthening endeavors must be considered as members of his *mu-fu*: they were technically competent; they were personally hired by him; and they owed their positions to his provincial authority. His generals and admirals, the directors of his steamship, mining, railway, and telegraph companies and his cotton mill, and the staffs of his schools were all his *mu-yu*, as were his private secretaries and advisers. They all owed him personal allegiance and were dependent on him and on his official position for their protection, rewards, and punishments. Although most of his commercial and industrial enterprises fitted the accepted business pattern of official supervision and merchant management ( *kuan-tu shang-pan* ), and their respective directors held official rank, it was Li who was the principal official. He secured court approval for a venture and protected it from the inroads of the metropolitan officials. He hired and fired, with and without the court's approval, and was the final arbiter of company policy, despite statements in the articles of incorporation regarding the responsibility of management to directors and stockholders. His entire organization was built on the principle of personal loyalty, and, although Li believed in loyalty to the state, in a hierarchical world his *mu-yu*'s fundamental loyalty was due to him. He in turn would take care of the greater loyalty.

In his recruitment of *mu-yu*, Li was primarily concerned with talent, ability, and mental attitude. Although he adhered to the Confucian principle that men are adaptable and can be educated,[8] still he was not as orthodox in his beliefs as most of his contemporaries, in that he did not place morality above ability. His thinking seems to have been more in harmony with that of Ch'i-ying, who in 1851, in a suggestion to the new Hsien-feng Emperor, said, "If a man be employed in a capacity for which his talents do not fit him, though he be the 'good man' [*chün-tzu*], he will too probably

---

[8] J. O. P. Bland, *Li Hung-chang* (New York: Henry Holt and Co., 1917), p. 301; Li Hung-chang, *Li Wen-chung-kung ch'üan-chi* (The Complete Works of Li Hung-chang), ed. by Wu Ju-lun (Nanking, 1908), P'eng-liao han-kao Letters to Friends and Colleagues), *chüan* 20, pp. 8a, 11b; *chüan* 9, pp. 19b, 29b; *chüan* 17, p. 29a; *chüan* 4, p. 26a; *chüan* 1, pp. 24a, 37a (hereafter cited as *LWCK-PL*).

mar his undertaking; if he be employed to do what he is able to perform, though 'the worthless' [*hsiao-jen*], he may still be turned to account."[9] Ch'i-ying was rebuked by the emperor for this heretical statement, and Li was criticized by many of his contemporaries for his hiring policies. Nonetheless, the members of Li's *mu-fu* were capable, if not always moral.

The supply of capable personnel was, however, limited. The examination system was still the guiding force in regard to education, and people who were willing to learn about the West and its techniques were scarce. Those men who, despite their literary training, could adapt to new ideas and learn new techniques were assiduously sought after, and Li was continually bemoaning this lack of talent.[10] In his eyes, men of talent were the key to the preservation of China. "Even if we have an abundance of wealth, but do not have an abundance of talent, then not only will we be humbled by the Westerners, but we will not even be equal to Japan."[11] In his search for talent, Li ranged far and wide, and his *mu-yu* included representatives from both the traditional and the foreign sectors of the Chinese world.

The Ch'ien-lung and Chia-ch'ing emperors had proscribed the use of family members and relatives in the *mu-fu* (see Chapter II). Although this regulation had lost its force by the latter part of the nineteenth century, the requirement of competency tended to act as a self-imposed restriction. Li Hung-chang was the second of six sons, yet the role played by his brothers in his *mu-fu* was very limited. His elder brother, Li Han-chang, after serving nine years in Tseng Kuo-fan's *mu-fu* (see Chapter IV), began his official career in 1862 when he was appointed the Kwangtung Grain Taotai. At no time during his subsequent career, which saw him achieve the rank of governor-general, did he ever serve in his younger brother's *mu-fu*.[12] The third and sixth brothers, Li Ho-chang and

---

[9] Mary C. Wright, *The Last Stand of Chinese Conservatism. The T'ung-Chih Restoration, 1862–1874* (Stanford: Stanford Univ. Press, 1957), p. 68.

[10] *LWCK-PL, chüan* 17, p. 7b; *chüan* 1, p. 43b; *chüan* 14, pp. 31a–b; *chüan* 19, p. 13b; *chüan* 16, pp. 31a–b; *chüan* 3, pp. 14a–b, 40a; *chüan* 16, p. 15b.

[11] *Ibid., chüan* 12, p. 3b.

[12] Li Han-chang: After serving in Tseng Kuo-fan's *mu-fu* for nine years (see Chapter IV), Li Han-chang was transferred to Kwantung Province in 1862 to assist in supervising *likin* affairs. On his way to Canton, he passed through Shanghai and was commissioned by his younger brother, Li Hung-chang, to buy "foreign cannon, powder, and caps" at Hong Kong. Hung-chang also in-

Li Chao-ch'ing, respectively, served under the second brother as commanders in the *Huai-chün*. In 1853 and after, Ho-chang had fought with Hung-chang and their father against the rebels in An-hwei; from 1859 until 1862 he commanded troops under Tseng Kuo-fan and then joined the newly created *Huai-chün*. Ho-chang

tended to use him as a source of information about conditions in the South. Through Han-chang's efforts, the *likin* revenue was virtually monopolized by Tseng Kuo-fan and was used to support his troops. At the end of the year he was made the Kwangtung Grain Taotai (*tu-liang-tao*), and in the next year became the Provincial Judge (*an-ch'a-shih*) in that province. In 1864 he was made Kwangtung Provincial Treasurer (*pu-cheng-shih*) and early in the next year was raised to the position of Governor of Hunan. At the beginning of 1867, when his younger brother, Hung-chang, was made Governor-General of Hu-kuang but replaced Tseng Kuo-fan to fight the Nien rebels, Han-chang substituted for him as the Acting Governor-General of Hu-kuang. He held this post until the end of 1867, when he was made the Governor of Chekiang and awarded the Button of the First Rank (*t'ou-p'in ting-tai*). At the end of 1869, when Hung-chang was ordered to investigate the anti-Christian riots in Kweichow, Han-chang was shifted back to Hu-kuang as the Acting Governor-General to substitute for his brother. He became the substantive Governor-General of Hu-kuang in the following summer, when his younger brother was made the Chihli Governor-General, replacing Tseng Kuo-fan.

For the next twelve years, Li Han-chang held the post of Governor-General of Hu-kuang, except for one period of a little over a year. This interlude began in the summer of 1875 when he was transferred to be the Governor-General of Szechwan. At the end of the year he was detached from this post and assigned to investigate the murder of the Englishman, Augustus Margary, in Yunnan, while Hung-chang negotiated with the British in Chefoo. After the case was settled, in September, 1876, Li Han-chang was reassigned to the Hu-kuang Governor-Generalship. When his mother, who had been living with him for over ten years, died in 1882, he was forced to give up his post and go into mourning.

Between 1884, when he came out of mourning, and 1888, Han-chang was unable to secure an official appointment. Finally he was granted an audience with the emperor and assigned to the post of Director General of Grain Transport (*ts'ao-yün tsung-tu*) and two months later was given the concurrent rank of President of the Board of War (*ping-pu shang-shu*). In the summer of the next year (1889) he was shifted to be the Liang-kuang (Kwangtung and Kwangsi) Governor-General. He held this post until the spring of 1895, when, due to illness and, no doubt, to the debacle of his brother's forces against the Japanese, he was allowed to retire. In 1894 he had been granted the honorary title of Junior Guardian of the Heir Apparent (*t'ai-tzu shao-pao*), on the occasion of the Empress Dowager's sixtieth birthday. He died at the family estates in Ho-fei on September 11, 1899, at the age of about eighty. *LWCK-PL, chüan* 2, pp. 14a, 27a, 35b; *chüan* 3, p. 12b; *chüan* 5, p. 27a; *chüan* 6, p. 9a; Stanley Spector, "Li Hung-chang and the Huai-chün (unpublished Ph.D. Dissertation, University of Washington, 1953), p. 227; *Ch'ing-shih lieh-chuan* (Taipei, Taiwan: Chung-hua shu-chü, 1962), *chüan* 59, pp. 24a–26b; *Ch'ing-tai cheng-hsien lei-pien* (Taipei, Taiwan: Shih-chieh shu-chü, 1961), *shang*, Tsung-tu nien-piao, *chüan* 3, pp. 8a–11b.

served as one of Hung-chang's commanders until the end of the Taiping Rebellion, when he retired because of illness. From 1865 until his death in 1880 he lived in retirement in Ho-fei.[13] Chao-ch'ing was ten years younger than Hung-chang and was considered the baby of the family. He began his military career with the creation of *Huai-chün* and served in it until the end of the Taiping Rebellion, when he went into retirement. A year later, however, he was recalled to serve under Tseng Kuo-fan, who had taken over the *Huai-chün* to fight the Nien rebels. Chao-ch'ing remained with his

[13] Li Ho-chang: The career of Li Ho-chang, the third brother, was closely connected to that of Li Hung-chang, up to the close of the Taiping Rebellion. He achieved the first of the literary degrees, *hsiu-ts'ai*, but was never able to pass the examination for the next higher degree, although he did purchase the rank of senior licentiate (*ling-kung-sheng*). In 1853 he raised and led local militia troops in Anhwei with his father and Hung-chang, and in 1855, for his efforts in the fighting at Lu-chou, he received the Blue Plume (*lan-ling*). In the next year he was raised to the 5th official rank for assisting in the capture of Wu-wei. In 1859 he joined Tseng Kuo-fan's *mu-fu* as a military commander, and, for his part in the recovery of An-ch'ing in 1861, he was awarded the Single-Eyed Peacock Feather (*hua-ling*) and appointed an Expectant District Magistrate. When Li Hung-chang took the main body of his newly created *Huai* army by ship to Shanghai in 1862, Ho-chang brought another contingent by land to join his brother in Shanghai. For the next three years he served in his brother's *mu-fu* in various military capacities. At first he was in command of Li's personal troops, and later he commanded a mobile force. During his military career, he commanded troops in conjunction with such famous *Huai* generals as Ch'eng Hsüeh-ch'i, Liu Ming-ch'uan, Kuo Sung-lin, and Huang I-sheng, and with Ward and Gordon of the Ever-Victorious Army. His efforts were rewarded by gradual increases in rank and honors. After the recovery of Ch'ang-chou in 1864, he was appointed the Kansu, Kan-liang Taotai and awarded the Yellow Riding Jacket (*huang-ma-kua*), but he stayed on with Li's armies in Kiangsu. In the next year, because the Kansu Moslems were in rebellion, he was ordered to proceed to his post, but he refused to go because of illness. Li backed him up and asked Tseng Kuo-fan to intercede. Tseng also requested in a memorial that the post be kept open for him until he recovered from his illness. Although Ho-chang did not go to Kansu, he made a liberal contribution to the Shansi relief fund and, as a result, was raised to the 2nd official rank. Between 1865 and his death in 1880 he lived in retirement in Ho-fei, *Ching shih-kao* (Draft History of the Ch'ing Dynasty), ed. by Chao Erh-hsün, *et al.* (Hong Kong: Hsiang-kang wen-hsüeh yen-chiu she [1960?], *lieh-chuan* 220, *hsia*, p. 1373; *Ch'ing-shih lieh-chuan, chüan* 65, p. 48a; Yü Yü-ti, "Tseng Kuo-fan mu-fu pin-liao nien-p'u" (A Chronological Record of Tseng Kuo-fan's *Mu-fu* and Its Members) (unpublished Bachelor's Thesis, National Taiwan University, Taipei, Taiwan, 1960), p. 23; *LWCK-PL*, *chüan* 2, pp. 16a, 50b; *chüan* 6, pp. 5a–b; *chüan* 1, p. 41b; interview with Li Kuo-ch'ao, San Francisco, California, April 4, 1962; Li Hung-chang, *Li Wen-chung-kung i-chi* (Posthumous Collection of the Writings of Li Hung-chang), *in* Li Kuo-chieh, ed., *Ho-fei Li shih san shih i-chi* ([no place]: The Li Family of Ho-fei, 1904), *chüan* 4, p. 4a (hereafter cited as *LWCK-IC*).

second brother's army as a commander until his death in 1873 at the age of thirty-nine.[14]

The fourth brother, Li Yün-chang, and the fifth brother, Li Feng-chang, were never active in military or political affairs and never served in Hung-chang's *mu-fu*. Yün-chang was blind and spent his entire life in Ho-fei. Feng-chang was a banker and something of a miser. He was, according to Li Hung-chang's late grandson, the richest of all the brothers, with an estate in Ho-fei and many pawnshops and other businesses in Ho-fei and Shanghai.[15]

Of the six Li brothers, Hung-chang was obviously the most outstanding, and his career influenced the lives of the others, for better or for worse. Although Han-chang was the eldest and achieved high official position, his timid and cautious character resulted in his relinquishing the leadership in the family to Hung-chang, who was much more forceful and ambitious. Han-chang was reported to have acknowledged that his success as an official was due to his younger brother.[16] The exigencies of the times permitted Hung-chang to utilize the military attributes of two of his brothers in his *mu-fu*, but the power of the throne, the character of his brothers,

---

[14] Li Chao-ch'ing: The youngest brother, Chao-ch'ing, who was ten years younger than Li, began his career with the creation of the *Huai-chün* in Anhwei. He is first mentioned in Li's letters in November, 1862 as being in charge of drilling the five *Shu* character battalions, which Tseng Kuo-fan retained for the defense of Wu-wei (see Chapter IV). When these battalions were finally released by Tseng to go to Shanghai in the spring of 1863, Chao-ch'ing accompanied them to serve under his elder brother. In 1864 he served as a Detachment Commander (*t'ung-ling*) in the army of Liu Ming-ch'uan, leading his own four battalions. With the end of the Taiping Rebellion, he returned to Anhwei but was again called to military service when Tseng Kuo-fan was given command of the campaign against the Nien rebels in 1865. Chao-ch'ing requested duty in the newly created cavalry units and became a commander of a mobile force. When Li replaced Tseng as commander of the campaign, his youngest brother continued to serve under him. After the suppression of the Nien rebels in 1868, Chao-ch'ing continued to serve in the *Huai* army as a commander in the Chiang-huai region. For his work in the Nien campaign, he was recorded to be a Salt Controller (*yen-yün-shih*) and awarded the Single-Eyed Peacock Feather. In 1873 he went north for an audience with the emperor and died in Tientsin at the age of forty (*sui*) from illnesses contracted during his military service. *LWCK-PL, chüan* 2, p. 25b; *chüan* 6, p. 34a; *chüan* 13, p. 14a; Spector, p. 68; *Ch'ing shih-kao*, lieh-chuan 220, *hsia*, p. 1373; Huang Yün-hsiu, *Hsü-hsiu Lu-chou fu-chih* (Revised edition of the Lu-chou Prefecture Gazetteer) (1885), *chüan* 58, p. 6a; Mrs. Archibald Little, *Li Hung-Chang. His Life and Time* (London: Cassell and Company, Ltd., 1903), p. 83.

[15] Interview with Li Kuo-ch'ao, San Francisco, California, April 4, 1962.

[16] W. A. P. Martin, "Li Hung Chang," *The Independent*, LIII, No. 2763 (November 14, 1901), 2688.

and illness and death prevented the formation of a family clique. Li Hung-chang, thus, received no substantial help from any of his brothers and was forced to rely on his own efforts. He had to wait until his sons had reached maturity before he could utilize the services of any of the members of his family in his *mu-fu* to any real advantage.

Li Hung-chang had six sons (one was adopted) and three daughters. Three of the sons and a son-in-law served in his *mu-fu*. The adopted son, Li Ching-fang, who was the eldest son of his youngest brother, was born in 1860 and in 1878 was attending his adoptive father in the latter's *yamen* in Tientsin.[17] Although he became a *chü-jen* in 1882, he was also learning English and preparing for a diplomatic career. In 1886 he was sent to Europe as a Secretary of Legation under Liu Jui-fen, the Chinese Minister to England, who was an Anhwei man and had served under Li during the early days of the *Huai-chün*.[18] Ching-fang returned to China in 1889 and in the next year became the Chinese Minister to Japan (1890–1892). After the required period of mourning for his adoptive mother, beginning in 1892, he served his adoptive father during the negotiations for the Treaty of Shimonoseki (1895), during his trip around the world (1896), and during the Boxer settlement negotiations (1900).[19] Li's other two sons who reached maturity, Ching-shu and

[17] *LWCK-PL*, *chüan* 17, pp. 44b–45a.

[18] Spector, p. 310; Ch'ien, *Ch'ing-chi hsin-she chih-kuan nien-pao*, p. 19.

[19] Li Ching-fang: Li Hung-chang's first son was born to his first wife, *née* Chou, who was also from Ho-fei. However, this child died when about one year old, and its mother soon passed away, overcome by grief over the loss of her only son. Because there were no surviving sons to carry out the worship to their mother's spirit, Li's mother decided that he should adopt the eldest son of his youngest brother, Chao-ch'ing, who was about the same age as Li's recently deceased son. This adopted son, Li Ching-fang, born in 1860, was to be considered the eldest true son and receive all the rights and privileges pertaining thereto. Throughout Li's lifetime, Ching-fang remained the first son, despite the fact that Li had other sons born to his second wife.

About 1863 Li Hung-chang married his second wife, *née* Chao, who was from T'ai-hu *hsien* in Anhwei and the daughter of a famous family of scholars. This wife, who was about thirteen years his junior, bore him three sons and three daughters. The first son of this marriage was Ching-shu, who was born in 1864 and survived his father by only three months, dying in January, 1902. Then came Ching-yüan, who lived for only a couple of years and was followed in 1877 by Ching-mai, who died in 1938. Li's last son was Ching-chin, who was born to Li's concubine, Mo, in 1877, but he died when he was sixteen (*sui*), one day before Li's 70th birthday, on February 14, 1892. Of the three daughters we know little more than whom they married. In 1888, the second daughter married Chang P'ei-lun, who was a former Acting Senior Vice-Presi-

Ching-mai, never achieved any position of real importance under their father. Although Ching-shu, Li's first natural son, became a *chü-jen* in 1885, he was never active in politics, because he was a cripple and in poor health. He did emerge briefly from obscurity in 1896 when he accompanied his father on his trip to Europe and

dent of the Censorate (*tso-fu tu-yü-shih*) and a Hanlin Expositor (*shih-chiang hsüeh-shih*). The eldest daughter married Kuo En-hou, a First Class Sub-Prefect (*t'ung-chih*) in Shantung, and the youngest married Jen Te-ho, a Second Class Secretary of a Board (*chu-shih*). Li's youngest daughter, Ching-p'u, was still living in China, being over eighty years old, as of 1963.

In a letter written in 1878, Li mentioned that both Ching-fang and Ching-shu were with him in his *yamen* in Tientsin and were preparing for the examinations. He was trying to find a suitable tutor for them, one whose conduct and virtue were in keeping with the teachings of the sages, but whose writings were in accord with the prevailing times. Ching-fang became a *chü-jen* in 1882 and Ching-shu in 1885. Yet at the same time Ching-fang was also learning English and preparing for a diplomatic career. In 1886 Li said that although Ching-fang had a "rough knowledge" of Western speech and writing, he had not handled any diplomatic negotiations, and he would thus be sent abroad for further training. Shortly thereafter he went to Europe where he served as Secretary of Legation in both London and Paris. He returned to China in 1889. In 1890 he was given the official position of Expectant Taotai and sent to Japan as the Chinese Minister. When his adoptive mother, *née* Chao, died in 1892, he returned home from Japan and went into full mourning, although he had only been allowed one hundred days of mourning when his real mother had died the previous year. Ching-fang was called back to duty in 1895 when he accompanied his adoptive father to Shimonoseki for the peace negotiations. When Li was wounded by an assassin's bullet, Ching-fang became the plenipotentiary and continued the negotiations. He was also the Chinese representative at the ceremony on board a Japanese warship off Keelung, Formosa, when that island was formally turned over to Japan in 1895. In the next year, when Li made his trip around the world, at his father's request and with the Court's approval, Ching-fang accompanied him as consulting commissioner to assist him in any diplomatic negotiations. During his father's period of eclipse, Ching-fang was in official retirement. He assisted his father as a *mu-yu* during the Boxer Uprising in 1900, but was not called to duty again until he became the Chinese Minister to England, 1907–1910. He died in Dairen about 1934. Interview with Li Kuo-ch'ao, February 21, 1962, September 20, 1962, and March 5, 1964; Wu Ju-lun, "Li Wen-chung-kung shen-tao-pei," *in Li Wen-chung-kung ch'üan-chi,* chüan-shou, p. 64b; interview with Li Chia-wei, Hong Kong, November 2, 1961; Fan Yin-nan, *Tang-tai Chung-kuo ming-jen lu* (Shanghai: Liang-yu t'u-shu yin-shua kung-ssu ch'u-pan, 1931), p. 106; Yang Chia-lo, *Min-kuo ming-jen t'u-chien* (A Survey of the Famous Men of the Chinese Republic), *chüan* 13, p. 53; Li Chia-huang, correspondence, Hong Kong, February 28, 1962; Little, pp. 161, 188, 190; Bland, *Li Hung-chang,* p. 70; Huang, *Hsü-hsiu Lu-chou fu-chih,* chüan 30, p. 55b; LWCK-PL, chüan 17, p. 44b; chüan 20, pp. 63b–64a; Ch'ien, *Ch'ing-chi hsin-she chih-kuan nien-pao,* p. 78; Hosea Ballou Morse, *The International Relations of the Chinese Empire* (Taiwan Reprint), III, 43; U.S. Library of Congress, Asiatic Division, *Eminent Chinese of the Ch'ing Period (1644–1912),* ed. by Arthur W. Hummel (Wash-

America.[20] Ching-mai, the younger of Li's surviving sons, never passed any of the official examinations but became very adept at English and frequently served as an interpreter for his father, who never learned any foreign languages. He did not become actively engaged in his father's *mu-fu* until 1900, one year before Li's death, when he accompanied him from Shanghai to Peking for the Boxer negotiations.[21]

The only other member of Li's immediate family who served in his *mu-fu* was his son-in-law, Chang P'ei-lun, who in 1888 married his second daughter. Why Li accepted Chang as a *mu-yu* and later as a son-in-law is one of the perplexing questions of his career. Chang was a *chin-shih* of 1871, a Hanlin, and during the 1880's a member of the *Ch'ing-liu* ("Pure Flowing") Party, which vociferously and trenchantly opposed any compromise with the West. He was scathing in his denunciations of those officials, such as Ch'unghou, whom he felt were giving in to the foreigners, and hot-headedly demanded that China use force against the Japanese in 1882 during the Liu-ch'iu dispute, and against the French when Sino-French relations became strained in the same year.[22] Yet despite his political views, which were directly opposed to Li's, Chang served in

ington, D.C.: U.S. Gov't Printing Office, 1943), I, 469 (hereafter cited as Hummel); Hosea Ballou Morse, "Letter-books of H. B. Morse Containing Copies of His Correspondence While Commissioner with the Chinese Maritime Customs, 1886–1907" (MS, Houghton Library, Harvard University), Morse to Hart, June 3, 1895, Tamsui; Paul King, *In the Chinese Customs Service*, rev. ed. (London: T. Fisher Unwin, Ltd., 1930), p. 155; Hsü I-shih, "T'an Li Chingfang," *Kuo-wen chou-pao*, XI, No. 44 (November, 1934), 4.

[20] Huang, *Hsü-hsiu Lu-chou fu-chih, chüan* 30, p. 55b; interview with Li Kuo-ch'ao, February 21, 1962, June 7, 1962; Wu Ju-lun, *Li Wen-chungkung shih lüeh* (An outline of the Career of Li Hung-chang) (Tokyo: Sanseidō Shoten, 1902), p. 2a; T'ao-ch'i-yü-yen and Hsing-hsing-an-chu, eds., "Li Fuhsiang yu-li ko-kuo jih-chi" (A Diary of Li Hung-chang's journey to Various Countries), *in* Tso Shun-sheng, comp., *Chung-kuo chin-pai-nien shih tzu-liao hsü-pien* (Taipei, Taiwan: Chung-hua shu-chü, 1958), pp. 387–388.

[21] Robert K. Douglas, *Li Hungchang* (London: Bliss, Sands and Foster, 1895), p. 231; Sarah Pike Conger, *Letters from China* (London: Hodder and Stoughton, 1909), p. 56; interview with Li Kuo-ch'ao, February 21, 1962, April 4, 1962, March 5, 1964; Wu Ju-lun, *Li Wen-chung-kung shih-lüeh*, p. 2a; Fan Yin-nan, p. 106; Yang Chia-lo, *chüan* 13, p. 53.

[22] Hummel, I, 48; Lloyd Eric Eastman, "Reactions of Chinese Officials to Foreign Aggression: A Study of the Sino-French Controversy 1880–1885" (unpublished Ph.D. Dissertation, Harvard University, 1962), p. 117, cited with the author's permission; T. F. Tsiang, "Sino-Japanese Diplomatic Relations, 1870–1894," *Chinese Social and Political Science Review*, XVII, No. 1 (April, 1933), 77.

Li's *mu-fu* from 1879 to 1881, while in mourning for his mother, as a military adviser. In 1884, his cowardly defection during the French bombardment of Foochow resulted in his banishment. He was recalled from exile through Li's intercession in 1888, and in the same year was invited to rejoin Li's *mu-fu* and became his son-in-law. Chang continued to serve in Li's *mu-fu*, despite differences of opinion, until 1894.[23] The only explanation for his long service under Li is that Li admired his outspoken nature and excellent scholarship. Other possible reasons are that Li and Chang's father, Chang Yin-t'ang, had served together in Anhwei under Chiang Chung-yüan in 1853, although there is no record of any close relationship between the two men, and also that Li might have felt it was better to have Chang in his *mu-fu* where he could keep an eye on him.

The qualification of competency was no doubt the reason why more of Li's relatives and close family friends did not serve in his *mu-fu*. He was probably compelled by reasons of filial piety to hire some of them, but he tried to keep the deadwood at a minimum. There are vague reports that some of his nephews served as his *mu-yu*, but none of them ever achieved any position of importance.[24] On the other hand, he was more than willing to hire a capable family friend. In 1876 when Li was arguing for the establishment of a cotton spinning mill in Shanghai to undercut the importation of English cotton cloth, he wrote to Shen Pao-chen (Yu-tan) as follows: "As to the Taotai Wei Wen-yün, the intertwining of his ancestors with mine has been good for many generations. In accounting he is most skilled, and in the details of commerce he is most experienced. I have requested him to come out to head up the management." [25] Even though Li hired members of his family, relatives, and family friends as his *mu-yu*, the regulations of the Ch'ing against nepotism still had enough life and the censors were still vociferous enough to force him to do it with caution. In a sense he probably welcomed the lingering force of these regulations because they provided him with a convenient excuse to refuse the

[23] Hummel, I, 48. Service in a *mu-fu* seems to have been permissible during the period of mourning, while holding an active official post was not.
[24] Bernhard Menne, *Blood and Steel; The Rise of the House of Krupp*, transl. by G. H. Smith (New York: L. Furman, Inc., 1938), pp. 196–197; Morse, *The International Relations of the Chinese Empire*, III, 33–34; Chiang Siang-tseh, *The Nien Rebellion* (Seattle: Univ. of Washington Press, 1954), p. 146.
[25] *LWCK-PL, chüan* 16, p. 3b.

countless requests he must have received from friends and relatives to join his *mu-fu*.

The composition of Li's *mu-fu* naturally varied from time to time and included literally hundreds of people during his long career. However, certain individuals continually reappeared in various capacities and formed a comparatively small, hard-core group. Their origins and educational backgrounds varied, as did their reasons for serving under Li, but in general they were all concerned with the problem of preserving China from its internal or external enemies. They came from scholarly, military, merchant, and "returned-student" backgrounds and acted as advisers, generals, secretaries, diplomats, and directors of commercial and industrial enterprises. Up to about the mid-1880's, this group was mainly composed of men with a more traditional background who had begun their service under Li during the years of the rebellions (1862–1870), but after that time the leadership was gradually dominated by men who were either "returned students" or who had lived in the West at some time. Of Li's advisers, the three who had the most influence on his thinking regarding the West and the needs of self-strengthening were Feng Kuei-fen, Kuo Sung-t'ao, and Hsüeh Fu-ch'eng.

Li had known Feng Kuei-fen (1809–1874) during his Hanlin days in Peking (1847–1853), but it was not until 1861, when the Soochow gentry beseeched Tseng Kuo-fan to send an army to protect Shanghai, that the two men renewed their acquaintance.[26] Feng had written the petition for the Soochow gentry, which resulted in Li forming the *Huai-chün* and becoming the Kiangsu Governor (see Chapter IV). Feng was a *chin-shih* of 1841 and a Hanlin from Soochow. Although he was a scholar, he was, nonetheless, active in the local militia in his native area. When the Taiping rebels captured Soochow, he fled to Shanghai where he saw at firsthand the strength and power of the West. In 1862 Li Hung-chang memorialized that Feng be attached to his staff, and from then until 1865 he served Li as an independent adviser and part-time *mu-yu*, leaving an indelible imprint on Li's future thinking, In 1870, in a memorial to the throne, Li acknowledged his great debt to Feng.[27]

[26] *LWCK-TK, chüan* 9, p. 24a.

[27] Hummel, I, 242; Teng Ssu-yü and John K. Fairbank, *China's Response to the West, A Documentary Survey, 1839–1923* (Cambridge: Harvard Univ. Press, 1954), pp. 50–51; William T. DeBary, ed., *Sources of Chinese Tradition*

Feng Kuei-fen, who became one of the leading theorists of the T'ung-chih Restoration, was probably the originator of the term "self-strengthening" (*tzu-ch'iang*). He was also one of the first Chinese to see the need to learn Western techniques if China was to survive, and his ideas anticipated the later famous phrase "*Chung-hsüeh wei-t'i, Hsi-hsüeh wei-yung*" (Chinese studies for the base, Western studies for use). He saw clearly that the West was far superior to China but felt that this did not have to be so. The situation could be corrected within the Chinese context if the emperor would put morals aright, and if China obtained from the West the much-needed ships and guns. He further felt that mathematics formed the basis of Western knowledge, and that translation bureaus should be established in Shanghai and Canton to train students in Western languages, so that foreign mathematical and scientific texts could be translated into Chinese. On the basis of his suggestions, Li set up such a school in Shanghai in 1863. Feng was also an advocate of reforming the examination system to include scientific subjects. He further believed that the foreigners should not be despised but treated honestly and fairly. He was a prime mover in the rehabilitation of the Soochow area at the end of the Taiping Rebellion and was the author of the tax reduction program initiated by Li and Tseng in 1865. Many of Li's proposals for reforms during this period were actually written, or at least directly influenced, by Feng Kuei-fen.[28]

The second of Li's advisers, Kuo Sung-t'ao (1818–1891), was a *ting-wei* classmate of Li's and a fellow-Hanlin, who had also served in Tseng Kuo-fan's *mu-fu*. Although Kuo only served in Li's *mu-fu* for a few months in 1862, Li remained his close friend, confidant, and protector throughout his life. It was on Li's recommendation that Kuo was appointed the Soochow and Sungkiang Grain Taotai (1862). He subsequently became the Acting Governor of Kwangtung (1863–1866) and, in 1875, the first Chinese Minister to England. As early as 1859, when he was assigned to the staff of Seng-ko-lin-ch'in,

(New York: Columbia Univ. Press, 1960), p. 707; *LWCK-TK, chüan* 16, p. 24a; Spector, p. 84; *LWCK-PL, chüan* 1, p. 31a.

[28] Hummel, I, 242; Teng and Fairbank, pp. 50–55; DeBary, *Sources of Chinese Tradition*, pp. 707–711; Mary C. Wright, p. 66; Hsiao Kung-ch'üan, "Weng T'ung-ho and the Reform Movement of 1898," *The Tsing Hua Journal of Chinese Studies*, New Series 1, No. 2 (April, 1957), pp. 120, 150–151; Immanuel C. Y. Hsü, *China's Entrance into the Family of Nations* (Cambridge: Harvard Univ. Press, 1960), p. 142.

who was defending the approaches to the capital against the Western armies, Kuo was outspoken in his condemnation of the use of force against the foreigners. His position was that the foreigners desired only the right to trade with China, and that, if the Chinese government would use reason instead of force, the empire would have a century of peace. As the most outspoken advocate of compromise with the West, Kuo became the prime target of the conservatives. Their attacks against him became even more violent after he went to England in 1876 and after his diary was published in which he said that the West had a long and respectable civilization which was superior to that of other barbarians. He advocated long-range reforms, even to the extent of changing China's basic institutions, and wished to see iron and coal mines opened and railways built in every part of the empire. Although Li agreed with him and protected him as best he could, still the intensity of the attack by the traditionalists compelled Li to caution him to be more discreet. Kuo was recalled to China in 1879; fearing for his life if he went to Peking, he returned to his home in Hunan, where he lived in retirement. However, he continued to write letters and memorials in support of Li's policies until his death in 1891.[29]

The third adviser was Hsüeh Fu-ch'eng (1838–1894), a *hsiu-ts'ai* of 1857 from Kiangsu, who served in Tseng Kuo-fan's *mu-fu* from 1865 to 1872. In 1875 he was invited to join Li's *mu-fu* as a secretary and served him until 1884, when on Li's recommendation he was appointed a Taotai in Chekiang. He later became the Chinese Minister to England (1890–1894). During the years he was in Li's *mu-fu*, Hsüeh served as an adviser on current national problems. His views on diplomatic representation had helped persuade the court to send envoys to the Western countries in 1875. At that time he stated that it was necessary to create a new branch of examinations which should deal with foreign subjects and serve as an incentive to get capable men to study foreign affairs. China was being victimized, he felt, because of her lack of knowledge of international law and modern diplomacy.[30] Many of his ideas were incorporated into the Chefoo Convention of 1876; he drew up a set of regulations for a

[29] Hummel, I, 438; David Hamilton, "Kuo-Sung-tao; A Maverick Confucian," Harvard University, Center for East Asian Studies, *Papers on China*, Vol. 15, pp. 1, 3, 4, 19, 20; Hsiao Kung-ch'üan, "Weng T'ung-ho and the Reform Movement of 1898," p. 131; Eastman, pp. 59–61; Spector, pp. 155–156.
[30] Immanuel C. Y. Hsü, pp. 175–176, 121.

modern Chinese navy in 1881; and it was on his suggestion that Chinese troops were sent to Korea in 1882 following the riots in Seoul.[31] At first Hsüeh had considered Kuo Sung-t'ao's reform ideas to be too radical, but when he became the Chinese Minister to England in 1890, he had a chance to see for himself what Kuo had been talking about and in general came to agree with him.[32] He felt that the parliamentary system of government was the best, and that science, compulsory education, government encouragement of commerce and industry, and the use of machinery to produce wealth and feed the people were the reasons behind European prosperity and strength.[33]

Of the three advisers, Hsüeh was the last to appear and also the most practical. All three had had their eyes opened by contact with Westerners — Feng in Shanghai, and Kuo and Hsüeh in Europe — and had passed their ideas on to Li. They all continued to work with Li even after they had left his *mu-fu*. During the course of his long career, Li was an advocate of compromise with the West and one of the leading self-strengtheners; he favored diplomatic representation and the training of Chinese in foreign languages and sciences, and on several occasions he spoke out for reforms in the examination system to include a knowledge of the West so that there would be a reason for talented people to pursue these subjects. Feng Kuei-fen probably had the greatest influence on Li's thinking because of their early association, whereas Kuo and Hsüeh no doubt supplemented and supported his ideas and, at the same time, provided him with a source of knowledge about the West.

Li Hung-chang used his *mu-fu* and his bureaucratic position as a means of training personnel in foreign techniques. He did not approve of his generals resting on their laurels, but encouraged them to keep an open mind and to study Western innovations. He criticized Ch'eng Hsüeh-ch'i and Kuo Sung-lin for being "obstinate, rustic, self-satisfied, and not willing to seek instruction," whereas he praised Liu Ming-ch'uan for his desire to improve himself and hoped that while the *Huai-chün* was stationed in Shanghai (1862–1864), Liu would be able to learn the superior military methods of the foreigners.[34] This policy paid dividends for Li and for China in that a number of his generals eventually attained high official position

---

[31] Teng and Fairbank, p. 141.
[32] Hamilton, p. 22; Teng and Fairbank, pp. 143–144.
[33] Teng and Fairbank, pp. 141–146.    [34] *LWCK-PL, chüan* 2, p. 47a.

and became active in self-strengthening enterprises. Under Li's tutelage, Liu Ming-ch'uan rose from a local militia leader in Anhwei with a smuggler's background to be the most famous general of the *Huai-chün*. Later, as the first Governor of Taiwan (1885–1891), Liu completely reorganized the island's military defenses, administration, and tax structure. He established schools, paved streets, installed electric lights, introduced a Westernized postal system, extended the previously installed telegraph lines, laid a submarine cable between Taiwan and Foochow, and built one of the first railways in China — 62 miles long.[35]

As for Li's other generals, Chang Shu-sheng, who had been a local militia commander in Ho-fei and one of Li's original *Huai-chün* commanders, rose to the rank of governor-general, as did Liu Ping-chang, a *chin-shih* of 1860 from Anhwei and a Hanlin who had served under Li in the early days of the *Huai-chün*.[36] Ting Shou-ch'ang, an old friend of Li's from Ho-fei, was one of the commanders of the *Ming-chün* during the post-Nien Rebellion period and then went on to become the Tientsin Military Taotai in the 1870's. He was also one of a committee which drew up the regulations for the establishment of the Kaiping Mining Company, in compliance with Li's instructions, in late 1877.[37]

For the establishment and operation of his commercial and industrial enterprises, Li relied heavily on men from the merchant or compradore classes of Shanghai and Kwangtung. Chu Ch'i-ang, the first Manager of the China Merchants Steam Navigation Company, was from a merchant family in Shangai which owned junks and had interests in the tribute rice trade.[38] His replacement in 1873, T'ang T'ing-shu (Tong King-sing), and T'ang's assistant, Hsü Jun, were both ex-compradores from Kwangtung who had settled in Shanghai. Cheng Kuan-ying, the founder of the first Chinese-owned cotton mill, who was later associated with the Imperial Telegraph Adminis-

[35] Hummel, I, 526–528.

[36] Ch'ien Shih-fu, *Ch'ing-chi chung-yao chih-kuan nien-piao* (A Table of the Important Officials at the End of the Ch'ing) (Peking: Chung-hua shu-chü, 1959), p. 246; LWCK-PL, *chüan* 1, p. 37a.

[37] *LWCK-IC*, *chüan* 3, p. 16a; Ellsworth C. Carlson, *The Kaiping Mines (1877–1912)* (Cambridge: Harvard Univ. Press, 1957), p. 29; LWCK-PL, *chüan* 9, pp. 20a–b; *Ta-Ch'ing chin-shen ch'üan-shu*, 1872, 1873, 1874, Vol. 2, p. 14b. This Ting Shou-ch'ang should not be confused with another man by the same name (same characters), who was a *ting-wei* classmate of Li's but who was from Kiangsu.

[38] Feuerwerker, p. 108.

tration, was also an ex-compradore from Kwangtung. Through these men Li was able to secure the financial support of the Shanghai and Cantonese merchant and compradore groups for his enterprises.[39]

The career of Sheng Hsuan-huai is illustrative of how the gulf between the old China and the new could be spanned in Li's service. Sheng had started his career in the orthodox fashion by taking the official examinations but had never succeeded in becoming more than a *hsiu-ts'ai* (1866) — a fact he regretted to the end of his life. On the recommendation of a friend, who was one of Li's *mu-yu*, he was invited to join Li's army in 1870. Sheng stayed with the *Huai-chün* when Li was transferred to Tientsin and continued to serve Li as a *mu-yu* dealing with supply problems. In 1871 he left the military service and was engaged by Li in flood and famine relief in Chihli. Up to this point his career had followed lines which were well within the traditional Chinese framework. When Li established the China Merchants Steam Navigation Company in 1872, Sheng assisted in the planning, and it was at this point that he undertook his role as Li's chief economic adviser, which only ended with Li's fall from power in 1895. During this period, Sheng became the Director-General of the China Merchants Company and at the same time was the Director-General of the Imperial Telegraph Administration. He was also involved in mining and textile ventures. He had been assigned to these posts by Li Hung-chang and was directly responsible to him for the operation and success of the ventures. His duties in these companies, however, did not prevent him from holding the substantive post of Customs Taotai first at Chefoo and later (1892–1895) at Tientsin. Sheng, thus, was able to keep a foot in both the old and the new worlds,[40] as well as in the *mu-fu* and the bureaucracy.

Of those in Li's *mu-fu* who were committed to the ways of the West, the "returned students" were by far the largest group. In his official capacity, Li sponsored sending students to America and Europe to study naval and military sciences, mining engineering, communications, and so forth. When these students completed their education and returned to China, many of them found service in his *mu-fu*. Li was one of the few officials who recognized the value

[39] *Ibid.*, pp. 112–113, 116.

[40] *Ibid.*, pp. 60–62, 24; *Ta-Ch'ing chin-shen ch'üan-shu*, 1892–1895, Vol. 2, p. 14b.

of the training which the boys of the Chinese Educational Mission had received in the United States. He had been a co-sponsor of the mission, and when the boys were abruptly ordered to return to China in 1881, he placed many of them in his organization. A large portion of them were sent to his newly established Naval College and Torpedo School at Tientsin, while others went to the Telegraph School. A few were sent to the Kaiping coal mines north of Tientsin, and some were attached to the hospital Li had founded in that city. In time many of them also found their way into the diplomatic service.[41] The boys of the Chinese Educational Mission were too young to become more than junior members of Li's *mu-fu* during his period of power; however, three returned students who were old enough to play a major role in Li's affairs after the early 1880's were Ma Chien-chung, Lo Feng-lu, and Wu T'ing-fang.

Ma Chien-chung (1844–1900) came from a gentry family in Kiangsu and attracted Li's attention in Shanghai during the Taiping Rebellion. His experiences in that treaty port city had made him an advocate of "Westernization," and during the 1870's he studied in France, where Li had sent him to learn more about the West. For a time he served as a Secretary in the Chinese Legation in Paris and then returned to China in the late 1870's.[42] Shortly after his return, Li mentioned in a letter that Ma was giving lectures on the foreign laws of diplomacy, was doing translations, and was being groomed for diplomatic missions.[43] In 1881 Li sent him to India as an unofficial envoy to discuss the opium question, and in the same year he drew up a tentative treaty which was to serve as the basis of the negotiations between the United States and Korea. He also served as Li's representative during the negotiations for the Korean treaties with the United States, England, and Germany in 1882.[44] Ma was back in Korea later in the same year as Li's agent during the suppression of the rebellion of the Tai-Wön-Kun. In 1884 Li switched him to the commercial side of his operations and made Ma the Manager of the China Merchants Company, a position he held until

---

[41] Thomas E. LaFargue, *China's First Hundred* (Pullman, Wash.: The State College of Washington Press, 1942), pp. 60, 72.

[42] Feuerwerker, p. 117.

[43] *LWCK-PL*, *chüan* 18, p. 5b.

[44] Stanley F. Wright, *Hart and the Chinese Customs* (Belfast: Wm. Mullan and Son, Ltd., 1950), p. 561; Tsiang, p. 66; Albert Philip Ludwig, "Li Hung-chang and Chinese Foreign Policy, 1870–1885," (unpublished Ph.D. Dissertation, University of California, 1936), p. 368.

1891. He accompanied Li to Shimonoseki in 1895 and in the next year on his trip around the world.[45] In the years before his death, he combined his knowledge of his classical heritage and his training in modern languages to write the first modern grammar of classical Chinese, which was published in 1898 as *Ma-shih wen-t'ung* (Mr. Ma's Grammar).[46]

Li's Naval Secretary and close confidant for years was Lo Feng-lu, a Fukienese. Lo had graduated at the head of the first class of naval students from the Foochow Arsenal in 1871 and subsequently was a member of Kuo Sung-t'ao's suite in England.[47] Exactly when he joined Li's *mu-fu* is not known, but in October, 1881 Li spoke of him as having a good education and being very industrious.[48] Lo served Li as confidential secretary, Naval Secretary, interpreter, and general factotum until 1897, when through Li's influence he became the Chinese Minister to England (1897–1901). He had an excellent command of both spoken and written English, as well as impeccable European manners.[49] Much of the praise which the public gave to Li for his wise sayings and apt expressions during his visit to England in 1896 belonged to Lo, who translated into English the various speeches that Li gave at receptions in his honor. Lo's use of a Shakesperian passage to translate a classical Chinese poem which Li had written in Queen Victoria's guest book gained him the favor of the English queen.[50] Yet, despite his Western education, he hastened his own death by refusing to have Western medical care for a malignant growth on his lip. He had no fear of death and whimsically explained that it was probably because he was not a

---

[45] Feuerwerker, p. 117; U.S. Department of State, *Despatches from United States Consuls in Tientsin, 1868–1906* (Washington, D.C.: The National Archives, 1947), Read to Uhl, June 13, 1895.

[46] Feuerwerker, p. 118; Wen Ching (Lim Boon-keng), *The Chinese Crisis From Within* (London: Grant Richards, 1901), pp. 24–25.

[47] Prosper Giquel, *The Foochow Arsenal and Its Results*, transl. by H. Lang (Shanghai: The Shanghai Evening Courier, 1874), p. 30; "The Visit of Li Hung-Chang to England," *The Illustrated London News, Supplement*, CIX (August 15, 1896), 193.

[48] *LWCK-PL, chüan* 20, p. 19b.

[49] "The Visit of Li Hung-chang to England," p. 193; Henry Norman, *The Peoples and Politics of the Far East* (London: T. Fisher Unwin, 1900), pp. 251–253; Bland, *Li Hung-chang*, p. 267.

[50] John Watson Foster, "The Great Chinese Viceroy and Diplomat," *International Monthly*, II (November, 1900), 588; interview with Li Kuo-ch'ao, April 4, 1962.

Christian and therefore knew nothing of the joys of Heaven or the penalties of Hell.[51]

The third of Li's principal "returned-student" *mu-yu* was Wu T'ing-fang, who served as the Chinese Minister to the United States from 1890 to 1903 and again from 1908 to 1909. Wu can be aptly described as "made in England."[52] He was born in Canton to the same family as the famous "Howqua" of the Co-hong days, and before his fifteenth year, when he started his English language studies, had already spent a good part of his life in Singapore. In 1873 his family sent him to England to study law, and he was the first Chinese to be admitted to the English bar. Kuo Sung-t'ao tried to persuade him to stay in England as a Secretary in the Chinese Legation, but he declined and returned to China in 1877. Wu opened law offices in Hong Kong, where he developed an extensive practice, but in 1882 he accepted Li Hung-chang's invitation to come to Tientsin to join his *mu-fu* as a legal adviser and Deputy for Foreign Affairs.[53] Aside from the obvious reasons for desiring to have a man of Wu's caliber in his *mu-fu*, Li also said he did not want him to become a servant of the British in Hong Kong.[54] While in Li's service, Wu also became interested in railway development and promoted the development of the Kaiping Railway Company in 1886 and became its chief Director.[55] Wu also accompanied Li to Shimonoseki along with Ma and Lo. Of these three close advisers, Wu was the only one to become active in the affairs of the early Chinese Republic.

Of all Li's *mu-yu*, the one who served him the longest was Chou Fu (1837–1921). He was an Anhweinese and began his career in Li's *mu-fu* in 1861, while Li was still one of Tseng Kuo-fan's *mu-yu*. Chou had not passed any of the official examinations but had had about ten years of formal schooling and prior to 1859 had, on occasion, taught children. From 1861 to 1901 Chou was continuously in Li's service, except for short periods when he was in mourning (1878–

---

[51] King, p. 90.

[52] La Fargue, pp. 148–149.

[53] U.S. Department of State, *Despatches from United States Consuls in Tientsin, 1868–1906*, Read to Rockhill, December 19, 1896; Edward Harper Parker, *John Chinaman and a Few Others*, 2nd ed. (London: John Murray, 1902), pp. 213–214.

[54] *LWCK-PL*, chüan 17, pp. 7b, 29a–b.

[55] U.S. Department of State, *Despatches from United States Consuls in Tientsin, 1868–1906*, Read to Rockhill, December 19, 1896; Carlson, p. 23.

1881), was in retirement (1895–1898), or was assigned to a post outside of Li's jurisdiction (Szechwan Provincial Treasurer, 1899). While Li was off fighting rebels between 1867 and 1870, Chou remained in Nanking in the service of first Tseng Kuo-fan and then Ma Hsin-i, both close friends of Li's. His duties in Li's *mu-fu* followed a conventional pattern; he was involved in reconstruction work at the close of the Taiping Rebellion and in flood control and river conservancy in Chihli. While in Chihli he served as the Tientsin Customs Taotai from 1881 to 1888, and from 1888 to 1895 was the Chihli Provincial Judge. Even though these were substantive offices, and by early Ch'ing standards he would no longer have been considered a member of Li's *mu-fu*, he continued to help Li by rendering him valuable assistance in establishing the Telegraph Office and the Tientsin Naval and Military Academies, among other projects. From time to time he concurrently held posts in the Chihli military organization and acted as Li's principal diplomatic adviser; when the war with Japan broke out in 1894, he headed the military secretariat at the front and, in conjunction with Yüan Shih-k'ai, was in charge of transporting military supplies. Chou Fu's career is illustrative of that large group of Li's *mu-yu* who never achieved any national importance during their lifetimes. They were the workhorses of his *mu-fu*, who served him loyally and well, but their greatest rewards were middle-level official positions. They were the career *mu-yu*, who served where they were ordered and, in general, were content with their lot. It was only after Li died, and they no longer had a host, that some of them, such as Chou Fu and Cheng Hsiao-hsü, achieved national recognition. Chou Fu became the Szechwan Governor-General in 1901, and when he was forced to retire in 1907 due to his age — he was seventy years old — he was the Liang-kuang Governor-General.[56] Cheng Hsiao-hsü, a Fukienese who had served Li to the end, remained loyal to the last of the Ch'ing emperors, and when P'u-i escaped from Tientsin to Manchuria in 1932 to become the puppet Emperor of Manchukuo, Cheng went with him as his new Prime Minister.[57]

Li was not averse to providing sinecures for old friends in need and often went out of his way to find them an official position which

[56] Lienche Fang, "Chou Fu," draft MS prepared for the Men and Politics in Modern China Project, Columbia University, 1959, cited with permission of the author; *Ta-Ch'ing chin-shen ch'üan-shu*, 1884–1895, Vol. 2, pp. 7a, 14b.
[57] Interview with Li Kuo-ch'ao, June 13, 1963.

would not tax their strength but would provide them with a living. However, in his own organization, every *mu-yu* seemed to be there for a purpose. Li was a strong believer in the value of education, and the scholars he supported helped, in turn, to support his projects. One scholar of note who served in his *mu-fu* was Wu Ju-lun (1840–1903), who was also his biographer. Wu was from Anhwei and a *chin-shih* of 1865. He was in Tseng Kuo-fan's *mu-fu* from 1865 to 1871, and from 1879 to 1889 he served in Chihli as the Acting Tientsin Prefect and later as a *chou* Magistrate. He had secured both of these positions through Li's recommendation. In 1889 Li dissuaded Wu from retiring and put him in charge of the Lien-ch'ih Academy in Pao-ting, where he held sway until 1899. Although Wu had started his career as a scholar in the orthodox fashion, through the influence of Tseng and Li he became interested in Westernization and devoted his time during his later years in Chihli to the problem of modern education. He gathered a group of brilliant scholars about him, read Chinese translations of Western works, and established a language school in Pao-ting, to which he invited teachers from Japan and England. It was estimated that Wu educated about 1,200 students in Chihli, some of whom no doubt found their way into Li's organization.[58] Wu was able to pursue his career as a scholar and educator in Li's service, but he was also helping Li to train people for the job of preserving China.

Li Hung-chang's *mu-yu* were trained for the immediate task of saving China, and in the process he drew to his side people of foreign as well as traditional backgrounds. However, their common interest in self-strengthening permitted a fusion of ideas, which in turn made Li's *mu-fu* a focal point for change — change which would not only radically affect the nature of the *mu-fu* system itself, but also the course of late Ch'ing and early Republican history. This process of gradual fusion and change can be seen in two widely separated chains of events and personal relations, one a "foreign force" and the other a "traditional force," which eventually intertwined in Li's *mu-fu* and then continued on together after his death.

The roots of the "foreign force" can be traced to Macao in 1841, when Yung Wing (Jung Hung), at the age of thirteen and through the aid of a medical missionary, was enrolled in the first classs of the Morrison Educational Society School (see above, Chapter III).

[58] Hummel, II, 870.

Of the five other boys in the class, one of them was Tong Chik, who was later known as Tong King-sing (T'ang T'ing-shu or T'ang Ching-hsing).[59] Both boys were from districts near Macao and represented that class of people in Kwangtung who looked to a knowledge of English and the West, rather than to the Confucian *Classics* and the bureaucracy, as a means of advancement. After six years of schooling in Macao and Hong Kong, where the school was moved in 1842, Yung Wing went to the United States to continue his education. Tong stayed in China and subsequently served as an interpreter for the Hong Kong colonial government and as an interpreter and chief secretary for the Shanghai customs house; in 1863 he became the Shanghai compradore for the English firm of Jardine, Matheson and Company.[60] Yung Wing returned to China in 1854 and spent his first few months back in his native land relearning his mother tongue. In 1863 Tseng Kuo-fan commissioned Yung Wing to go to America to buy machinery for a machine shop. By the time this machinery was shipped to Shanghai in the spring of 1865, Li Hung-chang, who was the Kiangsu Governor, and Ting Jih-ch'ang, the Su-sung-t'ai Taotai, had already set up a small machine shop in Shanghai. The American machinery and Li's machine shop were the beginnings of the Kiangnan Arsenal and also of the relationship between Yung Wing and Ting Jih-ch'ang.[61]

Unlike Yung Wing, Ting Jih-ch'ang (1823–1882), who was also a native of Kwangtung, had started his official career in the more orthodox fashion. However, by virtue of his interest in and appreciation for the West, as well as his contacts with Tseng Kuo-fan and Li Hung-chang, he served as an important link in the sequence of events in the "foreign force." Ting had passed the examination for the *hsiu-ts'ai* degree when he was about twenty *sui*. He joined Tseng Kuo-fan's *mu-fu* in about 1862, and soon after that Tseng sent him to Kwangtung on an errand concerning *likin* — at about the same time that Li's elder brother was sent there. While in Kwangtung, Ting was also asked to supervise the manufacture of firearms and ammunition. In 1863 Ting came back to Kiangsu at Li's request, joined his *mu-fu*, and became engaged in arsenal work. On Li's

---

59 *Ibid.*, I, 403; La Fargue, p. 19; Feuerwerker, p. 110.

60 Feuerwerker, p. 110.

61 Hummel, I, 403; Gideon Chen, *Tseng Kuo-fan, Pioneer Promoter of the Steamship in China* (Peiping: Yenching University, 1935), pp. 44–45.

recommendation, he was made the Su-sung-t'ai Taotai late in 1864.[62] In addition to his efforts on behalf of the Kiangnan Arsenal, Ting in 1865 also founded the Lung-men Academy in Shanghai.[63] Sir Edmund Hornby, in his *Autobiography*, described his visit to this school in 1865 on the occasion of an examination given by Ting.

It was not an examination for high honours, but a mere provincial affair. There was also a noticeable feature in it, for which the Taotai (Ting) deserves high praise. There was an examination in foreign history and in geography. Several coloured school maps, such as may be seen in national schools in England, were hung on the walls — the principal countries, towns, rivers, and mountains being marked in Chinese characters — and at one end was a scroll on which was inscribed the names of the reigning rulers of civilized countries. I hope the novelty may be productive of benefit, but although the Taotai was sanguine, he admitted that it was an innovation upon the curriculum which had not been received with favour either by the students or the higher provincial authorities.[64]

By 1867, when Ting Jih-ch'ang was made the Kiangsu Governor on the recommendation of Tseng and Li, he and Yung Wing had become old friends. It was at Yung Wing's suggestion that a language school for the translation of Western scientific works was established in conjunction with the Kiangnan Arsenal, and he also discussed at length with Ting his idea of sending Chinese boys to the United States to acquire a Western education.[65] Through Ting's good offices, Yung Wing's plan was brought to the attention of Tseng and Li. Under their auspices the idea received Imperial sanction in 1871, and the first group of students of the Chinese Educational Mission sailed for the United States in the summer of 1872 (see above, Chapter III).[66] Among the students who went to America as members of the mission were T'ang Kuo-an and T'ang Shao-i, the son and nephew, respectively, of Tong King-sing, who had been chosen on the basis of Tong's old friendship with Yung Wing.[67]

While the students were in America, Tong King-sing resigned

---

[62] Hummel, II, 721.

[63] Mary C. Wright, p. 130.

[64] Edmund G. Hornby, *Sir Edmund Hornby, An Autobiography* (Boston and New York: Houghton Mifflin Company, 1928), p. 211.

[65] Yung Wing, *My Life in China and America* (New York: Henry Holt and Co., 1909), p. 170; Hummel, I, 403.

[66] La Fargue, pp. 29–30; Hummel, I, 403–404.

[67] La Fargue, pp. 117–118.

his post with Jardine, Matheson and joined Li Hung-chang's *mu-fu* as the Manager of the China Merchants Steam Navigation Company — a post he held from 1873 to 1884. Westerners who knew him admired Tong for his administrative abilities, his honesty and integrity, and for his "progressive" ideas and desire to see China adopt Western civilization. Li, on the other hand, when considering him as a possible candidate for the post of American Minister in 1877, said that his knowledge of Chinese was not very profound.[68] In regard to his relationship to Li, Tong said, "The viceroy [Li] leads, but I am the man that pushes."[69]

By the mid 1870's those Chinese who had received their training and become interested in things Western either by serving the foreigners as compradores, by studying abroad, or by associating with the Westerners in the treaty ports, and who were, thus, members of the "foreign forces," were still not influential enough to lead. Instead they were forced to rely on personal connections with men like Tseng Kuo-fan, Li Hung-chang, and Ting Jih-ch'ang, who had high provincial office and were interested in self-strengthening, in order to get their ideas implemented. They could push, but the leadership remained in the hands of those who had been trained in a more orthodox manner. Confucian amateurism was still the ideal, even though self-strengtheners, such as Li Hung-chang, were staffing their *mu-fu*'s with experts rather than nourishing scholars. Nonetheless, a chink had been made in the dike, and the conflict between Western experts and Confucian amateurs, which would survive the passing of the *mu-fu* system and result in the triumph of the former in the twentieth century, was already vaguely apparent. For the time being, however, expertise, whether Chinese or Western, was still subsidiary to the Confucian end.

The roots of the second chain of events, the "traditional force," can be traced back to 1853, when an Imperial Decree sent Li Hung-chang back to Anhwei from Peking to fight the rebels. This decree also sent Yüan Chia-san (1803–1863), a Junior Metropolitan Censor, with him as a fellow *mu-yu* on the staff of Lü Hsien-chi (see Chapter V). Later in the same year, Li's father, Wen-an, who had also returned to Anhwei to fight the Taipings, joined the *mu-fu* of Yüan Chia-san for a few months to recruit "braves" to fight the rising

[68] Carlson, pp. 30, 33; *LWCK-PL*, *chüan* 17, p. 18a.
[69] W. A. P. Martin, *A Cycle of Cathay* (London: Oliphant Anderson and Ferrier, 1896), p. 351.

Nien rebels.[70] These events in 1853 were the beginning of the long and close relationship between the Li family of Anhwei and the Yüan family of Honan. Approximately three years after Yüan Chia-san's death in 1863, one of his nephews, Yüan Pao-ch'ing, who had fought under Chia-san and later became a well-known military official, because he had no sons of his own, adopted the 4th son of Yüan Pao-chung, his own elder brother. The six or seven year old boy, who thus became the heir to a famous scholarly and military tradition, was Yüan Shih-k'ai.[71] Yüan Chia-san had started his career as a scholar and an official but had been forced by circumstances to become a military leader, as had Li Hung-chang, and it was

[70] Li Wen-an: During the rebellious period at the end of the Ming, the Hsü family of Hu-k'ou in Kiangsi moved to Ho-fei, Anhwei. In Ho-fei, the father of the family became friends with Li Hsin-chuang, who had no sons, and ordered his son, Fu-shan, to become Mr. Li's adopted son. This was the beginning of the Li family of Ho-fei. No one in the family achieved any notable success until Li Hung-chang's father, Wen-an, became a *chin-shih* in 1838. The youngest of four brothers, he is best remembered by his fellow *hsien* members as having built the Lu-chou examination halls, under imperial decree. The highest official post he achieved was that of a Department Director in the Board of Punishments (*hsing-pu lang-chung*), and he was registered for the Censorate. On December 10, 1853, the Junior Vice-President of the Board of Revenue (*hu-pu yu-shih-lang*), Wang Mao-yin, memorialized that, because of the seriousness of the rebellion in Anhwei, officials from that province should be sent home from the capital to organize the local militia in order to resist the Taipings. As a result of this memorial, Li Wen-an was ordered to return to Lu-chou to work under Fu-chi, the Governor. He set out from the capital in the 12th month (December 30, 1953–January 28, 1854), which was almost a year after his son, Hung-chang, had returned to Anhwei. However, Yüan Chia-san memorialized to detain Wen-an in Lin-huai to assist him in enrolling militia to fight the Nien rebels. Later he continued his journey to Lu-chou to fight against the Taipings. On July 6, 1855, as the result of illness contracted while fighting the rebels, he died in his fifty-fourth year (fifty-five *sui*). He left a wife, who was also surnamed Li (the Li's would marry Li's but never Hsü's), and six sons and two daughters. Of the daughters, we only know that the elder married Chang Shao-t'ang, who was registered to be a provincial commander-in-chief, and the younger married a Kiangsu expectant prefect, Fei Jih-ch'i. Interview with Li Kuo-ch'ao, June 7, 1962; Huang, *Hsü-hsü Lu-chou fu-chih*, *chüan* 58, p. 1b; *chüan* 34, pp. 12a, 12b–13a; Wu Ju-lun, "Li Wen-chung-kung shen-tao-pei," *in Li Wen-chung-kung ch'uan-chi*, chüan-shou, p. 62a. Hummel, I, 464; *LWCK-IC*, *chüan* 4, p. 4b.

[71] Hummel, II, 950; Jerome Ch'en, *Yuan Shih-k'ai, 1895–1916* (Stanford: Stanford Univ. Press, 1961), p. 14. Mr. Ch'en's account of Yüan's early life states that he was adopted by the adopted son of Yüan Chia-san in about 1860. On the basis of my own investigation of Yüan Chia-san's biography in the *Ch'ing-shih lieh-chuan* and the known record for careful scholarship by the author of the Hummel account, Fang Chao-ying, I have chosen to abide by the Hummel version.

through the military that Yüan Shih-k'ai would become the first President of the Republic of China.

Yüan Shih-k'ai never succeeded in passing any of the official examinations, despite several attempts. He did, however, become very adept at the arts of the soldier and, in 1880, after purchasing his first title, went to Shantung to join the army of Wu Ch'ang-ch'ing, one of the original commanders in the *Huai-chün* and an old friend of his adoptive father. When Yüan's adoptive father had died in Nanking in 1873, Wu and Liu Ming-ch'uan had arranged his funeral, and the fourteen year old Yüan had escorted the coffin back to the family shrine.[72] Yüan was twenty-one when he joined Wu Ch'ang-ch'ing, but, instead of becoming a soldier, he was ordered by Wu to pursue his studies under the direction of Chang Chien, who was also in Wu's *mu-fu* and later became one of China's leading industrialists. Under Chang's tutelage, Yüan studied poetry and prose, but his military attributes were so far superior to his literary ones that, on Chang's recommendation, he was put in charge of training and discipline in Wu's brigade. Chang also informed him that he should give up any hopes of a civil career.[73]

Yüan Shih-k'ai's first opportunity for recognition came in 1882, when Wu Ch'ang-ch'ing was ordered by the Acting Chihli Governor-General, Chang Shu-sheng (Li was in Anhwei attending his mother's funeral), to take 3,000 troops to Korea to suppress the rebellion. The order had been given at the suggestion of Hsüeh Fu-ch'eng and Wu was accompanied by Ting Ju-ch'ang, a fellow-Anhweinese and the Admiral of Li's navy, and Ma Chien-chung, who was in charge of the diplomatic aspects of the mission. As a member of Wu Ch'ang-ch'ing's *mu-fu*, Yüan Shih-k'ai also went along, and, because of his swiftness and efficiency in carrying out his military assignments during the suppression of the revolt, he was brought to the attention of Li Hung-chang and was made an Expectant Sub-Prefect.[74] When the king of Korea proposed to train a corps of 500 soldiers in modern warfare, Li Hung-chang gave Yüan the task. Yüan stayed in Korea training troops, ingratiated himself with the king and queen of Korea, and acted as the Quartermaster for the Chinese garrison.[75]

[72] Jerome Ch'en, pp. 14, 15; Hummel, II, 950.
[73] Jerome Ch'en, p. 15.
[74] Hummel, II, 950; Ralph L. Powell, *The Rise of Chinese Military Power, 1895–1912* (Princeton: Princeton Univ. Press, 1955), p. 73.
[75] Jerome Ch'en, pp. 19, 23; Tsiang, p. 80.

When the Japanese-inspired riot broke out in Seoul in 1884, Yüan's prompt action quelled the outbreak. During the fighting, Yüan met T'ang Shao-i, who was guarding the residence of the Commissioner of Korean Customs, P. G. von Mollendorff, and from this meeting developed a close and lasting friendship.[76]

T'ang Shao-i had left China in 1874 in the third contingent of students of the Chinese Educational Mission and had graduated with honors from the Hartford (Connecticut) high school in 1880, the same year that Yüan Shih-k'ai had joined Wu Ch'ang-ch'ing's *mu-fu*. When the mission was abruptly ordered home in the summer of 1881, T'ang had completed his first year at Columbia University. Like so many of the other boys of this mission, T'ang was taken into Li Hung-chang's service on his return to China, and in 1883, when Li sent Baron P. G. von Mollendorff to Korea as the Commissioner of Korean Customs, T'ang was sent with him as an assistant.[77] The chance meeting of T'ang and Yüan Shih-k'ai, who were both nominally in Li's service, in Seoul during the riot of 1884 was also the meeting of the two "forces" which had begun so many years before in different parts of China.

For his meritorious service in putting down the disturbance in Seoul, Yüan was called back to China and recommended by Li for the post of China's Commissioner of Commerce in Korea, with the rank of Prefect and the powers of a Resident. When Yüan returned to Korea in 1885 to take up his new post, T'ang went with him as his confidential secretary.[78] Yüan served as China's (and Li's) representative in Korea until 1894, and, all during this period of nine years, T'ang Shao-i was his confidential assistant, acting for him whenever Yüan was away from his post.[79] This association, which began in Korea, continued into the twentieth century, and, as Yüan's fortunes rose, he brought T'ang Shao-i up with him. The culmination of this relationship came with the establishment of the Republic of China. Yüan Shih-k'ai became its first President, and T'ang Shao-i its first Prime Minister. Yüan, who had come up through the more traditional military was the leader, and T'ang, who was a "returned student," was dependent upon him for his position.

By pre-Taiping standards, Yüan Shih-k'ai and T'ang Shao-i were

---

[76] Jerome Ch'en, p. 26.
[77] La Fargue, pp. 117–118.
[78] Hummel, II, 951; Tsiang, pp. 92–93; La Fargue, pp. 117–118
[79] Jerome Ch'en, p. 39.

members of Li Hung-chang's *mu-fu* for only very short periods of time — Yüan in 1894, when he helped Chou Fu supply Li's forces against the Japanese, and T'ang between 1881 and 1883, and again from 1899–1900, when he acted as interpreter for Li in Canton. During the rest of their respective careers, they were either in the *mu-fu* of one of Li's *mu-yu* or held official position. The *mu-fu* system in its early form consisted of small groups of advisers centered around single officials. Under Tseng Kuo-fan it began to expand its operation, and the *mu-yu* began to have *mu-yu*. When Li Hung-chang further expanded the system in order to handle his multifarious enterprises, it lost its small and intimate quality, and the dividing line between *mu-yu* and official, between private and public hiring, became blurred. Yüan actually served in Wu Ch'ang-ch'ing's *mu-fu*, but took his orders from Li and looked to him for recommendation and support. The same situation prevailed when he was the Chinese Resident in Korea. He was appointed by the throne, but took his orders from Li, who was in charge of Korean affairs. Sheng Hsuan-huai was the substantive Chefoo, and later Tientsin, Taotai yet at the same time he was the Director-General of the China Merchants Steam Navigation Company, a position he owed directly to Li.

Under the early Ch'ing *mu-fu* system, the *mu-yu* were not supposed to become involved in affairs outside the host official's *yamen* and, therefore, had no need for official rank. However, when *mu-yu* began running steamship companies, commanding armies and navies, and helping in diplomatic negotiations, it was imperative that they have recognizable official status in order to be able to communicate as equals or near equals with the responsible officials. The civil ranks of the bureaucracy were the accepted norm and the criteria for association, but the traditional bureaucratic structure made no provisions for shipping company managers, directors of arsenals, *Huai-chün* commanders, and the like. Therefore, of necessity, this type of personnel was hired privately by Li Hung-chang, but they were permitted to purchase orthodox rank, or else it was granted to them on Li's recommendation. The experts were thus accomodated and "taken into camp," and the ideal of social mobility within the Confucian structure was preserved. The experts willingly accepted this, because they still believed that the way to fame and fortune was through the orthodox bureaucracy. Their unorthodox skills, and not their classical knowledge, had made it possible for them to enter the ranks of officialdom, but, once having obtained this foothold, they became staunch supporters of orthodoxy.[80] Most of Li's key personnel, such as Chu Ch'i-ang, Ma Chien-chung, Tong King-sing, and Li Ching-fang, held the rank of Taotai. These ranks, however, were usually either "expectant" or did not entail any substantive responsibilities.

Because Li's *mu-yu* held official rank, and some of them substantive posts, the criteria for *mu-yu* became blurred in the late nineteenth century, and, through the power of recommendation, Li and other provincial leaders were able to compete with the central government itself as sources of official patronage. Personal loyalty replaced private hiring as the basis of the *mu-fu* system, and because of their more pervasive nature, such loyalties made the system a greater corrosive of central authority. The "Laws of Avoidance" were thus even further circumvented by the Chinese proclivity to organize both government and society on the basis of personal relationships. Even though he had been appointed to his post in Korea by the throne, Yüan Shih-k'ai was loyal to Li, and his loyalty redounded to Li in the enhancement of Li's personal power. Li used the right of recommendation to reward loyalty, to bind his followers to him, and to extend the scope and depth of his power network. *Mu-fu's* thus became enmeshed in the provincial bureaucracy and almost assumed the proportions of cliques.

The greater opportunities, both in rank and wealth, which had become available to *mu-yu*, made the host official's right to recommend much more important to *mu-yu* than the salaries he could pay. Whereas early Ch'ing *mu-yu* had not availed themselves of the opportunity to enter the ranks of officialdom because of the obstacles involved, those who were ambitious or whose talents were unorthodox during the late Ch'ing, as in T'ang times, looked to the *mu-fu* as a means of rapid promotion and wealth.

The growth of the *mu-fu* system under Li Hung-chang, both in size and responsibilities, which in effect made it a private bureaucracy, resulted in a gradual breakdown of efficiency and permitted the evils of the bureacratic system, corruption and nepotism, to appear. Modern sociological studies on organization have shown that an executive can deal effectively, depending on the situation, with

---

[80] John Lang Rawlinson, "The Chinese Navy, 1839–1895" (unpublished Ph.D. Dissertation, Harvard University, 1959), pp. 354, 360. Cited with permission of the author.

only from five to fifteen subordinates. As the number increases beyond that point, the degree of efficiency declines.[81] Within Li's
organization literally hundreds of people were employed. Li could
not personally hire every employee and could only approve the
actions of his managers. Sheng Hsuan-huai's relatives were spread
throughout the China Merchants Company, and Tong King-sing's
and Ma Chien-chung's brothers acted in their stead on occasion.[82]
Li's enterprises had grown so large that there was ample opportunity for graft and corruption.

Li approached the whole matter of nepotism and corruption in
his organization, not as a reformer, but as a man who accepts things
as they are and tries to work with them. He also appears to have
had a deep understanding and appreciation for human frailty.
Whereas Tseng Kuo-fan had been morally rigid and correct, Li
was willing to be more flexible and make allowances for human
weakness. He realized very clearly that corruption and nepotism
were a part of the social and political mores of China, and being a
realist, he did not seek to change them. Besides, men qualified in
the Western techniques were hard to find, and he could not afford
to dispense with their services just because they wanted to fatten
their own purses and employ their relatives. When the Imperial
Censors criticized the conduct of Sheng Hsuan-huai and Chu Ch'i-ang
in the management of the China Merchants Company, Li came to
their defense.[83] He invariably was able to clear his subordinates of
of charges of bribery, extortion, and the like, because the memorials
were customarily referred to him for investigation, and his recommendations were usually followed by the court.[84] Li's job was to
defend China against the encroachments of the West and internal
rebellion. In order to do this, he had to work with the tools at hand,
and he would not let considerations of moral character outweigh
talent and ability.

Because of the shortage of qualified Chinese to run his enterprises
and his need to train men as quickly as possible, Li was forced to
introduce a new element into the indigenous *mu-fu* system — the
use of foreigners as *mu-yu*. The foreigners acted as advisers, teach-

[81] Chester I. Barnard, *The Functions of the Executive* (Cambridge: Harvard
Univ. Press, 1956), pp. 106–107.
[82] Feuerwerker, pp. 63, 145; Morse, "Letter-books," Morse to Detring, August 16, 1886.
[83] Feuerwerker, p. 444.                    [84] *Ibid.*, pp. 89, 155.

ers, naval officers, ship captains, warehouse managers, directors of arsenals, military instructors, and even as his representatives in diplomatic negotiations. One thing was certain though; no foreigner ever stayed in Li's employ for long who did not acknowledge him as the master. His conflict with Charles Gordon during the Taiping Rebellion was occasioned by Gordon's desire to lead the Ever-Victorious Army as an independent military force. Li would have no part of the Lay-Osborn Flotilla because its British commander, Captain Osborn, refused to recognize Li's authority and looked to the emperor as his immediate superior. Those foreigners, however, who acknowledged Li's position and served him loyally were treated with respect and paid very well.

In the organization of Li's *mu-fu*, the foreigners occupied a special position and had their own informal hierarchy. There were two men who more or less stood at the apex — Gustav Detring and William N. Pethick. All the foreigners in Li's *mu-fu* usually directed their communications to one of these two men, not so much because they were ordered to do so, or because Li had formally established a chain of command, but because both of them were in close personal contact with Li on an almost day-to-day basis and could speak Chinese. Detring was the liaison for those in Li's commercial and industrial enterprises and also a liaison for those in foreign affairs. Pethick handled foreign naval personnel and foreigners in general. There also was an informal division on the basis of Western regional and language affinity. Detring held sway among the Europeans in Li's employ, while Pethick attracted the Americans and, at times, the English. Constantin von Hanneken, who seems to have stood just below these two, was Li's military liaison, but he usually worked through Detring and did not enjoy as close a relationship with Li as did the other two men. However, these lines of communication were not rigid, and any foreigner in Li's employ could deal with him directly.

Gustav Detring, a German and the Tientsin Commissioner of Customs, although technically not a part of Li's *mu-fu* because he was hired by the Customs Service under Robert Hart, maintained his close connection with Li during almost the entire period of Li's career in Chihli. He advised Li on all sorts of local, national and international affairs and was in constant contact with him. When H. B. Morse was transferred, at Li's request, to the China Merchants Company from the Customs Service in 1885 to assist in the retrans-

ferring of the company ships and warehouses back from the American company after the Sino-French War, it was through Detring
that Morse reported to Li. During the two years that Morse served
the China Merchants Company (1885–1887), he wrote to Detring
concerning warehouses, docks, design of steamships and costs, routes,
Yellow River control, the opening-up of Formosa, disposal and acquisition of property, collision cases, coaling, railway trains, draw-
bridges, personnel problems, international disputes, opium smug-
gling, ship repairs, the Korean loan, and so forth. Morse used Detring
as a sounding board and as a direct channel to Li. He kept Detring informed of almost everything that went on in the China Merchants
Company and thus also served as a private source of information
for Li.[85] When H. F. Merrill was the Inspector of Korean Customs
during the latter part of the 1880's, many of his letters were directed
to Detring, who would relay the information on to Li and then
transmit Li's orders to Merrill.[86]

William N. Pethick, an American, had served in a New York cavalry regiment at the close of the Civil War. He came out to China
shortly thereafter for the purpose of learning all he could about
China in order to help her and, at the same time, to foster Sino-
American relations. He became an accomplished scholar of Chinese
literature and could read, write, and speak Chinese fluently. In
1872 he was appointed Vice Consul and Interpreter at the American Consulate in Tientsin, a post which he held until 1894, except
for the period between 1880–1884. Pethick was discharged from
the U.S. Consular Service in 1894 because the Consul at Tientsin
felt his services to Li as a private secretary would not permit him
to be impartial in his consular duties.[87] Pethick's service under Li
was not a secret in Tientsin as he had held this position since before
1879. He had begun his service under Li by tutoring his children
in English and had gained Li's confidence and friendship. He was
one of the few men who had access to Li at all times and was an
invaluable aid to his employer in foreign affairs. He continued to
serve Li until the latter's death in 1901 and survived his employer and

85 Morse, "Letter-books," Morse to Detring, 1885 to 1887.
86 Robert Hart, "Letters to Various Westerners in the Chinese Customs
Service," MS. Typed transcripts, 1865–1910 (Houghton Library, Harvard University), Detring to Merrill, August 20, 1886, September 3, 1888.
87 U.S. Department of State, Despatches from United States Consuls in
Tientsin, 1868–1906 file consulted from 1872 to 1894.

friend by only a month or so.[88] Pethick had been writing a biography of Li which was still in manuscript when he died. The publication of this book was eagerly anticipated by many persons, primarily because its author knew Li better than any other foreigner. However, the manuscript was not found among Pethick's personal effects after his death, nor has it been found since.[89] Although Pethick's position in Li's *mu-fu* was that of a private secretary, he also acted as an interpreter, escorted foreign guests, read (in Chinese translation) no less than 800 English, French, and German books to Li, searched out likely candidates for Li's service among the foreign community, accompanied foreign engineers or technicans on mining surveys and the like, accompanied Li to Shimonoseki in 1895, and in general kept him informed about what was going on in the foreign and diplomatic community in Tientsin.[90]

The third most important foreign member of Li's *mu-fu*, and one who was completely in his employ, was Constantin von Hanneken, a German who had served in the German Army as an artillery and a cavalry officer. He was engaged to join Li's service in 1879 as an aide-de-camp through the Chinese Legation in Berlin.[91] In addition to his service as a military adviser, von Hanneken also supervised the construction of the fortifications at Port Arthur and Weihaiwei.[92] At the outbreak of the Sino-Japanese War, he was with the Chinese troops as their military instructor, on board the ill-fated "Kowsing" but managed to save himself by swimming ashore. During the course of the war, he served in both Li's navy and army, being at one time Co-Admiral of the Fleet.[93] Li was prone to use

[88] Tsiang, p. 40; Lewis Charles Arlington, *Through the Dragon's Eyes* (London: Constable and Co., Ltd., 1931), pp. 12–13; James Harrison Wilson, *China: Travels and Investigations in the Middle Kingdom*, 3rd ed. revised (New York: D. Appleton and Co., 1901), pp. 90–91; U.S. Department of State, *Despatches from United States Consuls in Tientsin, 1868–1906*, Regsdale to Hill, December 28, 1901.

[89] Martin, "Li Hung chang," p. 2688; Little, p. 329; Bland, *Li Hung-chang*, p. 302.

[90] Demetrius C. Boulger, *The Life of Sir Halliday Macartney* (London and New York: J. Lane, 1908), p. 255; Conger, p. 74; Foster, p. 589; Arlington, pp. 12–13; U.S. Department of State, *Despatches from United States Consuls in Tientsin, 1868–1906*, Denny to Seward, November 20, 1878; James Harrison Wilson, p. 340; Tsiang, p. 41.

[91] Bland, *Li Hung-chang*, p. 242, footnote 1.

[92] Rawlinson, pp. 637–638; William Ferdinand Tyler, *Pulling Strings in China* (London: Constable and Co., Ltd., 1929), p. 39.

[93] Rawlinson, p. 739; Tyler, p. 39.

men wherever he felt they were needed, despite their previous training; his Chinese Admiral was also an ex-cavalryman.

Li Hung-chang's first foreign *mu-yu* was Halliday Macartney, a
British surgeon, formerly in the 99th Regiment. In 1862, on the death
of Frederick Townsend Ward, Commander of the Ever-Victorious
Army, Macartney resigned his commission in the British Army and
joined Li's service. For a time he was Li's personal assistant, drilled
troops, gave advice, instructed Li on foreign matters, and served
as a liaison between Li and foreigners, as well as a mediator between
Li and Gordon.[94] It was at Macartney's instigation that Li established his first arsenal at Sungkiang in 1863. Macartney served Li
faithfully as the Director of his arsenals in Sungkiang, Soochow,
and then in Nanking until 1875, when he resigned over a dispute
with his Chinese Co-Director. In almost every case of a conflict
between a foreign and a Chinese *mu-yu*, despite the validity of the
foreigner's complaints, Li invariably sided with the Chinese. H. B.
Morse resigned from the China Merchants Company and Captain
Lang from Li's fleet under similar conditions. The foreigner might
be right, but he was still a foreigner. However, Li did not completely desert Macartney but secured for him the position of Secretary to the Chinese Legation in London. Macartney accompanied
Kuo Sung-t'ao to England in 1876 and faithfully served the legation
and Li for thirty years.[95]

In almost every phase of his operation, Li was forced to rely on
foreign technical advisers. In the China Merchants Company, he
had a foreign Supervisory Director and a foreign Marine Superintendent. On board the ships of the company, according to the regis-
ter of 1885, not one of the 144 captains, mates, and engineers was a
Chinese.[96] In the Kaiping Mines, foreign engineers were employed
from the start, and the same was true of Li's railway company.[97]
His cotton mill secured the services of A. W. Danforth to erect the

[94] Andrew Wilson, *The "Ever-Victorious Army"* (Edinburgh and London:
W. Blackwood and Sons, 1868), p. 165; Bernard M. Allen, *Gordon in China*
(London: Macmillan and Co., Ltd., 1933), p. 103; Demetrius C. Boulger,
*The Life of Gordon* (London: T. Fisher Unwin, 1896), p. 90.

[95] Boulger, *The Life of Sir Halliday Macartney*, p. 146; Rawlinson, pp.
422–423; Stanley F. Wright, p. 495, footnote 53.

[96] Feuerwerker, pp. 114–115, 140, 184.

[97] Carlson, pp. 7, 11–12; W. L. Langer, *The Diplomacy of Imperialism,
1890–1902*, 2nd ed. (New York and London: A. A. Knopf, 1951), I, 171.

plant, purchase machinery, and organize the production of the mill.[98] Li's navy relied on foreigners as instructors, advisory commanders, engineers, and gunnery officers.[99] He maintained the services of a foreign physician, Dr. Irwin, to treat the members of his family, after foreign doctors had successfully cured his wife's illness in 1879. Li also appointed Dr. Irwin as the physician for his fleet.[100] John Dunn (an Englishman in Tientsin whom Li used as his envoy to the Pope regarding the establishment of diplomatic relations with the Vatican), Detring, and Alexander Michie all served Li at various times in diplomatic negotiations.[101]

However, Li used foreigners only where he could not use Chinese. He had been in contact with them ever since 1862, when he arrived in Shanghai, and had learned to respect them for their good qualities and to dread them for their bad ones.[102] Although Li felt that the Westerners were chiefly responsible for all of China's problems,[103] he still used them to increase his own knowledge of the West and to train Chinese who could replace them.

Li's knowledge of foreigners and their world was extensive and had been acquired through "pumping" visitors, through reading Western books in translation, and through the instruction of his native and foreign *mu-yu*. He could talk knowledgeably about almost everything from the technical details of ships and guns to the latest gossip in the foreign settlement in Tientsin.[104] Knowledge was power, and in his *mu-fu* Li Hung-chang surrounded himself with men from China and the West who could supply him with the knowledge he needed to carry out his self-imposed task of saving China.

[98] Feuerwerker, p. 221.

[99] Arlington, p. 14; Tyler, p. 44; Rawlinson, p. 797, footnote 72.

[100] Little, pp. 188, 192; U.S. Department of State, *Despatches from the United States Consuls in Tientsin, 1868–1906*, Denny to Seward, August 12, 1879.

[101] King, p. 84; Douglas, *Li Hungchang*, pp. 221–222; A. Gervais, "Diplomatie Chinoise: Li-Hung-chang et le commandant Fournier," *Revue Politique et Littéraire (Revue Bleue)*, XXI, No. 15 (October 11, 1884), 451; Little, p. 225.

[102] Morse, *The International Relations of the Chinese Empire*, II, 208; Bland, *Li Hung-chang*, p. 19; Alexander Michie, *The Englishman in China* (Edinburgh: W. Blackwood and Sons, 1900), II, 190.

[103] *LWCK-PL, chüan* 4, p. 17a.

[104] Alfred Cunningham, *The Chinese Soldier and Other Sketches* (Hong Kong: The "Daily Press" Office, n.d.), pp. 88–89; Douglas, *Li Hungchang*, p. 109; Little, p. 186; Andrew Wilson, p. 284; Wu Ju-lun, "Li Wen-chung-kung mu-chih-ming," *in Li Wen-chung-kung ch'üan-chi*, chüan shou, p. 66b; Rawlinson, pp. 324, 444–445.

# VII. Li Hung-chang's Network of Power

During the thirty-three years, between 1862 and 1895, that Li Hung-chang held the position of governor-general or governor, he gradually built up a network of power that spread out from his parochial seat and assumed national proportions. It reached upward toward the throne, became entrenched in Chihli, and infiltrated the other provinces of the empire. It was based on his formal position within the bureaucracy and on his informal *mu-fu* but, in the final analysis, was subject to the whims of the court, the strength of the conservative opposition, and the gravity of the foreign situation. Even so, it survived as the paramount constructive force in China until the debacle of 1895.[1]

Li Hung-chang's commitment was to China, not just to Chihli or Anhwei, and instead of shirking national responsibilities, he reached out for power and resolutely shouldered the problems of the nation. His statements in regard to the national situation closely approached those of a ruler, who, in his insularity, expresses concern for the safety of the nation: "It may be all right for you people not to take an interest [in foreign matters], but if I too do not talk about them, by what method is the ship of state to be steered?"[2] "The riches of the Empire were originally supplied for the Empire's use. If we must say that such and such an army looks only to such and such a province for its supplies and support, then Tso's [Tsung-t'ang] entire army ought to have starved to death a long time ago."[3]

---

[1] Alexander Michie, *The Englishman in China* (Edinburgh: W. Blackwood and Sons, 1900), II, 386; John Lang Rawlinson, "The Chinese Navy, 1839–1895" (unpublished Ph.D. Dissertation, Harvard University, 1959), p. 267. Cited with the author's permission.

[2] Immanuel C. Y. Hsü, *China's Entrance into the Family of Nations* (Cambridge: Harvard Univ. Press, 1960), pp. 203–204.

[3] Li Hung-chang, *Li Wen-chang-kung ch'üan-chi* (The Complete Works of Li Hung-chang), ed. by Wu Ju-lun (Nanking, 1908), P'eng-liao han-kao

"Within our country there are not many talented generals left, and the current affairs become more and more difficult. My strength is small, but my responsibilities are heavy, and I lack people to help me."[4] "China and the foreign countries demand and expect too much of me."[5]

The task of saving China, which Li Hung-chang imposed upon himself, stemmed not only from his genuine patriotism, but also from his ego and his perception. He was egotistical enough to believe that he alone had the foresight and the ability necessary for real leadership, and perceptive enough to recognize the weaknesses of the court and the officials: "The Court's plans appear even more vague, like catching the wind."[6] "[In regard to the Court] . . . already we can see that there are no fixed opinions and, also, seldom a constant heart. . . . Those who hear of this, can they not be ashamed, depressed, and wish to die?"[7] "The decision of the morning is changed in the evening. I really do not dare to estimate what will be the final outcome."[8] "In our land it is not that there are no smart and capable people, but that the upper classes all waste their time in literary pursuits and do not really try to help in strengthening the country."[9] "No one dares to take the direction of it [Tsungli Yamen], and consequently it merely comes to naught. This then is the evil of having too many high officials."[10]

Although there is no denying that Li enjoyed power and was firmly convinced of his own capabilities, still his primary aim was to save China. An analysis of his policies, ideas, actions, and character, however, indicates that he believed China's only salvation was a strong, unified state, and his methods of achieving this goal, if carried to their logical conclusion, would have created a totally new and revolutionary centralized government. In effect, what Li was unconsciously advocating was the replacement of the existing bureaucratic system, based on the examinations, by a corps of professionally trained experts in government, who would be selected on the basis of ability and personal connections. The professionals of the *mu-fu* system would replace the time-honored amateurs.

(Letters to Friends and Colleagues), *chüan* 14, p. 26a. Hereafter cited as *LWCK-PL*.

[4] *LWCK-PL*, *chüan* 19, p. 13b.
[5] *Ibid.*, *chüan* 12, p. 14b.
[6] *Ibid.*, *chüan* 15, p. 23a.
[7] *Ibid.*, *chüan* 14, p. 23b.

[8] *Ibid.*, *chüan* 12, p. 3b.
[9] *Ibid.*, *chüan* 13, p. 8b.
[10] *Ibid.*, *chüan* 13, p. 13a.

There is no evidence to prove that Li consciously advocated the overthrow of the existing central government, but his lack of confidence in or respect for most officials, his conviction that he alone could do the job, and his firm belief that power in China must be centralized all indicate that the trend was in this direction. In 1872 in a letter to Tseng Kuo-fan, he said: "To begin building steamships and warships actually is one method of self-strengthening. But in China's system of government, the officials and the people, the center and the provinces, all are difficult to unite as one. Although we make plans in the beginning, we definitely are not able to make them good in the end. . . . Japan, because of its monarch's support and the ministers and the people being of one heart, is altogether strong. Its wealth and talent daily increase, and it does not become impoverished." [11] In his discussions with Itō Hirobumi in 1895, during the negotiations preceding the Treaty of Shimonoseki, Li said that the reason for China's defeat was provincialism, and he compared China to Japan during its feudal period, when there were too many conflicting centers of regional power. He went on to say that there were too many provinces in China and no unified power. [12] Such a penetrating analysis of China's need for centralization from one who had built his power on decentralization strikes an ironic, if not tragic, note.

Li received his ideas on the need for centralized power early in his career from Tseng Kuo-fan and Feng Kuei-fen. Tseng had stressed the need for a centralized and unified command in military operations, and Li had followed these teachings in his own operations. Feng Kuei-fen had emphasized the centralization of power in order to keep the vast empire from breaking up into warring states, [13] and Li's words to Itō in 1895 reflected Feng's ideas. Alexander Michie, a close friend and adviser of Li's, stated the case very clearly in his book, *The Englishman in China*: "The personal authority wielded by the Grand Secretary [Li] in provinces beyond his own government was really a step towards centralization of the executive, and with time and an adequate succession of followers in the same path

---

11 *Ibid.*, *chüan* 12, pp. 3a–b.

12 Chang Te-ch'ang, "Li Hung-chang chih wei-hsin yün-tung," (Li Hung-chang's Reform Movement), *Ch'ing-hua chou-k'an*, XXXV, No. 2 (1931), 110–111.

13 Mary C. Wright, *The Last Stand of Chinese Conservatism. The T'ung-Chih Restoration, 1862–1874* (Stanford: Stanford Univ. Press, 1957), p. 57.

there is no telling what changes in the government system might not have been evolved from such a nucleus." [14]

The above conclusion raises the question of whether or not Li ever sought to set himself up as emperor. There is no evidence to indicate that he ever actively planned such a step. However, the idea did cross his mind, but he was too much of a realist and too loyal to the throne to attempt to carry it out. In 1880 there was a rumor afoot that Russia contemplated setting Li up as a puppet emperor and that Li was being urged to rebel. [15] When Charles Gordon paid him a visit, in the same year, he suggested to Li that since he had the only effective army in China, he should lead a force to Peking and assume the supreme power. Li is reported to have replied, " 'All very well, but, you see, I have never been a traitor to the Throne,' and to have added, 'Besides, it wouldn't succeed, and I should get my head taken off.' " [16] Instead he chose to work within the system and gradually build up his own little empire which would serve China and the throne. The crux of the situation was that Li regarded the throne as distinct from the central government. His organization could supplant the inefficient central boards, but his extreme loyalty would not permit him to replace the emperor. The inconsistencies of this arrangement indicate that Li never had a carefully thought-out program of change in mind, but merely reacted to the threat of the West and, on the basis of his character, ideas, and the existing conditions, improvised as best he could.

In the late nineteenth century, the real power in China resided in the provinces, and Li Hung-chang's power was founded on his provincial position. Although he was the Governor-General of the Metropolitan Province (Chihli), he made certain that he did not become a captive of the court by maintaining his headquarters in Tientsin — far enough away from Peking to preserve his semi-independent provincial status, yet close enough to the capital to exert his influence. In Tientsin, the main port of entry to Peking, Li met the foreign envoys before they reached the court, discussed his ideas with the foreign consuls, who would pass on his words to their

[14] Michie, *The Englishman in China*, II, 391–392.

[15] E. V. G. Kiernan, *British Diplomacy in China 1880 to 1885* (Cambridge: Cambridge Univ. Press, 1939), p. 64.

[16] Paul King, *In the Chinese Customs Service* (London: T. Fisher Unwin, Ltd., 1924), pp. 51–52. This statement by Li was told to King by Gordon in 1880 at Chefoo, after Gordon's visit to Li in Tientsin.

respective legations in the capital, and was free to run his provincial operation with a minimum amount of interference from the central government officials. In the capital he would have been just another high official with titles but no real power.

The basis of Li's power was his army — the *Huai-chün*. This army, which was originally a provincial one but which later assumed national proportions, had its beginnings in 1853 when Li's father, Wen-an, was sent back to Anhwei from the capital to organize the local militia around Ho-fei. Li had returned to Anhwei earlier in the same year, and, when his father arrived, he joined him to help lead the local corps. Li Wen-an died in 1855, and Hung-chang left Anhwei to join Tseng's *mu-fu* in 1858, but the Li family's popularity persisted in the Huai area. When Li returned home in 1861 to recruit his new army, he turned to his father's old local corps commanders to help him in his task.[17]

The initial five battalions (*ying*) which Li recruited in Anhwei totaled 2,500 men. When this force arrived at Tseng Kuo-fan's headquarters in An-ch'ing, Anhwei, on February 22, 1862, it was aug-

---

17 Wu Wei-p'ing, "The Rise of the Anhwei Army," Harvard University, Center for East Asian Studies, *Papers on China*, Vol. 14, pp. 32–33; Stanley Spector, "Li Hung-chang and the Huai-chün" (unpublished Ph.D. Dissertation, Univ. of Washington, 1953), pp. 50–51; Li Hung-chang, *Li Wen-chung-kung i-chi* (Posthumous Collection of the Writings of Li Hung-chang) *in* Li Kuo-chieh, ed., *Ho-fei Li shih san shih i-chi* ([no place]: The Li Family of Ho-fei, 1904), *chüan* 4, p. 3a (hereafter cited as *LWCK-IC*); Huang Yün-hsiu, *Hsü-hsiu Lu-chou fu-chih* (Revised edition of the Lu-chou Prefecture Gazetteer) (1885), *chüan* 96, pp. 1a–2a. Li's five original battalions were designated by the personal name of their respective commanders. The *Shu-tzu-ying* (Shu-character battalion) was commanded by Chang Shu-sheng and his younger brother, Chang Shu-shan, who were from Ho-fei and had both led local militia units against the Taipings since 1853. The *Ting-tzu-ying* was led by P'an Ting-hsin, a native of Lu-chiang, a District within Lu-chou Prefecture, and a *chü-jen* of 1849. His father had been a local militia leader and was killed in action against the rebels, so his son swore vengeance and joined the local corps in 1857. Wu Ch'ang-ch'ing, also from Lu-chiang, commanded the *Ch'ing-tzu-ying*. His father had created a local corps in 1854 and was later granted an hereditary title for meritorious service, which his son inherited. In 1855 Wu was put in charge of all the local corps in Shu-ch'eng and Lu-chiang, Anhwei, by the Governor Fu-chi. The *Sheng-tzu-ying* was first commanded by Chou Sheng-po and later by his younger brother, Chou Sheng-ch'uan, who were from Ho-fei and had formed a local corps in 1853. The youngest of the group, and the one who became the most famous, was Liu Ming-ch'uan, who led the *Ming-tzu-ying* and was also from Ho-fei. He had led a band of salt smugglers and at 18 was reported to have committed at least one murder. When the Taipings advanced on Lu-chou, he formed a strong local corps, probably composed of his former gang. He is reported to have fought directly under Li's father.

mented by about 5,500 men from Tseng's army.[18] During the next two years the number rapidly increased so that by November, 1864, it had reached its maximum strength of 60,000 or 70,000 men.[19] With the suppression of the Taiping Rebellion, the *Huai-chün* was only reduced to about 50,000 men, because it was needed to fight the Nien rebels.[20] However, when the Nien Rebellion was finally crushed in 1868, there was serious talk of completly disbanding the army.

During the fall and winter of 1868, Li carried on lengthy discussions with Tseng Kuo-fan and other officials about disbanding the *Huai-chün*. At first he wished to disband the army entirely, but Tseng asked him to keep 20,000 or more men to guard against future contingencies. Tso Tsung-t'ang, Mao Ch'ang-hsi (Hsü-ch'u), and Ying-han (Hsi-lin) repeatedly requested that the army be retained to guard the northern frontier and that Liu Ming-ch'uan be given command of it, because they did not trust the effectiveness of the *lien-chün* in guarding the Imperial Domain (Chihli).[21] Finally in January, 1869, Li wrote to Ho Ching (Hsiao-sung), the Governor-General of Fukien and Chekiang, who was also his *ting-wei* classmate:

After I arrived at Ning [Nanking], I met with the Marquis and Grand Secretary Tseng [Tseng Kuo-fan] and the Commander Ma Ku [-shan, Ma Hsin-i, a *ting-wei* classmate] to discuss the matter of partially disbanding the Huai Army. We have already dismissed 50 battalions

[18] Spector, p. 69; Wei Hsi-yü, *Li Hung-chang* (Shanghai: Chung-hua shu-chu, 1931), p. 18; William James Hail, *Tseng Kuo-fan and the Taiping Rebellion* (New Haven: Yale Univ. Press, 1927), p. 242; Andrew Wilson, *The "Ever-Victorious Army"* (Edinburgh and London: W. Blackwood and Sons, 1868), pp. 229–230. Tseng assigned Ch'eng Hsüeh-ch'i, a native of Anhwei and a general who had served the Taipings but had returned to allegiance in 1861, with 1,000 men, and Kuo Sung-lin, a Hunanese, and his *Sung-tzu-chün* from Tseng's *Hsiang-chün*, 4,000 men, to help train and organize Li's recruits and mold them into what came to be known as the *Huai-chün*, a total force of about 8,000 men.

[19] Wu Wei-p'ing, pp. 37–38. During the course of the Taiping Rebellion, the *Huai-chün* was augmented by additional recruits from the Huai area, men selected from the disbanded Chinese defense forces in the Shanghai area, recruits from the Huai-yang area in Kiangsu, surrendered rebels, and an artillery unit from the disbanded Ever-Victorious Army. By June, 1863, the army had grown to 40,000 men and by November, 1864 had reached its maximum growth of about 60,000 or 70,000. In addition to soldiers, there were also naval forces led by Li Chao-pin and Huang I-sheng, which were part of the total.

[20] Spector, p. 68.

[21] *LWCK-PL, chüan* 18, pp. 51a, 51b–52a.

[25,000 men] of cavalry and infantry, but the Central Plain has just now been settled, and in the North and South there are still bandits. We must use our discretion to keep the battle-seasoned troops for suppression. I have memorialized explaining that the Ming Army, 20 battalions [10,000 men], is defending the Chihli–Shantung contiguous border and is being prepared to be transferred [to Chihli] after the Marquis and Grand Secretary arrives at his post [in Chihli]. The Ch'ing and Hsün Armies, 20-plus battalions, are stationed in the Kiangsu area and have been turned over to the Commander Ku [Ma Hsin-i] to be under his direction. I intend to take Kuo Tzu-mei's [Kuo Sung-lin] five battalions [2,500 men], Chou Hsin-ju's (Sheng-ch'uan) thirteen battalions [6,500 men], T'ang Yüan-pu's cavalry, and my personal army's artillery section and go to Hupeh.[22]

The *Huai-chün* was thus reduced to about 30,000 men and distributed over North and Central China, but it was still under the control of Li and his friends.

At the conclusion of earlier rebellions and wars during the Ch'ing period, such as the White Lotus Rebellion and the Opium War, it had been the standard practice for the militia units to be disbanded and for the Green Standard to be solely responsible for national defense. However, in 1868 this practice was no longer possible. The country had been fighting rebellions for eighteen years. Of the original Green Standard troops, more than half of them were dead and, of the remainder, many had deserted to join the militia, because "braves" were treated better than "soldiers." As a result, the ranks of the Green Standard were depleted by about ninety percent. Even though this force was soon restored, it was no longer capable of assuming the responsibility for major military operations and was relegated to local patrol duty, its role being much the same as that of a modern police force. The *Huai-chün* and the other militia battalions bore the responsibility of national defense and were stationed in the important cities and towns as the "Defense Army" (*fangchün*). What had originally been purely provincial forces became, in fact, the regular army of China. However, there was no unity among these militia armies in training, equipment, or general organization. Each local force was a private army under the control of a provincial leader, and the Board of War did not even know their total strength.[23]

22 *LWCK-PL, chüan* 8, p. 56a.
23 Lo Erh-kang, "Ch'ing-chi ping wei chiang-yu ti ch'i-yüan" (The Origin of the Personal Armies at the End of the Ch'ing), *Chung-kuo she-hui ching-chi*

When Li was shifted to Chihli in 1870, his army went with him and for the next twenty-five years was the principal fighting force in China. It was maintained at a strength of about 30,000 men, drilled in modern military techniques, and equipped with the latest European weapons. Li had hoped to make it into a national army, which would have been supported by all the provinces,[24] but local jealousies and loyalties prevented this. However, his army did achieve a supra-provincial magnitude and dominated China from north of the Yangtze to Southern Manchuria. In addition, it was used in times of crisis in South China and abroad. During the Sino-Japanese incident of 1874, 6,500 troops from the *Huai-chün* were sent to Formosa under the command of Shen Pao-chen, an old friend of Li's who had been appointed Special Imperial Commissioner for Formosan Affairs on Li's recommendation. Throughout this entire incident, the initiative lay with Li, who was the Northern Commissioner, even though the military operations were in the Southern Commissioner's area of jurisdiction; that official did not even concern himself with the affair.[25] During the entire course of Korean affairs from 1882 to 1895, whatever Chinese troops were used to keep order, to put down riots and rebellions, and to oppose the Japanese came from the *Huai-chün*.

In a feeble attempt to reduce its complete reliance on the *Huai-chün* and to return the control of the military to the central authority, the court, in the post-rebellion period, established the *lien-chün*, a special foreign-drilled army whose members were recruited from the Green Standard. It was hoped that it would absorb the various regional armies, such as the *Huai-chün*, and that, along with the Eight Banners and the Green Standard, it would form the national military establishment. However, the various units of the *lien-chün* were assigned to the provinces and placed under the control of the provincial commanders-in-chief. Because the bulk of these units were

*shih chi-k'an*, V, No. 2 (June, 1937), 249; Li Chien-nung, *The Political History of China, 1840–1928*, transl. and ed. by Teng Ssu-yü and J. Ingalls (Princeton: D. Van Nostrand Company, Inc., 1956), p. 141; Ralph L. Powell, *The Rise of Chinese Military Power, 1895–1912* (Princeton: Princeton Univ. Press, 1955), p. 36.

[24] Rawlinson, pp. 267–268; Li Hung-chang, *Li Wen-chung-kung ch'üan-chi* (The Complete Works of Li Hung-chang), ed. by Wu Ju-lun (Nanking, 1908), Tsou-kao, *chüan* 16, pp. 20 ff. (hereafter cited as *LWCK-TK*).

[25] Albert Philip Ludwig, "Li Hung-chang and Chinese Foreign Policy, 1870–1885" (unpublished Ph.D. Dissertation, University of California, 1936), p. 187; Rawlinson, p. 265.

assigned to Chihli, and because Li made certain that his men held the post of Chihli Provincial Commander-in-Chief, he had the actual, as well as the theoretical, control of the *lien-chün*. In addition, the Peking *lien-chün* and the northern Banner and Green Standard forces were supplied from the Tientsin Arsenal, which Li controlled. Also, the regulations and organization of the *lien-chün* were patterned after those established by Tseng Kuo-fan for his army, and thus the element of personal loyalty became an integral part of a national organization. Therefore, through various devices, Li was able to subvert the intentions of the central government and perpetuate its dependence on the *Huai-chün*, which was loyal to him. Li's army insured his provincial position, but his loyalty to the throne guaranteed that it would serve China.[26]

In the devious world of Chinese politics, it took more than just an army, important as it was, in order to succeed and maintain one's position. Powerful friends were indispensable. During the years between 1862 and 1872, when Li Hung-chang was becoming an important provincial official, he was to a large degree dependent on Tseng Kuo-fan and Tseng's friends among the high provincial and central government officials. For seven of these ten years, Tseng was the Liangkiang Governor-General, whose area of jurisdiction included the three provinces of Anhwei, Kiangsi, and Kiangsu. Li or Ma Hsin-i, who had been the Prefect in Ho-fei when Li was serving there under Fu-chi, held the post for the balance of the period. Thus, during these ten crucial years, either Tseng, Li, or a close friend held this all-important governor-generalship of the richest area of China. This was not by accident but by design. When Tseng was ordered to command the Nien campaign in 1865, he made sure that Li would be in Nanking to support his operation, and it was on Tseng's recommendation that he and Li switched places late in 1866. In 1868 when Tseng was ordered to Chihli, Li was already the Governor-General of Hupeh and Hunan, so Ma Hsin-i was assigned to the Liangkiang post. From 1868 to 1870, the three most important provincial posts in China were held by Li, his teacher, and his friend. The shuffling of personnel caused by the Tientsin Massacre and the assassination of Ma Hsin-i resulted in Li's bringing pressure to bear on the court to have Tseng

[26] Rawlinson, pp. 269, 420; Spector, pp. 428–429; 365–366; Lo Erh-kang, p. 249; Powell, p. 36.

returned to the Nanking post, instead of being retired to the Grand Secretariat in Peking.[27] Even though he was now in Chihli, Li still had interests in the Yangtze Valley and wanted someone there on whom he could rely.

During this same ten-year period, his elder brother, Li Han-chang, was the Acting Hu-kuang Governor-General (1867, 1869–1870), holding the office for Hung-chang who was campaigning first against the Nien rebels and later against the rebels in Kweichow and in the northwest. Han-chang was also the Governor of Hunan (1865–1867), and later of Chekiang (1867–1869). When Hung-chang became the Chihli Governor-General in 1870, Han-chang was made the substantive Hu-kuang Governor-General, a post he held until 1882.[28]

The governors of Kiangsu, who succeeded Li after he relinquished that post in 1865, were, in order, Liu Hsün-kao (1865–1866), a *ting-wei* classmate of Li's and an ex *mu-yu*;[29] Kuo Po-yin (1866–1867), an ex-*mu-yu* of Tseng's and the Kiangsu Provincial Judge under Li;[30] Ting Jih-ch'ang (1867–1870), an ex-*mu-yu* of Li's; Chang Chih-wan (1870–1871), a *ting-wei* classmate; and Ho Ching (1871–1872), another *ting-wei* classmate.[31] Ch'iao Sung-nien, the Governor of Anhwei (1863–1865), had served under Li as the Soochow Salt Controller, a post which Li had secured for him.[32] Ying-han, who was the Anhwei Governor from 1865–1874, had been an Expectant District Magistrate in Anhwei in 1854 when Li was a *mu-yu* of the Governor of Anhwei, and in 1859 Ying was made the Acting Ho-fei District Magistrate.[33] Tso Tsung-t'ang, Tseng Kuo-ch'üan, and Ma Hsin-i all served as the Governor of Chekiang, and Shen Pao-chen,

---

[27] Chiang Siang-tseh, *The Nien Rebellion* (Seattle: Univ. of Washington Press, 1954), p. 115, footnote 209.

[28] *Ch'ing-shih lieh-chuan* (Taipei, Taiwan: Chung-hua shu-chü, 1962), *chüan* 59, pp. 24a–25a; *Ch'ing-tai cheng-hsien lei-pien* (Taipei, Taiwan: Shih-chieh shu-chü, 1961), *shang*, Tsung-tu nien-piao, *chüan* 3, pp. 8a–10a.

[29] *Ch'ing-tai cheng-hsien lei-pien*, *shang*, Hsün-fu nien-piao, *chüan* 4, p. 2a; Fang Chao-ying and Tu Lien-che, *Tseng-chiao Ch'ing-ch'ao chin-shih t'i-ming pei-lu*, Harvard-Yenching Institute Sinological Index Series, Supplement No. 19 (Peiping: Harvard-Yenching Institute, 1941), p. 180; *LWCK-PL*, *chüan* 1, p. 23a.

[30] *Ch'ing-shih lieh-chuan*, *chüan* 55, p. 22a; *Ch'ing-tai cheng-hsien lei-pien*, *shang*, Hsün-fu nien-piao, *chüan* 4, pp. 2a–b.

[31] *Ch'ing-tai cheng-hsien lei-pien*, *shang*, Hsün-fu nien-piao, *chüan* 4, p. 3b.

[32] *LWCK-PL*, *chüan* 2, pp. 4a–b; *Ch'ing-tai cheng-hsien lei-pien*, *shang*, Hsün-fu nien piao, *chüan* 4, pp. 1b–2a.

[33] *Ch'ing-shih lieh-chuan*, *chüan* 56, p. 5b.

a *ting-wei* classmate, and Liu K'un-i, who had served in Tseng's army, practically monopolized the Governorship of Kiangsi during this period.[34] Other friends and classmates of Li's or Tseng's who held governorships were: Ch'ien Ting-ming (Honan: 1871–1875), Shen Kuei-fen (Shansi: 1863–1865), Li Tsung-hsi (Shansi: 1869–1870), Pao Yüan-shen (Shansi: 1871–1876), Kuo Sung-t'ao (Kwangtung: 1863–1866), and Ch'iao Sung-nien (Shensi: 1866–1868).[35]

At the governor-general level, in addition to the Liangkiang and Hu-kuang posts mentioned above, Liu Ch'ang-yu, a Hunanese and former general in the *Hsiang-chün*, held the Chihli post from 1862 to 1867, and Tso Tsung-t'ang was the Shensi-Kansu Governor-General from 1866 to 1880 and before that had held the Fukien-Chekiang post from 1865 to 1866. Chang Shu-sheng, a *Huai-chün* commander, was the Director-General of Grain Transport from 1871 to 1872, and Ch'iao Sung-nien was the Director-General of Conservation of the Yellow River and the Grand Canal from 1871 to 1875. Ma Hsin-i held the Fukien-Chekiang governor-generalship from 1867 to 1868.[36]

When Tseng Kuo-fan died in 1872, Li Hung-chang lost a powerful patron and ally. Tseng had had a wide circle of friends in Peking, stemming from his years of service there, on whom he and his protégés could rely, and, although Li had been forming friendships in the capital since 1862, especially with Prince Kung, he appears to have relied to a large extent on Tseng and his powerful position. However, two years after Tseng's death, there began for Li an association which was to last the rest of his life and which insured his position in the face of extreme opposition — his friendship with the Empress Dowager Tz'u-hsi.

There is no conclusive evidence as to how this friendship began, but it seems to have developed out of events that took place in 1874 and 1875. In 1874, when the two empress dowagers paid a visit to the tombs of the Ch'ing rulers, Tz'u-an, the senior Empress Dowager, summoned Li to escort the imperial procession. This event provided Tz'u-hsi, the junior Empress Dowager, with an opportunity to judge the character of Li Hung-chang. In the next year,

---

[34] *Ch'ing-tai cheng-hsien lei-pien, shang,* Hsün-fu nien-piao, *chüan* 4, pp. 1a–4a; U.S. Library of Congress, Asiatic Division, *Eminent Chinese of the Ch'ing Period (1644–1912),* ed. by Arthur W. Hummel (Washington, D.C.: U.S. Gov't Printing Office, 1943), I, 523 (hereafter cited as Hummel).

[35] *Ch'ing-tai cheng-hsien lei-pien, shang,* Hsün-fu nien-piao, *chüan* 4 pp. 1a–4a.

[36] *Ibid., shang,* Tsung-tu nien-piao, *chüan* 3, pp. 7a–9a.

the events surrounding the death of the T'ung-chih Emperor and Tz'u-hsi's *coup d'état*, which put the Kuang-hsü Emperor on the throne, provided another opportunity for her to test Li's loyalty and ability. There are conflicting reports regarding Li's role in these events, but the most commonly accepted version, both at the time and since, places Li and his loyal Anhwei troops in Peking as active participants in the *coup d'état*. The story goes that, owing to the extreme opposition from within the court to Tz'u-hsi's plan to put her nephew on the throne, she appealed to Li, as the Governor-General of Chihli and, therefore, the legitimate protector of the Imperial Household, to bring his troops to Peking to support her move. Tz'u-hsi's candidate for the throne was from the same generation as the recently deceased T'ung-chih Emperor, and thus his enthronement would have been in direct violation of the Manchu laws of succession, which held that a new emperor should be from the next younger generation. Li purportedly responded to the Empress-Dowager's appeal by moving his troops on a forced march from Tientsin to Peking, where they arrived at midnight. Having muffled their horses' hooves and with chop-sticks clenched between their teeth to guarantee complete silence, his men surrounded the Forbidden City. The Manchu guards of questionable loyalty were bound and hauled off to prison; the leaders of the opposition were arrested; and by morning the Forbidden City was in Li's hands. The Empress Dowager Tz'u-hsi, having thus reduced all opposition, proclaimed her four-year-old nephew emperor. Having achieved their purpose, Li and his troops quietly returned to Tientsin.[37]

H. B. Morse and J. O. P. Bland both state, however, that Li himself did not lead his troops to Peking, but that the contingent of Anhwei troops which he sent was under the command of Tz'u-hsi's faithful ally, the commander of the bodyguard, Jung-lu.[38] According to Li's own letters, he appears to have been surprised by the *coup d'état* and did not arrive in Peking until January 28, 1875, about two weeks

[37] Wen Ching (Lim Boon-keng), *The Chinese Crisis from Within* (London: Grant Richards, 1901), pp. 95, 96; Mrs. Archibald Little, *Li Hung-Chang. His Life and Time* (London: Cassell and Co., Ltd., 1903), pp. 92–93; P. W. Sergeant, *The Great Empress Dowager of China* (London: Hutchinson and Co., 1910), pp. 106–107; Daniele Varé, *The Last Empress* (Garden City, New York: Doubleday, Doran and Co., Inc., 1936), p. 137.

[38] Hosea B. Morse, *The International Relations of the Chinese Empire* (Taiwan reprint), II, 280; J. O. P. Bland and E. Backhouse, *China Under the Empress Dowager* (London: William Heinemann, 1911), p. 123.

after the death of the T'ung-chih Emperor and the *coup d'état*.[39] Despite the conflicting reports regarding Li's role, Li did have three audiences with the Empress Dowager (January 29, 30, and February 2, 1875) and was ordered back to Chihli so that she could rely on his keeping the Metropolitan Province under control during the crisis of the change of emperors.[40] In his letters relating to these events, Li expressed his confidence and respect for the strong-handed policies of Tz'u-hsi and his belief that they would lead to peace and stability for China.[41] It was out of this matrix that the long and loyal relationship which existed between these two extremely capable and powerful figures apparently developed.

Both Tz'u-hsi and Li were noted for their loyalty to their friends, but the real basis of their association was that they recognized each other's abilities, needed each other, and also feared each other. Tz'u-hsi had the power to dismiss Li, and there was sufficient conservative opposition to him to back her up, but she was clever enough not to oppose openly the man who had the Huai Army, the Pei-yang Navy, and a loyal following of men versed in commercial and foreign affairs. She feared his vast powers but also was forced to rely on them.[42] Li is reported to have said, "The Empress-Dowager is always interfering with my schemes. She thinks I am too pro-foreign. She is afraid that I will become too powerful."[43] In order to restrict Li's aggrandizement of power, she used the device of playing him off against the Conservatives and pretended to listen to the "public opinion" of the literati. She permitted, and even secretly fostered, the clamor of the antiforeign faction so that the proposals of Li and similar-minded men met opposition on all sides. However, once she had made up her mind as to a course of action, she quickly and effectively cut off the hue and cry. Although Li held a great deal of power and, at times, was able to defy openly the orders of the court, still he was Tz'u-hsi's instrument, and she manipulated him, not vice-versa.[44]

[39] *LWCK, chüan* 14, pp. 37b, 38b. The T'ung-chih Emperor died on January 12, 1875 (TC 13/12/5).

[40] *Ibid., chüan* 15, p. 2a.

[41] *Ibid., chüan* 14, p. 38b; *chüan* 15, pp. 2a–3b, 8b.

[42] Immanuel C. Y. Hsü, p. 205.

[43] Lewis Charles Arlington, *Through the Dragon's Eyes* (London: Constable and Co., Ltd., 1931), p. 25.

[44] Immanuel C. Y. Hsü, pp. 205–206; Lloyd Eric Eastman, "Reactions of Chinese Officials to Foreign Aggression: A Study of the Sino-French Contro-

Li, for his part, never went against Tz'u-hsi's wishes, once she had made up her mind, and remained loyal to her throughout his lifetime. He chafed at her restrictions but never hinted at rebellion. His loyalty paid off because she stood by him in times of crisis when it appeared that all hands were turned against him. During the furor created by the terms of the Sino-French Treaty of 1885, her backing permitted him to survive and ignore the accusations of his enemies, and in 1895 she saved his life when the officials demanded his head to pay for China's defeat by Japan. Although their methods may have differed, both Tz'u-hsi and Li Hung-chang had a common goal — the preservation of China and the Imperial household. Because of this they respected each other, and Tz'u-hsi, although a conservative at heart, supported many of Li's self-strengthening measures and turned to him for advice.

Through his self-strengthening endeavors, Li also achieved the support of the two most important Manchu princes — Prince Kung and Prince Ch'un. Prince Kung, the sixth son of the Tao-kuang Emperor, had played a major role in the government during the reign of the T'ung-chih Emperor, but under the Kuang-hsü Emperor his influence began to decline, partly because it was his son that the opposition had supported for the throne at the time of the *coup d'état* in 1875. Nevertheless, in the late 1870's he was still an important figure in the court, and his interest in self-strengthening measures and foreign affairs brought him into contact with Li.[45] The real power, however, was Prince Ch'un, the seventh son of the Tao-kuang Emperor and the father of the Kuang-hsü Emperor. As the father of a boy emperor, it was in his name that things were sanctioned and legitimized.[46] His wife was the younger sister of the Empress Dowager Tz'u-hsi, and, through her, he enjoyed special favors and was raised to high office. Li Hung-chang became a close friend of the prince and sought to interest him in matters of national defense. In this way, what Li initiated at a provincial level could become a national concern. Through the prince, Li was able to imbue the court, to a considerable extent, with his own ideas and to assure it that there was no danger in adopting foreign meth-

versy 1880–1885" (unpublished Ph.D. Dissertation, Harvard University, 1962), pp. 279–280, 197, cited with the author's permission.

[45] Hummel, I, 380; Sergeant, p. 111.

[46] Alexander Michie, "Li Hung-chang," *The Nineteenth Century*, XL (August, 1896), 239.

ods. Prince Ch'un became genuinely interested in naval matters and
in 1885 was appointed to head up the newly created Board of the
Admiralty, with Li as his colleague. Despite his weak character
and the fact that he was a tool of his sister-in-law, he stood by Li,
as best he could, and supported the expansion and development
of the navy and the introduction of foreign enterprises into China.
His death, early in 1891, robbed Li of a valuable support at court.[47]

During his twenty-five years in Chihli, Li maintained the network
of friendships and acquaintances with other high provincial officials
that he had begun in 1862. As his older colleagues died or retired,
their places were taken by younger men, some of whom had served
in the *Huai-chün* or in other capacities in his *mu-fu*. Between 1872
and 1894, the post of Liangkiang Governor-General, probably the
second most important provincial post in China, was held successively by Ho Ching, a *ting-wei* classmate; Chang Shu-sheng, an
ex-military *mu-yu*; P'eng Yü-lin, an ex-general in the *Hsiang-chün*;
Li Tsung-hsi, another *ting-wei* classmate; Liu K'un-i, a friend of
Tseng's; Shen Pao-chen, a *ting-wei* classmate and former fellow-
*mu-yu* in Tseng's *mu-fu*; Tso Tsung-t'ang; and Tseng Kuo-ch'üan,
who was Tseng Kuo-fan's brother. In Szechwan, Ting Pao-chen, the
ex-Governor of Shantung with whom Li had worked during the
Nien campaign, served as Governor-General, as did Liu Ping-chang,
an ex-military *mu-yu* and fellow-provincial. Ho Ching also served
as the Fukien-Chekiang Governor-General, and Liu K'un-i, Chang
shu-sheng, Tseng Kuo-ch'üan, and Li Han-chang, in order, practically monopolized the Liang-kuang post during this period, except
for the years from 1884 to 1889 when Chang Chih-tung, one of Li's
arch rivals, was the incumbent.[48]

At the governor level, during this same twenty-three-year period,
many of the same names appear. Tseng Kuo-ch'üan served as Governor in Shansi, as did Pao Yüan-shen, a *ting-wei* classmate. Ch'ien
Ting-ming, an ex-*mu-yu*, was the Honan Governor, and Ting Jih-
ch'ang served as the Governor of Fukien, as did Ho Ching and Liu
Ming-ch'uan. Liu Ping-chang was the Kiangsi Governor and, later,

---

[47] Hummel, I, 384; Michie, *The Englishman in China*, II, 314, 316; Rawlinson, p. 579; James Harrison Wilson, *China: Travels and Investigations in the
Middle Kingdom*, 3rd ed. revised (New York: D. Appleton and Co., 1901),
p. 315.

[48] *Ch'ing-tai cheng-hsien lei-pien, shang*, Tsung-tu nien-piao, *chüan* 3,
pp. 9a–11b.

Chekiang Governor, and P'an Ting-hsin, an ex-military *mu-yu*, was the Governor of Yunnan. Liu Ming-ch'uan also became the first Governor of Taiwan, a post he held from 1885 to 1891.[49]

Even though some of these governors and governors-general had served in Li's *mu-fu* and others were old friends, it did not necessarily mean that they were under his control. Shen Pao-chen and Ting Jih-ch'ang were probably more amenable to his wishes than any of the others, especially in naval matters, since they were both close friends of his, and he had taken a personal interest in their careers.[50] On the other hand, Chang Shu-sheng, who was one of the original *Huai-chün* commanders and whom Li had requested to replace him as the Acting Chihli Governor-General in 1882 when Li was allowed 100 days of mourning for his mother, reportedly tried to get rid of Li's *mu-yu* when he took over the post and planned to denounce Li to the throne in a grab for power. However, Li's *mu-yu* informed him of the plot, and he was able to nip it in the bud.[51] Personal connections and friendships with other governors and governors-general were necessary in order to carry out official business, but they could not be relied upon to build a network of power. Each of his colleagues seems to have been looking out primarily for his own interests and would switch from one side to the other as the occasion demanded. Li had many friends and acquaintances in high provincial office throughout the empire, but he did not have any of them "in his pocket."

Within Chihli, however, Li held the power and could bind men to himself through favors and recommendations. In 1870, at the instance of Li, the court created the post of Tientsin Customs Taotai. The creation of this post marks the beginning of the gradual trend towards professionalism, as opposed to scholarly amateurism, in the orthodox ranks of the bureaucracy in China during the late nineteenth and twentieth centuries. Heretofore, provincial posts within the orthodox bureaucracy were normally based on territorial responsibility, but this taotaiship was organized on the basis of specific duties, and its incumbent was limited in his responsibilities to the conduct of foreign affairs, defense measures, and customs col-

---

[49] *Ibid.*, *shang*, Hsün-fu nien-piao, *chüan* 4, pp. 4a–10b.
[50] Rawlinson, pp. 402–403, 270–273; Albert Feuerwerker, *China's Early Industrialization: Sheng Hsuan-huai (1844–1916) and Mandarin Enterprises* (Cambridge: Harvard Univ. Press, 1958), p. 13; LWCK-PL, *chüan* 15, p. 17a.
[51] Little, pp. 145, 148–149.

lection, functions which gave it a foreign and professional tinge.
Through this office, which was to supplement his own position as
the Commissioner for Northern Trade, Li gained control of the
commerce and revenue of the major port serving the capital area.[52]
Needless to say, it was essential to Li that a trusted and technically
qualified follower hold this new office. Thus, everyone who held the
post of Tientsin Customs Taotai between its creation in 1870 and Li's
fall from power in 1895 was handpicked by Li, was often an old follower, and was experienced in foreign affairs. The first incumbent
was Ch'en Ch'in. Ch'en had been the Acting Tientsin Prefect and
was highly recommended by Tseng Kuo-fan. He had also had considerable experience in the Tsungli Yamen and was, thus, well acquainted with the problems confronting China. Because Ch'en's
services were also requested by the Tsungli Yamen, Li had agreed
to use him only to get things started and then replace him with
Shen Pao-ching. Shen was a Kiangsu chü-jen, who had served Li
in Shanghai, Anhwei, and Hupeh since 1862, and whom Li had
brought north to head up the Tientsin Arsenal.[53] However, as it
turned out, Shen Pao-ching was ordered to the Kiukiang Customs
Taotai post in 1872, and Ch'en Ch'in continued to serve in Tientsin
until 1874, when he retired due to illness.[54] Li then appointed Sun
Shih-ta as the Acting Taotai, pending imperial approval of his request to make Li Chao-t'ang the substantive Taotai. Li Chao-t'ang,
who held the post from 1874 to 1878, was a chin-shih from Kwangtung, had had years of service in foreign affairs, and was the Acting
Taiwan Taotai during the Japanese crisis in 1874, at which time
he had proven his ability to Li and to Li's classmate and friend,
Shen Pao-chen.[55] When Li Chao-t'ang was promoted in 1878 to be
the Superintendent of the Foochow shipyard, Li Hung-chang designated Ting Shou-ch'ang, the newly appointed Chihli Provincial
Judge and an ex-commander in the Huai-chün from Anhwei, as
the Acting Tientsin Customs Taotai, pending the approval of his
next candidate for the post, Cheng Tsao-ju. Li noted in his recommendation that Cheng had supervised the Arsenal in Shanghai for

[52] Feuerwerker, pp. 64–65; Spector, p. 318; *LWCK-TK, chüan* 17, p. 14a,
*chüan* 24, p. 6a, *chüan* 42, p. 47a.

[53] *LWCK-TK, chüan* 17, pp. 14a–15b, 5a; Spector, pp. 315–317; Rawlinson, pp. 322–323, 353–354.

[54] *LWCK-TK, chüan* 71, p. 36b, *chüan* 58, p. 5a, *chüan* 24, p. 6a.

[55] *Ibid., chüan* 24, pp. 6a–7a.

ten years, had been active in military affairs, and had built machinery.[56] Cheng served as the Tientsin Customs Taotai from 1878 until 1881, when he became, concurrently, the Chinese Minister to America, Japan, and Peru. Li then picked his trusted follower, Chou Fu, to fill the post, which he did until 1888.[57] Between 1888 and 1889, for some unexplained reason, the post was vacant, but in the latter year Li recommended Liu Ju-i for the office, and it was approved. Liu, who held the post from 1889 to 1891, was from Anhwei and had been in Li's service for twenty years, primarily in the Tientsin Arsenal.[58] After another vacancy of one year, between 1891 and 1892, the post was filled by Li's old *mu-yu*, Sheng Hsuan-huai, who held it through 1895.[59]

A clause in the regulations pertaining to the post of Tientsin Customs Taotai provided the loophole which made it possible for Li to handpick the candidates for this office. The clause stated that if among all of the various taotais, expectant-taotais, and prefects who were assigned to Chihli there was no one whom the governor-general felt was worthy of the post, then he could recommend someone else.[60] In his recommendations, Li stressed the unusual qualifications of the post and how difficult it was to find men who matched up to them. He did not belittle the more orthodox officials who were assigned to the province to await an opening, but stated that they could not be selected for this post because they did not have the necessary experience in foreign affairs. Because of the above clause, his arguments, and his powerful position, in every case Li was able to get his recommendations for this all-important office approved.[61]

Li was also fairly successful either in getting his candidates assigned to the other official posts within Chihli or in having these offices held by close friends. Chou Fu, while serving as the Tientsin Customs Taotai (1881–1888), also held at various times the concurrent posts of Tientsin Military Taotai (1883) and Acting Salt

[56] *Ibid., chüan* 33, pp. 19a–20a; Rawlinson, p. 379.

[57] *Ibid., chüan* 59, pp. 31a–b, *chüan* 42, p. 47a.

[58] *Ibid., chüan* 78, p. 57a; *Ta-Ch'ing chin-shen ch'üan-shu* (The Complete Record of the Officials of the Ch'ing), 1888–1891, Vol. 2, p. 14b (hereafter cited as *TCCSCS*).

[59] *TCCSCS*, 1891–1895, Vol. 2, p. 14b.

[60] *LWCK-TK, chüan* 24, p. 6a.

[61] *Ibid., chüan* 17, p. 14a; *chüan* 24, p. 6a; *chüan* 33, p. 19a; *chüan* 58, p. 5a; *chüan* 59, p. 31a; *chüan* 78, pp. 57a–b.

Controller at Ch'ang-lu (ca. 1887). From 1888 to 1895 he was the Chihli Provincial Judge and, for a short time in 1889, was the Chihli Provincial Treasurer. Earlier, between 1877 and 1878, he had served as the Acting Chihli River Taotai.[62] Ch'en Nai, Li's old classmate and fellow *mu-yu* from their Tseng Kuo-fan days, held the post of Chihli River Taotai (*Ch'ing-ho tao*) in 1872.[63] He was succeeded by Yeh Po-ying, who was from Anwei and who had been in military service under both Li and Tseng Kuo-fan. It was Li who had appointed him to this taotaiship in 1872; and in 1874, when Yeh was accused of "swindling and scheming" to get the post, it was Li who not only cleared him of the charges but also praised his ability.[64] Shih K'e-k'uan held the post from 1881 to 1884. Shih was also from Anhwei, had served in the *Huai-chün* in both the Taiping and Nien rebellions, and had been ordered to the post by Li.[65] Between 1889 and 1895 the post was held by another Anhwei man, P'an Chün-te.[66] The office of Chihli Provincial Treasurer was held, in 1870, by Ch'ien Ting-ming, an ex-*mu-yu*. Two years later Li's *ting-wei* classmate from Anhwei, Sun Kuan, assumed this position and held it until 1877.[67] In 1885 the treasurership went to K'uei-pin, a Mongol, whom Li had recommended in 1880 to handle the Chahar Mongol affairs under Li's direction.[68] The Tientsin Military Taotai between 1870 and 1875 was Ting Shou-ch'ang, who was from Li's home prefecture of Ho-fei and who had served in the *Huai-chün* since its inception in 1862. Ting was forced to give up his taotaiship in 1875 in order to go into mourning, but once this period was over, he returned to Li's service where he remained until his death in 1890. During this latter period, in addition to performing various military duties, he

[62] Fang Lienche, "Chou Fu," draft *MS* prepared for the Men and Politics in Modern China Project, Columbia University, 1959; *Ch'ing shih* (History of the Ch'ing Dynasty), compiled by Ch'ing-shih pien-tsuan wei-yüan-hui (Taipei, Taiwan: Kuo-fang yen-chiu yüan, 1961), Vol. 6, pp. 4970–4971; *TCCSCS*, 1870–1874, 1884–1895, Vol. 2, pp. 14b, 7a.
[63] *TCCSCS*, 1872, Vol. 2, p. 7a; *LWCK-TK, chüan* 7, pp. 35a–b.
[64] *LWCK-TK, chüan* 23, pp. 5a–6a.
[65] *Ibid., chüan* 72, pp. 39a–b; *TCCSCS*, 1884, Vol. 2, p. 7a.
[66] *TCCSCS*, 1889–1895, Vol. 2, p. 7a.
[67] *Ibid.*, 1870–1877, Vol. 2, p. 7a.
[68] *LWCK-TK, chüan* 36, pp. 20a–b; *TCCSCS*, 1885, Vol. 2, p. 7a. The Chihli Governor-General had superior jurisdiction over the Chahar Mongols in civilian questions and exercised this authority through the K'ou-pei Taotai, a post formerly held by K'uei-pin; see H. S. Brunnert and V. V. Hagelstrom, *Present Day Political Organization of China* (Taiwan reprint, 1961), No. 893, p. 459.

was, at times, the Chihli Provincial Judge.[69] Between 1886 and 1892 the Tientsin Military Taotai post was held successively by two men from Anhwei, Hu Yü-fen (1886–1891) and Chou Mao-ch'i (1891–1892).[70]

Despite his powerful and important position, Li was not a free agent when it came to selecting official personnel. He could recommend and use pressure, but the Board of Civil Appointments usually had the final say. However, Li was not above going over the head of the board and appealing directly to the emperor, especially when he wanted someone and had been refused on the basis of regulations and procedures. His standard arguments were the lack of men of talent and how badly he needed the individual in question. He insisted that the exigencies of the time made it necessary on occasion to adhere to the spirit rather than the letter of the law.[71]

During the Taiping Rebellion, his and Tseng's recommendations concerning the selection of official personnel were, for the most part, rubber-stamped by the board. The two men would discuss the qualifications of various candidates for a specific office and, having reached an agreement, would memorialize to that effect. However, after the situation had returned to normal and the court was no longer completely dependent on them, the power of the central government reasserted itself. It was a mark of Li's power and his knowledge of the workings of Chinese politics that he was able to get as many of his people in office in Chihli as he did.

Li Hung-chang had been able to build a strong provincial government in Chihli and a wide network of personal relationships in the other provinces, but the other provincial leaders did the same, even if to a lesser degree. Rampant provincialism, which was so endemic to China, was the rock on which Li's plans for a national navy, with himself at its head, foundered. Naval ships were considered the personal possessions of the provincial leaders and those from one area of jurisdiction could not enter another area without creating jealousy and being regarded in much the same light as a foreign force.[72] The crisis of 1874 over the Japanese expedition to Formosa

[69] LWCK-TK, chüan 25, pp. 1a–2b, chüan 33, pp. 19a–20a, chüan 68, pp. 37a–38a; LWCK-IC, chüan 3, p. 17b; TCCSCS, 1870–1877, Vol. 2, p. 14b.

[70] TCCSCS, 1886–1892, Vol. 2, p. 14b; Hummel, II, 951; The North China Herald, December 7, 1906, p. 550.

[71] LWCK-TK, chüan 20, p. 41a, chüan 21, pp. 45a–46a, chüan 23, p. 5b, chüan 42, pp. 1a–2b.

[72] Michie, The Englishman in China, II, 400.

brought home to responsible officials the need for centralizing the naval forces. As soon as the crisis was over, Ting Jih-ch'ang, an old friend of Li's who had helped him in founding the Kiangnan Arsenal, suggested in a memorial that the coastal defense be unified under a system of subregions. In the North, a Pei-yang Admiral would be responsible for Chihli and Shantung, with his headquarters at Tientsin; a Tung-yang (Eastern Ocean) Admiral would be in charge of Chekiang and Kiangsu with his base at Woosung; and a Nan-yang Admiral, stationed at Amoy, would oversee Fukien and Kwangtung. Wen-ping, the Acting Governor of Shantung, shortly thereafter proposed that Li Hung-chang be the Admiral of the North; that P'eng Yü-lin, a Hunanese and Tseng Kuo-fan's most famous general, be assigned to the Center; and that Shen Pao-chen, a *ting-wei* classmate of Li's and the Liangkiang Governor-General, be in charge of the South. All three admirals would report to a supreme naval commander. Li considered a single command the most preferable, but he realized that China was not yet ready for it; therefore, he supported the three-way split. The old system, whereby the coastal defense was divided between a Northern and a Southern Commissioner, had proven inefficient during the Formosa incident, and it would have been even worse if someone in opposition to Li, such as Tso Tsung-t'ang, had held the Southern post. With the coast divided into three sections, there was a chance that Li might be able to control one, if not both, of the other sectors.[73] However, this proposal was not accepted, and the two-Commissioner plan was confirmed in 1875, when the Northern Commissioner (Li) was formally given the responsibility of the defense of the Northern coast. The Southern Commissioner was not formally confirmed in his defense responsibilities until 1879, when Ting Jih-ch'ang was assigned that office.[74]

China was not to have anything approaching naval unity until October, 1885, when, as a result of the destruction of the Southern Fleet at Foochow by the French, it was decided to establish a Board of the Admiralty with Prince Ch'un at its head, and with Prince Ch'ing and Li serving as his colleagues.[75] During the intervening years several attempts had been made to straighten out the chaos of provincial navies; Shen Pao-chen suggested in 1877 that the

[73] Rawlinson, pp. 270–272.                [75] *Ibid.*, p. 579; Li Chien-nung, p. 125.
[74] *Ibid.*, p. 272.

Northern Commissioner be allowed to build his fleet first;[76] and in 1884 Chang P'ei-lun proposed the organization of a Naval Bureau under the Tsungli Yamen — a proposal which Prince Kung heartily approved, even hinting that Li should be placed in charge of it.[77] However, until 1885 the navies remained strictly provincial organizations.

As the Commissioner of Northern Defense and, at the same time, as a member of the Board of the Admiralty, Li was able to compound his power position. He was not only solely responsible for all naval affairs in the North, but, as the one really knowledgeable member of the Admiralty, he had a say in what went on in the southern defense area. This was as close as he ever came to achieving control of a national navy. Prince Ch'un died in 1891, and the control of the Admiralty fell into the hands of less sympathetic men who hindered, rather than helped, him. Also, with Prince Kung no longer in charge of the Tsungli Yamen, Li lacked the strong support he needed at court to assure him of a reliable source of funds. As a result, he was forced to fall back on his provincial position in order to keep his navy going.[78]

Li Hung-chang's provincial position had made it possible for him to establish his various commercial and industrial enterprises for the stated purpose of regaining for China the commercial rights that had been usurped by the foreigners and in order to prevent the foreigners from making new inroads into the Chinese economy. However, a corollary purpose had been to strengthen his regional power and to support his military and naval establishments. The income derived from these enterprises, when kept in Chinese hands, would enrich the country and make it possible to support a military force which would be capable of warding off the foreigners. At the same time, Li could also strengthen his own political position by using the profits from one enterprise either to start another or to buy the support he needed in Peking to insure his own position. These enterprises thus actually served two purposes: to strengthen China economically and militarily, and to strengthen Li.

His first venture in the manufacturing realm was in 1863, when he set up an arsenal in Sungkiang, Kiangsu, to make ammunition for his army. It was started at the instigation of Halliday Macartney,

[76] Rawlinson, p. 273.
[77] Li Chien-nung, p. 124.

[78] Rawlinson, pp. 585–586, 587.

an ex-British Army surgeon, who argued that Li was paying too
much for the arms and ammunition he bought from the foreigners.
In a temple in Sungkiang, Macartney set up a shop and proved to
Li that Chinese workmen under his supervision could turn out
quality goods.[79] When Soochow was recaptured in 1864, the operation was moved to that city and expanded. In 1865 when Li was
transferred to Nanking, he broke up his Soochow works and sent
part of it to Shanghai under Ting Jih-ch'ang, who had been added
to the Soochow staff in order to reduce Li's reliance on foreigners.
Ting had originally been sent to Kwangtung by Tseng Kuo-fan on an
errand relating to *likin* (1862), but while in that province he became
active in the manufacturing of munitions. Li felt that his services
could be put to better use in Kiangsu, and in 1863, after repeated
memorials and orders from Li, Ting came north to help in the
founding of the Soochow works. In Shanghai, Ting set up a small
machine shop which, when combined with the machinery Tseng
Kuo-fan had ordered from the United States through Yung Wing,
became the famous Kiangnan Arsenal. Under Macartney's supervision, the main bulk of the machinery and staff of the Soochow
Arsenal followed Li to Nanking.[80] Li's control of the Nanking
Arsenal remained a personal one long after he left Nanking, and
the plant continued to produce arms and ammunition for his troops
as late as 1876.[81] Although Li was listed as one of the four Directors
of the Kiangnan Arsenal until 1895, once he moved to Chihli, he
began to lose effective control of it, especially in the early 1880's
when Tso Tsung-t'ang was the Liangkiang Governor-General.[82]
Arsenals were political pawns or personal possessions, and control
of their output depended on keeping a close surveillance over them.
The provincial posts in the Yangtze Valley changed hands frequently,
but Li remained in Chihli for twenty-five years. Even though he

[79] Andrew Wilson, p. 165; Rawlinson, p. 244, footnote 91; Demetrius C.
Boulger, *The Life of Sir Halliday Macartney* (London and New York: J. Lane,
1908), p. 79.
[80] Boulger, *The Life of Sir Halliday Macartney*, p. 146; Robert K. Douglas,
*Li Hungchang* (London: Bliss, Sands and Foster, 1895), p. 87; Teng Ssu-yü and
John K. Fairbank, *China's Response to the West* (Cambridge: Harvard Univ.
Press, 1954), p. 64; Rawlinson, pp. 221–222, 289; *LWCK-TK, chüan* 4, pp.
44a–b.
[81] Boulger, *The Life of Sir Halliday Macartney*, p. 188; Douglas, *Li Hung-
chang*, p. 99; Rawlinson, pp. 420–422.
[82] Rawlinson, pp. 423–424.

lost out in the south, his long tenure in the north made it possible for him to build up the Tientsin Arsenal as his chief source of supply.

When Li established the China Merchants Steam Navigation Company in 1872, he informed the Tsungli Yamen that the basic purpose of the company was to recover China's economic rights.[83] Foreign shipping had been monopolizing the coastal carrying trade and also penetrating up the Yangtze and other Chinese rivers to syphon off a large portion of the inland business. By establishing a steamship company, Li hoped to cut into the profits of the foreign shipping companies and eventually drive them out of business.[84] His purpose in founding the Kaiping Mines in 1877 was to establish a cheap, local, and adequate source of coal for the steamers of the China Merchants Company and the warships of his growing navy.[85] The railway, which started out as a means of transporting the coal from the Kaiping Mines to Tientsin, was gradually developed for military reasons. Li consistently resisted all foreign offers to build and operate railways in China; the foreigners could build them, but it would be with Chinese money, and the control and operation of them would remain in Chinese hands.[86] The Imperial Telegraph Administration was established in 1881 for government and military purposes, but once again it was a Chinese endeavor. The Shanghai Cotton Cloth Company, established in 1882, was granted a ten-year monopoly to prevent foreigners from establishing similar mills and removing the profit from the country. The Moho Gold Mines (1887) provided gold to pay for Li's military establishment.[87] All of Li's commercial and industrial enterprises were financed with Chinese funds, with the exception of three foreign short-term loans, easily repaid, for the China Merchants Company.[88] Li was thus able to keep his enterprises free of the foreign financial entanglements which were to plague Chinese industrial development after 1895.

Even though the idea to establish a company usually came from someone other than Li, the money was raised by selling stock, the business was supposedly run on commercial principles, and the officers of the company were in theory responsible to the stockholders,

---

[83] Feuerwerker, p. 171.

[84] Harold C. Hinton, *The Grain Tribute System of China (1845–1911)* (Cambridge: Harvard Univ. Press, 1956), p. 99.

[85] Ellsworth C. Carlson, *The Kaiping Mines (1877–1912)* (Cambridge: Harvard Univ. Press, 1957), p. 3; Feuerwerker, p. 159.

[86] *LWCK-PL, chüan* 16, p. 20b.

[87] Feuerwerker, pp. 2, 210.        [88] *Ibid.*, pp. 133–136.

nevertheless all of the above-mentioned companies were under Li's control, and he alone had the power to appoint and remove top management. As their official sponsor, Li had obtained imperial approval for the establishment, but, more importantly, he furnished the protection without which none of these companies could have survived. In the absence of any system of commercial law, commercial companies in China were subject to the demands of officials for gifts, bribes, and so forth. However, Li's official position was strong enough and his personal connections extensive enough to prevent the metropolitan officials from taking any action against his companies. It was only after Li had been removed from the scene in 1895 that the China Merchants Company was forced to make sizable donations to the Imperial Treasury.[89]

This network of companies served to augment Li's political and military power. The ships and railways provided his army and navy with a controlled means of transportation for both troops and supplies. The coal mines gave him a source of power for his ships and locomotives and provided fuel for his arsenal. The telegraph lines gave him a fast means of communication between his military and naval units and also served as a source of information in his diplomatic negotiations. Copies of wires sent by foreign diplomats at the Chinese telegraph office in Tientsin were reported to have been in Li's hands within an hour.[90] Moreover, the connecting of his telegraph lines with the overseas cable in Shanghai, with the French lines in Yunnan and Kwangtung, and with the Russian lines on the Manchurian border gave him ready access to the capitals of the world. The China Merchants Company's tribute rice carrying trade provided Li with two advantages: on the one hand, because Peking was dependent on the rice, partial control of its transport through his steamship company gave Li a potential leverage in metropolitan politics, and, on the other hand, the profits from the trade could be used to buy military weapons. In 1880, Li secured permission to use Tls. 1,000,000 of the company's expected earnings from the tribute rice carriage to pay for the warships he was having constructed in England.[91]

One of the greatest political advantages Li derived from his network of companies was that they provided him with a source of pa-

[89] *Ibid.*, pp. 27, 156, 47, 48.        [91] Feuerwerker, p. 158.
[90] Douglas, *Li Hungchang*, p. 212.

tronage. Patronage, like wealth, was an important tool in the world of Chinese politics, and Li used it to enhance his own position. Officials had relatives, relatives needed jobs, and Li's companies were a source of lucrative employment. In return, Li gained support for his projects, the approval of government loans, and other favors. Unfortunately the caliber of men recommended by the officials was not very high, and their presence in his companies reduced the efficiency of his operation. Cheng Kuan-ying, who became the Manager of the China Merchants Company in 1879, stated that the men recommended for positions in the company by officials had no experience, they wanted to be secretaries or pursers but did not want to work, and they just sat back to wait for their share of the spoils.[92] Li was not blind to the evils which patronage engendered, but it was a fundamental part of the struggle for power, and Li sought not to change the system but to use it.[93]

Li also used his companies and their personnel for diplomatic purposes. The Shanghai office of the China Merchants Company was used as a clearing house for supplies and information during the Formosa crisis in 1874.[94] The same company's offices in Vietnam and its rice carrying trade with that country were used as a cover for Li's agents during the early years of the Sino-French conflict.[95] The first Chinese diplomatic personnel to go abroad after 1875 usually sent their dispatches back to China via the Shanghai office of the China Merchants Company. In 1878 this procedure was institutionalized when a central Office for the Transmission of Government Correspondence was officially established within the China Merchants Company.[96] Li thus had informal, as well as formal, access to all foreign dispatches.

Li's position in Chinese foreign affairs rested on his official post as the Commissioner of Trade for the Northern Ports. This office had been created in 1860 after China had agreed to allow foreign diplomatic personnel to reside in Peking. The Chinese were opposed to having foreigners live in the capital, but they had to permit it

---

[92] Liu Kwang-ching, "Steamship Enterprise in Nineteenth-Century China," *The Journal of Asian Studies*, XVIII, No. 4 (August, 1959), 444.

[93] *Ibid.*, p. 437.

[94] Rawlinson, p. 287, footnote 50.

[95] Eastman, pp. 65–66; A. Gervais, "Diplomatie Chinoise: Li-Hung-Chang et le commandant Fournier," *Revue Politique et Littéraire (Revue Bleue)*, XXI, No. 15 (October 11, 1884), 449.

[96] Immanuel C. Y. Hsü, p. 193.

under the terms of the Second Treaty Settlement (1858–1860). Prince Kung came up with the ingenious idea of arranging commercial and diplomatic affairs so that the foreigners would leave of their own free will. By establishing a new Trade Commissioner in Tientsin who would be responsible for all commercial matters with the foreigners, Prince Kung hoped to draw all business away from Peking, thus reducing the need for foreigners to visit the capital city. The court approved the idea, appointed another Commissioner in Shanghai, who would be in charge of the southern ports, and ordered the provincial authorities to handle foreign cases themselves and not refer them to the Tsungli Yamen. The post of Commissioner of Trade for Northern Ports was distinct from the Chihli Governor-Generalship and not very effective until 1870, when Li saw to it that the two offices were combined. As the energetic incumbent of both posts, Li was soon able to overshadow the Tsungli Yamen and become China's *de facto* Foreign Office.[97]

Li was strong, energetic, and keenly interested both in foreign affairs and in increasing his own power. He took pride in his ability to get the job done and had a following of like-minded people. Although the Tsungli Yamen was the official Foreign Office, most diplomatic questions were referred to Li in Tientsin for his opinion. In the normal course of events he could only advise and did not have the final say, but in times of crisis he was usually designated as China's diplomatic representative with full powers to negotiate. Korean affairs were normally handled by the Board of Rites, but in about 1880 the Tsungli Yamen memorialized to transfer the responsibility for Chinese relations with that country to Li. From that time on, Li was the guiding force behind China's policy in Korea.[98] His geographic position was another factor in his receiving these appointments: his headquarters in Tientsin where negotiations were held, were close enough to Peking to pass on information and receive instructions from the court, but far enough away to keep the foreign negotiators out of the capital.[99]

In the 1870's when China began to send diplomatic representatives abroad, Li was called upon by the Tsungli Yamen to make recommendations. He advised this body to send only men of high

[97] *Ibid.*, p. 107.
[98] Ludwig, p. 364.
[99] T. F. Tsiang, "Sino-Japanese Diplomatic Relations, 1870–1894," *Chinese Social and Political Science Review*, XVII, No. 1 (April, 1933), 8.

reliability and substantive positions to the various European powers so that they would not be slighted by the foreigners, but, because no one enjoyed going abroad, he was clever enough to leave the actual selection to the Tsungli Yamen.[100] The general feeling within the country was that to be sent abroad was worse than being banished and that no sensible man would volunteer; when the first Chinese diplomatic representative was appointed in 1875, he tried to decline the appointment.[101] Nevertheless, most of the Chinese diplomatic personnel during the first thirty or more years of China's foreign representation were friends or ex-*mu-yu* of Li Hung-chang, as the list of Chinese Ministers to England between 1875 and 1901 indicates: Kuo Sung-t'ao (1875–1878) was a *ting-wei* classmate and an ex-*mu-yu*; Tseng Chi-tse (1878–1885) was the son of Tseng Kuo-fan; Liu Jui-fen (1885–1889) was from Anhwei and had served under Li during the Taiping Rebellion; Hsüeh Fu-ch'eng (1889–1893) was an ex-*mu-yu*; Kung Chao-yüan (1893–1896) was from Ho-fei; and Lo Feng-lu (1896–1901) had been Li's personal secretary and interpreter for years.[102]

Because China's envoys were being sent to a foreign land to live among barbarians, it was considered only right that they should be allowed to select and pay their own staffs. In this way they would be surrounded by compatible people and would be able to expedite matters.[103] This was a government-approved extension of the *mu-fu* system, and it indirectly helped Li perpetuate his political power. With so many of his ex-*mu-yu* or friends serving as envoys, it was possible for him to place his own trainees in the legations. His son, Ching-fang, served as a Secretary of Legation in order to acquire experience and later became the Chinese Minister to Japan (1890–1892). In this fashion Li was able both to build up the number of his followers and to more or less monopolize the diplomatic service.

In theory, the envoys and the legations were under the jurisdiction of the court and Tsungli Yamen, and in 1877 the envoys were in-

[100] Immanuel C. Y. Hsü, p. 179.
[101] David Hamilton, "Kuo Sung-tao; Maverick Confucian," Harvard University, Center for East Asian Studies, *Papers on China*, Vol. 15, p. 8; Immanuel C. Y. Hsü, pp. 202–203.
[102] Ch'ien Shih-fu, *Ch'ing-chi hsin-she chih-kuan nien-piao* (A Table of the Newly Established Officials at the End of the Ch'ing) (Peking: Chung-hua shu-chü, 1961), pp. 16–23.
[103] Immanuel C. Y. Hsü, pp. 191–192.

structed by the court to report monthly to the Tsungli Yamen. However, this order was seldom obeyed, and in reality the Tsungli Yamen was allowed to concern itself with only the routine business. The customary procedure was for the envoys to bypass the Tsungli Yamen and memorialize the throne directly, but their dispatches were handled by the Shanghai office of Li's China Merchants Company, and he would undoubtedly receive a copy. The court's orders, on the other hand, were sent by the Board of War to Li in Tientsin for transmittal to the envoys. Thus, Li was kept fully informed of what was going on. In addition, the envoys usually maintained some sort of contact with Li and did not dare to neglect to provide him with information on guns, ships, new inventions, and political developments in the West.[104]

Despite his extensive network of power, Li Hung-chang lacked the one ingredient which was necessary in order to make his organization effective on a national scale — the supreme authority. He assumed a great many extraprovincial responsibilities, but in the final analysis it was up to the throne to decide on the course of action. It was his misfortune to have to rely on a ruler who was at heart antiforeign and at the same time fearful of the aggrandizement of power by internal factions, especially if they were Chinese. Because of this, Li was never able to obtain the whole-hearted support he needed to overcome the conservative opposition to his self-strengthening measures and the jealousy of his colleagues. Under the Ch'ing system of government, every grand secretary, governor-general, censor, governor, and other high official had the right to express his opinions on the various national problems. The throne was, therefore, subjected to a variety of opposing opinions and, by playing one faction off against another, was able to keep the provincial leaders from uniting behind one leader in a bid for the supreme power. Li Hung-chang was able to accomplish a great deal, but he could not suppress his enemies, who were ever on the alert to strike him down at a vulnerable moment.

Li Hung-chang was not a dictator, but just another governor-general, and his ideas and policies had a hated foreign tinge. Because of this he had not only to compete with other important officials who also had self-strengthening ideas, such as Tso Tsung-t'ang, Chang Chih-tung, and Weng T'ung-ho, but also to put up

[104] *Ibid.*, pp. 193, 194.

with the ever-present criticism of the conservative majority. His opinion of his adversaries was a combination of derision and healthy respect for their combined power. Although he referred to the censors and the other conservatives as "blind 'book-worms' who wanted to cure all diseases with the same ancient prescription"[105] and described their hue and cry as the "howling of dogs,"[106] he was keenly aware of what they could do. Their outcry against Kuo Sung-t'ao and the publication of his diary in 1877, as well as the viciousness of their invectives against Li himself during the Sino-French War, had impressed on him the magnitude of their power. The sheer weight of their numbers and the force of their combined voices was enough to bring about the downfall of lesser men. During the uproar caused by Ch'ung-hou's signing of the Treaty of Livadia in 1879 and his resulting imprisonment, Li, who worked with the foreigners to save Ch'ung-hou's life, is reported to have said that there were forty memorials demanding Ch'ung-hou's death, and that it was inconceivable how anyone could survive under such pressure. He went on to say that five memorials were enough to secure a man's dismissal, and fifteen or twenty his death.[107]

Li's basic policy in regard to China's relations with the West consisted of three points: (1) to reorganize the defenses of the empire on the basis of the lessons he had learned from his association with the foreigners and their previous military campaigns against China; (2) to observe scrupulously the treaties with the foreigners so as to give them no grounds for complaint; (3) when differences with the foreigners did arise, no matter whose fault or what the reason, to agree quickly with them. Li was not an appeaser or a pacifist at heart, but he was stalling for time in order to build up China's power to resist: despite what the war advocates claimed, his own experience and knowledge of the West had shown him that China was incapable of resisting a foreign attack.[108] Yet, in order to buy the time he needed, as well as the foreign weapons, he had to buck the conservative opposition and the political and social mores of the country.

Behind the studied civilities of the world of Chinese politics lay a partially exposed nether world of intense factional strife, per-

[105] *Ibid.*, p. 204.
[106] Michie, *The Englishman in China*, II, 329; Sergeant, p. 161.
[107] Kiernan, p. 53.
[108] Michie, *The Englishman in China*, II, 382–383.

sonal affiliations, shifting loyalties, and vicious infighting. Despite laws to the contrary, slanderous accusations embodied in secret memorials were the rule.[109] Political and moral principles were often combined with or overruled by selfish and jealous desires. Opportunists, as well as disgruntled or jealous office-seekers, would use a worthy cause as a convenient pretext to embarrass or ruin their enemies. What might appear on the surface as a close friendship was, in some instances, merely a camouflage for a deep-seated hatred.[110] The intense desire in Chinese society for wealth, position, and power made any successful official, no matter how much he had the interests of the state at heart, a fair target for those beneath him. The higher his position, the more he was subject to attack. As probably the most powerful provincial official in China, Li Hung-chang naturally became the chief target of the opportunists and social climbers, who rallied around the more powerful of the conservative leaders.

The two factions which led the attack on Li were the antiforeign group, whose hard core was composed of the *Ch'ing-liu* ("Pure Flowing") Party, and the war advocates. The members of the *Ch'ing-liu* Party, although small in numbers, were the unofficial spokesmen for the majority of the officials who were fanatically obscurantist and opposed to anything foreign. They were not only the self-appointed guardians of "pure" Confucian culture, but they also had a vested interest in the *status quo* and resisted any changes that might threaten their comfortable positions. Those who dared to try to change China were condemned as "sinners against the Confucian heritage." They argued that, although they had heard of transforming the barbarians by the Chinese way of life, they had never heard of changing Chinese culture by using barbarian ways. And to prove that reform was evil, they cited carefully chosen passages from the *Classics*. As the chief advocate of reform and the introduction of Western techniques, Li was labelled a traitor to Chinese culture and was likened to Ch'in Kuei, one of the most notorious appeasers in Chinese history.[111]

[109] Guy Boulais, S. J., *Manuel du Code Chinois*, Variétes Sinologiques, No. 55 (Shanghai: Imprimerie de la Mission Catholique, 1924), pp. 638–639.

[110] Hsiao Kung-ch'üan, "Weng T'ung-ho and the Reform Movement of 1898," *The Tsing Hua Journal of Chinese Studies*, New Series 1, No. 2 (April, 1957), p. 127.

[111] Immanuel C. Y. Hsü, pp. 201–202; Eastman, p. 177. Ch'in Kuei (1090–1155) has been execrated by Chinese for working for the Chin Tartars and

The war advocates were closely associated with the *Ch'ing-liu* Party, even though some of their members were also self-strengtheners. For example, Chang Chih-tung had been a member of the *Ch'ing-liu* Party, but he was also a self-strengthener and a war advocate. The common denominator in this seeming incongruity was Chang's concern for the preservation of Chinese culture. The obscurantists could support those who wanted to throw the foreigners out, even though they had to rely on Western weapons to do it.[112] The leader of the war advocates, until his death in 1885 was Tso Tsung-t'ang, who believed in fighting first and negotiating later. Although he and Li had served together in Tseng Kuo-fan's *mu-fu* and were both military leaders during the Taiping and Nien rebellions, they disliked each other intensely. Tso was, no doubt, Li's greatest single opponent, and the two men clashed on everything, from the timing of memorials to national defense policies.

Li Hung-chang was able to withstand the onslaught of his enemies for thirty-three years, thanks to the support of the Empress Dowager, his ability to play the game of Chinese politics, and his network of power. However, when the Japanese decided to move in 1894, the war advocates forced his hand and, against his wishes, he had to fight.[113] As just one man, whose power was based on his tenuous provincial position, his informal *mu-fu*, and a fluctuating network of personal relationships, Li had realized the futility of trying to change the Confucian mores of Chinese society and had relied on his own efforts to develop the sinews China needed to resist attack. He knew China and her weaknesses, and he also knew in 1894 that she was incapable of defeating even an Oriental nation that had embarked wholeheartedly on the path of Westernization. Nevertheless, the war advocates had the ear of the emperor, and it was Li's army and navy, the only ones available, that were sent to Korea — only to be crushed by the Japanese. Time had run out, and Li and his network of power came crashing to the ground.

arranging the peace which gave them the northern half of China. Herbert A. Giles, *A Chinese Biographical Dictionary* (Taiwan Reprint, 1962), I, 153.

[112] Tsiang, p. 49; Ku Hung-ming, *Chang Wen-hsiang mu-fu chi-wen* (A Record of Chang Chih-tung's *Mu-fu*) (Taipei, Taiwan: Shang-wu yin-shu-kuan, 1956), *shang*, p. 6a.

[113] Li Chien-nung, pp. 140–141; Sergeant, pp. 114–115.

# VIII. Conclusion

The paradoxes of the Confucian value system, as well as its strengths and weaknesses and its inability to stand up under the attacks of the West, can all be seen in the careers of Tseng Kuo-fan and Li Hung-chang and their use of the *mu-fu* system. They both relied upon this informal device in order to implement their policies and ideas, but it was a product of Chinese society and, as such, was prone to all of its inconsistencies. It also reflected the character of the host official and, thus, was subject to human strengths and failings. Tseng Kuo-fan, as the teacher and host official, had tried to guide and direct Li Hung-chang, the student and *mu-yu*, in the proper Confucian morality, but the human equation and the crisis situation deemed otherwise.

Although he inherited Tseng Kuo-fan's mantle and assumed the burden of preserving Chinese culture, Li Hung-chang strayed from the path set by Tseng. This deviation was caused by the absence of Tseng's guiding hand, a new and different set of circumstances, a more intimate association with foreigners, and a different personal character. Where Tseng drew back from power, Li reached out for it; where Tseng sought to preserve Confucian culture, Li sought to preserve China; and where Tseng aimed at a balance of power between the center and the provinces, Li's ultimate aim was to centralize the power in China in order to establish a new balance with the West. Tseng resurrected the military element in the *mu-fu* system in order to defeat China's internal enemies; Li modernized and expanded it in order to ward off China's external enemies. Tseng nourished scholars, whereas Li hired technicians and professionals.

In his early years, Li was firmly convinced of the universality of Confucian culture, but as he became more involved with the West and more frustrated in his attempts to strengthen China, he gradually became an advocate of change at a fundamental level. As early as 1863, he recognized the need for change in China when he said, "Since we Chinese thoroughly understand the principle that when one reaches a point of exhaustion, one must reform and then one can go on smoothly, we should also greatly change our plans."[1] In 1872 he wrote in a memorial, "Our scholar-officials have been indulging in the practice of writing in fancy and flowery language and are ignorant of the immense changes that have come about,"[2] and in the next year he wrote to Ch'ien Ting-ming (T'iao-fu), saying "The wisdom and strength of the people in former times were very deficient, yet their successors were content to follow them erroneously and to hand down their mistaken views. We do not realize that the situation today is not the same as it used to be. Is this not the reason for our downfall?"[3] Li was trying to free China from the enervating grip of the past, but he also realized the hopelessness of the task. In his conversations with Itō Hirobumi at Shimonoseki in March, 1895, Li is reported to have said, "My country's affairs are confined by custom. . . . My strength has not been enough to change them, and that is all. . . . You also deeply know that my country must change and reform in order to be independent."[4] His initial desire for change grew out of China's need to resist the encroachments of the West, which he felt could be countered simply through the acquisition of the military weapons of the West; but the frustrations created by the conservative opposition on the one hand, and his association with men like Kuo Sung-t'ao, who felt that a basic change in Chinese institutions was essential before China could compete with the West, on the other hand, tended to open his eyes to the deeper implications of self-strengthening. In a letter to Kuo in 1878, he remarked, "You said everything lacks a real foundation, so that even if the whole nation studied

[1] Teng Ssu-yü and John K. Fairbank, *China's Response to the West* (Cambridge: Harvard Univ. Press, 1954), p. 71.

[2] Li Chien-nung, *The Political History of China, 1840–1928*, transl. and ed by Teng Ssu-yü and J. Ingalls (Princeton: D. Van Nostrand Company, Inc., 1956), p. 106.

[3] Li Hung-chang, *Li Wen-chung-kung ch'üan-chi* (The Complete Works of Li Hung-chang), ed. by Wu Ju-lun (Nanking, 1908), P'eng-liao han-kao (Letters to Friends and Colleagues), *chüan* 13, p. 18a (hereafter cited as *LWCK-PL*).

[4] *Ma-kuan i-ho chung chih I Li wen-ta* (The Questions and Answers of Itō Hirobumi and Li Hung-chang During the Peace Negotiations at Shimonoseki), compiled by T'ai-wan yin-hang ching-chi yen-chiu shih (Taipei, Taiwan: T'ai-wan yin-hang, 1959), p. 3.

Western methods, it would be to no avail. I think you have hit the mark."[5]

When Li advocated a change in the examination system to include the study of Western mathematics, physics, geography, engineering, and the like, and when he advocated the granting of official ranks to "returned students" on the basis of their Western knowledge,[6] he was, in reality, thrusting at the heart of Confucianism and the Confucian bureaucratic system. Under such a change, the *Classics* would no longer provide the sole criterion for competency, and the expert would take his place alongside the amateur. Confucianism had been the universal criterion, but when men like Li, who had been raised in the Confucian tradition, recognized a foreign alternative, then Confucianism could no longer lay claim to universality and was doomed.

In their attacks on Li, the conservatives and the *Ch'ing-liu* Party were not as blind and unreasonable as they might appear. What was at issue was the age-old conflict between the Confucianists and the Legalists. Li was a practical man attempting to preserve China from a serious foreign threat, and he did not feel that he could afford the luxury of placing Confucian morality above practical ability. He was a hardheaded realist who saw that China must change, whether she liked it or not, if she was to survive in a world where might made right; and, in order to survive, she needed professionals, not amateurs. The *Ch'ing-liu* Party represented the Confucian side of the struggle, and, like their predecessors throughout ages of Chinese history, its members were concerned with the moral nature of man as exemplified in the teachings of Confucius. They appeared to be much more aware than Li of the cultural issues at stake. The case of the Confucianists was stated by Ku Hung-ming, an ex-*mu-yu* of Chang Chih-tung's: "During the T'ung-chih and Kuang-hsü periods the reason why the *Ch'ing-liu* Party opposed Li Hung-chang was not because it did not like Li personally, but . . . because he was concerned only with administration and not with [Confucian] education. Because he copied Tseng Kuo-fan and knew

[5] David Hamilton, "Kuo Sung-tao; A Maverick Confucian," Harvard University, Center for East Asian Studies, *Papers on China*, Vol. 15, pp. 11, 21.

[6] Wolfgang Franke, *The Reform and Abolition of the Traditional Chinese Examination System* (Cambridge: Harvard Univ. Press, 1960), p. 31; John Lang Rawlinson, "The Chinese Navy, 1839–1895" (unpublished Ph.D. Dissertation, Harvard University, 1959), p. 473; LWCK-PL, *chüan* 10, p. 32b.

nothing about education, therefore, in his employment practices he just took capabilities and benefits into account and did not bother with personality and morality. He was interested only in ability and not in conduct. This is what made the *Ch'ing-liu* Party angry and caused it to speak out."[7] After 2,000 years, the basic issue of the Confucian–Legalist controversy still had not changed — were men utensils or an end in themselves?

Li's desire for change, his practical concern for immediate problems, and his use of professionals, when coupled with the accusations of his critics, might well seem to place him in the camp of the Legalists, or at least in the company of men like Wang An-shih (1020–1086), who, like Li, wanted the examination system revised so that it would include subjects of a more practical nature, advocated that the salaries of the officials be raised in order to prevent corruption, and stressed the need for more specialization in office.[8] The Legalist and Confucian camps during the Warring States Period had been rather clearly defined, but during the succeeding centuries the lines of demarcation had become blurred so that by the late Ch'ing the criteria for what was Confucianism encompassed much of what had originally been Legalism. Despite the stress of Li's critics on personality, morality, and Confucian education, they were the staunch supporters of the orthodox bureaucracy, which was a basically Legalist structure in which men were selected for office on the basis of merit, and not on the basis of personality or personal relationships. The Confucianism of the late Ch'ing allowed room for many views, and, in his own way, Li was as much of a Confucian as were his accusers. The fine line of distinction which placed Li in the Confucian camp in the age-old Legalist-Confucian controversy was that, although he used professionals, he did not treat them as impersonal utensils. In a truly Confucian way, Li was deeply concerned with the human equation. Of all the basic Confucian tenets, the one which most deeply permeated Li's character and was evident throughout his entire career was his adherence to the Confucian concept of friendship. He had been willing to place all of his ambitions in jeopardy when, as a member of Tseng's

---

[7] Ku Hung-ming, *Chang Wen-hsiang mu-fu chi-wen* (A Record of Chang Chih-tung's *Mu-fu*) (Taipei, Taiwan: Shang-wu yin-shu kuan, 1956), pp. 40a–b. The *Ch'ing-liu* Party felt that even Tseng Kuo-fan had been too much of a statesman and not enough of a scholar.

[8] *LWCK-PL, chüan* 10, p. 33a.

*mu-fu*, he had resigned in support of this principle. Throughout his subsequent career and rise to fame and power, this principle guided Li in his official and personal relationships. In a memorial regarding the hiring of personnel, written in 1881, he supported his adherence to this principle by citing a passage from the *Analects* (*Lun-yü*): "Confucius said: 'Raise to office men of virtue and talents. Raise to office those whom you know.'"[9] Even when Li cited Kuan Chung (d. 645 B.C.), a noted statesman and forerunner of the Legalist school, the passage he chose was in support of the idea that friends and fellow-villagers should work together to fight a common enemy — the basic concept behind the *Hsiang-chün* and the *Huai-chün*.[10] Not once in all of his writings did Li suggest that impersonal law was the solution to China's problems — a concept that was central to Legalist thought. Despite his use of professionals in his *mu-fu*, his methods of selecting personnel and his relationships with them were personal and in keeping with the basic Confucian mores. Hence, Li must be regarded as a Confucian, although an extremely practical one.

Li Hung-chang was above all an official, but he resembled the active, dedicated professional official of the West more than he did his Chinese counterparts. In the process of the development in China from an elite of the scholar to an elite of the professional, during the late nineteenth and twentieth centuries, Li might well be considered as having taken the first step. He tried to provide China with the strength she needed to survive, but because he was opposed on all sides by the majority of the officials, he had to rely on his own efforts and based his operation on the power he derived from his provincial position and on the technical competency of his *mu-yu*. His contempt for the established bureaucracy and his desire to see China strong forced him down the path of centralization of power. However, had Li fully realized his dream, it would have meant the creation of a new type of central government in which, through necessity, professionals would supersede the amateur scholar-official, in which loyalty to the state would replace

[9] Li Hung-chang, *Li Wen-chung-kung ch'üan-chi* (The Complete Works of Li Hung-chang), ed. by Wu Ju-lun (Nanking, 1908), Tsou-kao, *chüan* 42, p. 1b. See also James Legge, *The Chinese Classics* (Taiwan reprint, 1962), I, 263.

[10] Li Hung-chang, *Li Wen-chung-kung i-chi* (Posthumous Collection of the Writings of Li Hung-chang) *in* Li Kuo-chieh, ed., *Ho-fei Li shih san shih i-chi* ([no place]: The Li Family of Ho-fei, 1904), *chüan* 5, p. 9a.

loyalty to the family, and in which the age-old conflict between a Confucian bureaucracy and a Legalist monarchy, which had already been diluted by the threat of the West, would cease to exist.

Whereas Tseng Kuo-fan had faced internal enemies, Li faced eternal enemies, and they had to be resisted by a new set of rules. Li learned the rules well and was able to contain China's external enemies until 1895. He had a modern army and navy which, although they had never been put to the test, appeared strong enough to give the Western nations second thoughts about grabbing Chinese territory. His commercial and industrial enterprises were kept free from entangling foreign loans and were able to hinder foreign economic penetration. In his diplomatic negotiations he was able to provide enough efficiency and reasonableness to keep the frustrations of the foreigners below the boiling point. Li stressed China in place of Chinese culture; in doing so, he was a forerunner of modern Chinese nationalism and paved the way for K'ang Yu-wei and the Reformers of 1898. His loyal service to China permitted her to remain intact during most of the late nineteenth century.

In the face of a heightened onslaught by Japan and the West, however, Li's efforts were no longer able to stem the rising tide. In his attempt to save China, he had relied on the traditional Chinese *mu-fu* system and had brought it to its latest and highest development, but this system was informal, personal, and provincial in nature and, as such, was not capable of dealing with a task of such national magnitude. The system worked well when it supplemented a firmly established government institution, but it was not capable of standing on its own. The impersonal nature of the Confucian bureaucratic system, despite its gradual ossification, had made it possible for it to survive from dynasty to dynasty as a continuing institution, but a *mu-fu* was held together by a network of personal relationships and, as a result, had no life expectancy beyond that of its host official. Li Hung-chang owed his position and his network of power to the *mu-fu* system, but when he fell, his *mu-fu* fell with him — as did China's defenses — and within three years the wolves of the West were preparing to devour China.

# A Genealogy
## of the
## Li Family

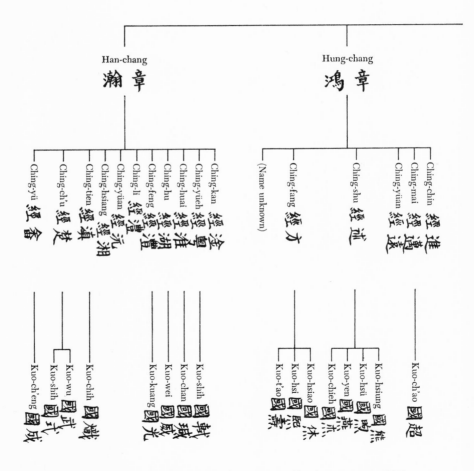

Han-chang 瀚章　　　Hung-chang 鴻章

Ching-yü 經畬
Ching-ch'ü 經楚
Ching-tien 經甸
Ching-hsiang 經湘
Ching-yüan 經沅
Ching-li 經澧
Ching-feng 經灃
Ching-hu 經瀚
Ching-huai 經淮
Ching-yüeh 經曾
Ching-kan 經淦

(Name unknown)
Ching-fang 經方
Ching-shu 經述
Ching-yüan 經遠
Ching-mai 經邁
Ching-chin 經進

Kuo-ch'eng 國成
Kuo-shih 國玉
Kuo-wu 國武
Kuo-chih 國燠
Kuo-kuang 國光
Kuo-wei 國殿
Kuo-chan 國藏
Kuo-shih 國輔

Kuo-t'ao 國燾
Kuo-hsi 國熙
Kuo-hsiao 國休
Kuo-chieh 國沐
Kuo-yen 國濂
Kuo-hsü 國烜
Kuo-hsiung 國熊

Kuo-ch'ao 國超

*Genealogy by Li Chia-huang (Hong Kong, 1962) and Li Kuo-ch'ao (San Francisco, 1963).

198

# Li Family of Ho-fei*

合肥李氏

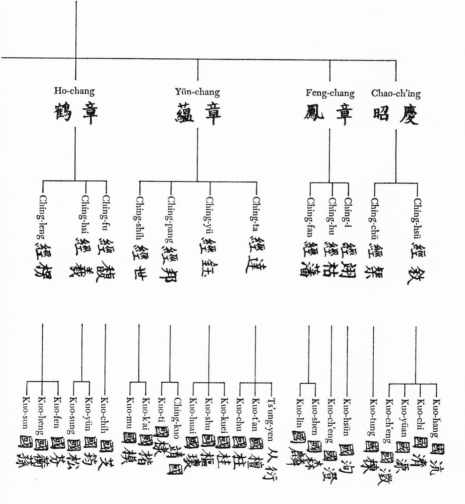

# Glossary

All Chinese personal names, place names, expressions, and the titles of books mentioned in the text and notes, with the exception of the names of provinces, are included in this list. Wherever possible, personal names are followed by the *tzu*, or style, in parentheses, and they have been cross-referenced to facilitate identification. The simplified Wade-Giles system of romanization has been used throughout, except for some of the more common place-name spellings.

Amoy (Hsia-men) 廈門
an-ch'a-shih 按察使
An-ch'ing 安慶
An-hua 安化
Anking *see* An-ch'ing
An-ti 安帝
an-tsung 案總

Chahar (Ch'a-ha-erh) 察哈爾
Chang Ch'ang 張敞
Chang Chen-hsien. *See* Chang Shu-sheng
Chang Chien 張謇
Chang Chih-tung 張之洞
　(Hsiao-ta 孝達)
Chang Chih-wan 張之萬
　(Tzu-ch'ing 子青)
Chang-ch'iu 張秋
Chang-chou 漳州
chang-fang 賬房
Chang Hai-k'o. *See* Chang Shu-shan
Chang Hsiao-ta. *See* Chang Chih-tung
Chang Liang-chi 張亮基

Chang Lien-ch'ing. *See* Chang Yü-chao
Chang P'ei-lun 張佩綸
　(Yu-ch'iao 幼樵)
Chang Shao-t'ang 張紹棠
Chang Shu-shan 張樹珊
　(Hai-k'o 海柯)
Chang Shu-sheng 張樹聲
　(Chen-hsien 振軒)
Chang Ssu-kuei 張斯桂
Chang Tzu-ch'ing. *See* Chang Chih-wan
Chang Wen-hu 張文虎
Chang Yin-t'ang 張印塘
Chang Yü-chao 張裕釗
　(Lien-ch'ing 廉卿)
Chang Yu-ch'iao. *See* Chang P'ei-lun
Ch'ang-chou 常州
Ch'ang-lu 長蘆
Ch'ang-sha 長沙
Chao 趙
Chao Hui-fu. *See* Chao Lieh-wen
Chao Lieh-wen 趙烈文
　(Hui-fu 惠甫)

Chao Shen-ch'iao 趙申喬
Ch'ao hsien 巢縣
Che-kao 柘皋
Chefoo (Chih-fu) 芝罘
Ch'en Ai 陳艾
(Hu-ch'en 虎臣)
Ch'en Ch'in 陳欽
Ch'en Ch'üan-ch'eng. See Ch'en
Shih-chieh
Ch'en Fan 陳蕃
Ch'en Hu-ch'en. See Ch'en Ai
Ch'en Lan-pin 陳蘭彬
(Li-ch'iu 荔秋)
Ch'en Li-ch'iu. See Ch'en Lan-pin
Ch'en Nai 陳鼐
(Tso-mei 作梅)
Ch'en Shih-chieh 陳士杰
(Ch'üan-ch'eng 雋丞)
Ch'en Tso-mei. See Ch'en Nai
Cheng Hsiao-hsü 鄭孝胥
Cheng Kuan-ying 鄭官應
cheng-pi 徵比
Cheng Tsao-ju 鄭藻如
Ch'eng Fang-chung. See Ch'eng
Hsüeh-ch'i
Ch'eng Hsüeh-ch'i 程學啓
(Fang-chung 方忠)
Ch'eng Hung-chao 程鴻詔
Ch'eng Jung-ching 成蓉鏡
Ch'eng Ming-piao 成名標
Ch'eng-ti 成帝
chi-shih-chung 給事中
Ch'i-men 祁門
Ch'i-ying 耆英
chia-ch'en 甲辰
Chia-ching 嘉靖
Chia-ch'ing 嘉慶
Chiang Ch'ang-ju. See Chiang
Chung-yüan

Chiang Chung-yüan 江忠源
(Ch'ang-ju 常孺)
Chiang Hsiang-ch'üan. See Chiang
I-li
Chiang-huai 江淮
Chiang I-li 蔣益澧
(Hsiang-ch'üan 薌泉)
Chiang-nan-pei 江南北
Chiang-ning (Nanking) 江寧
chiao-ch'ing 交情
chiao-i 交誼
chiao-yü 教諭
Ch'iao Ho-chai. See Ch'iao Sung-
nien
Ch'iao Sung-nien 喬松年
(Ho-chai 鶴儕)
chieh-tu-shih 節度使
Chien-ho 減河
ch'ien 謙
ch'ien-ku 錢穀
ch'ien-liang-tsung 錢糧總
Ch'ien-lung 乾隆
Ch'ien T'ai-chi 錢泰吉
Ch'ien T'iao-fu. See Ch'ien Ting-
ming
Ch'ien Ting-ming 錢鼎銘
(T'iao-fu 調甫)
Ch'ien Tzu-mi. See Ch'ien Ying-p'u
Ch'ien Ying-p'u 錢應溥
(Tzu-mi 子密)
chih-chi 知己
chih-chung 治中
chin-shih 進士
Chin Wu-lan 金吳瀾
ch'in-ch'ai ta-ch'en 欽差大臣
Ch'in-Kuei 秦檜
Ch'in Shih Huang-ti 秦始皇帝
ching 敬
ching-ch'ing 京卿
Ching-te-chen 景德鎮

Ch'ing, Prince 慶親王
Ch'ing-chün 慶軍
Ch'ing-ho-tao 清河道
Ch'ing-liu 清流
Ch'ing-liu tang 清流黨
Ch'ing-tzu-ying 慶字營
chiu-ti ch'ou-hsiang 就地籌餉
chou 州
Chou 周
Chou Fu 周馥
　(Yü-shan 玉山 )
Chou Hai-ling. See Chou Sheng-po
Chou K'ai-hsi 周開錫
Chou Hsin-ju. See Chou Sheng-
　ch'uan
Chou Mao-ch'i 周懋琦
Chou Sheng-ch'uan 周盛傳
　(Hsin-ju 薪如 )
Chou Sheng-po 周盛波
　(Hai-ling 海齡 )
Chou Yü-shan. See Chou Fu
chu 主
Chu Ch'i-ang 朱其昂
chu-mo 硃墨
chu-pu 主簿
chu-shih 主事
Chu Yün 朱筠
chü 局
chü-jen 舉人
Ch'un, Prince 淳親王
Ch'un-hsi 淳熙
chün 郡
chün-tzu 君子
chung 忠
Chung-ch'in 忠勤
Chung-hsüeh wei t'i, Hsi-hsüeh wei
　yung 中學爲體, 西學爲用
Ch'ung-hou 崇厚
　(Ti-shan 地山 )
Ch'ung Ti-shan. See Ch'ung-hou

Dairen (Ta-lien) 大連
Dorgon 多爾袞

fan-chen 藩鎮
fang-chün 防軍
Fang Chün-mu 方駿謨
fang-shih 房師
Fang Tsung-ch'eng 方宗誠
fang-yü-shih 防禦使
Fei Jih-ch'i 費日啟
Feng Kuei-fen 馮桂芬
　(Lin-i 林一 )
Feng Lin-i. See Feng Kuei-fen
Feng Tsun-kuang 馮焌光
Foochow (Fu-chou) 福州
fu 府
Fu-chi 福濟
　(Yüan-hsiu 元修 )
Fu Yüan-hsiu. See Fu-chi

Han-fei-tzu 韓非子
Han Hsin 韓信
Han-shan 含山
Han Yü 韓愈
Hankow (Han-k'ou) 漢口
Hanlin 翰林
Ho Ching 何璟
　(Hsiao-sung 筱宋 )
Ho-chou 和州
Ho-fei 合肥
Ho-fei hsien 合肥縣
Ho Hsiao-sung. See Ho Ching
Ho Shen-hsiu. See Ho Tzu-yung
Ho Tzu-yung 何子永
　(Shen-hsiu 慎修 )
hou 侯
"Howqua" (Hao-kuan) 浩官
　(Wu Kuo-ying 伍國瑩 )
Hsi-chiang 西江
Hsia 夏

Hsiang-chün 湘軍

Hsiang-hsiang 湘鄉

Hsiang Shih-ti 向師棣

Hsiang-yin 湘陰

Hsiao Ho 蕭何

hsiao-jen 小人

Hsiao-shan 蕭山

Hsiao Shih-pen 蕭世本

hsieh-pan ta-hsüeh-shih 協辦大學士

hsien 縣

hsien-ch'eng 縣丞

Hsien-feng 咸豐

hsin 信

hsing-ming 刑名

hsing-pu lang-chung 刑部郎中

hsiu-ts'ai 秀才

Hsiung-nu 匈奴

Hsü 許

Hsü Chen-wei 許振禕 (Hsien-p'ing 仙屏)

Hsü Hsi 徐晞

Hsü Hsien-p'ing. See Hsü Chen-wei

*Hsü-hsiu Lu-chou fu-chih* 續修廬州府志

Hsü Shou 徐壽

*Hsü tso-chih yao-yen* 續佐治藥言

Hsüan-te 宣德

*Hsüeh-chih i-shuo* 學治臆說

Hsüeh Fu-ch'eng 薛福成 (Shu-yün 叔耘)

Hsüeh Shu-yün. See Hsüeh Fu-ch'eng

hsün 勳

Hsün-chün 勳軍

hsün-li 循吏

Hu-k'ou 湖口

Hu-kuang 湖廣

Hu Lin-i 胡林翼

hu-pu yu-shih-lang 戶部右侍郎

Hu Tsung-hsien 胡宗憲

Hu Yü-fen 胡燏棻

Hua Heng-fang 華蘅芳 (Jo-t'ing 若汀)

Hua Jo-t'ing. See Hua Heng-fang

hua-ling 花翎

Huai 淮

Huai-chün 淮軍

Huai-nan 淮南

Huai-yang 淮揚

Huang Ch'ang-ch'i. See Huang I-sheng

Huang I-Sheng 黃翼升 (Ch'ang-ch'i 昌歧)

Huang Jun-ch'ang 黃潤昌

huang-ma-kua 黃馬褂

Huchow (Hu-chou) 湖州

Hui-chou 徽州

hui-kuan 會館

hui-pi 廻避

Hukow. See Hu-k'ou

Hung Ch'in-hsi. See Hung Ju-k'uei

Hung Fu 洪福

hung-hei pi 紅黑筆

Hung-hsi 洪熙

Hung Ju-k'uei 洪汝奎 (Ch'in-hsi 琴西)

Hung-wu 洪武

Huo-shan hsien 霍山縣

i 柳

i-teng su-i po 一等肅毅伯

Itō Hirobumi 伊藤博文

jen 仁

jen-ch'ing 人情

Jen Te-ho 任德龢

*Ju-lin wai-shih* 儒林外史

Jui Chung-lan 瑞仲蘭

Jung Ch'un-fu. *See* Jung Hung (Yung Wing)

Jung Hung (Yung Wing) 容閎 (Ch'un-fu 純甫)

Jung-lu 榮祿

Kaiping (K'ai-p'ing) 開平

Kan Chin 甘晉

kan-ch'ing 感情

Kan-liang 甘涼

K'ang-hsi 康熙

K'ang Yu-wei 康有爲

Kao Ti-chou 郜荻洲

Kao-tsu 高祖

Keelung (Chi-lung) 基隆

Kiangnan (Chiang-nan) 江南

Kiukiang (Chiu-chiang) 九江

K'o Yüeh 柯鉞

K'ou-pei tao 口北道

Ku Hung-ming 辜鴻銘

kua-hao 掛號

Kuan Chung 管仲

kuan-tu shang-pan 官督商辦

Kuang-hsü 光緒

kuei-mao 癸卯

K'uei-pin 奎斌

kung 功

Kung, Prince 恭親王

Kung Chao-yüan 龔照瑗 (Yang-ch'ü 仰蘧)

kung-pu shih-lang 工部侍郎

Kung Sun-hung 公孫弘

Kung-sun Yang 公孫鞅 (Shang Yang 商鞅)

kung-ts'ao 功曹

kung-tsui 公罪

Kung Yang-ch'ü. *See* Kung Chao-yüan

Kuo En-hou 郭恩垕

Kuo I-ch'eng. *See* Kuo K'un-t'ao

Kuo K'un-t'ao 郭崑燾 (I-ch'eng 意城)

Kuo Po-yin 郭柏蔭 (Yüan-t'ang 遠堂)

Kuo Sung-lin 郭松林 (Tzu-mei 子美)

Kuo Sung-t'ao 郭嵩燾 (Yün-hsien 筠仙)

Kuo Tzu-mei. *See* Kuo Sung-lin

Kuo Yüan-t'ang. *See* Kuo Po-yin

Kuo Yün-hsien. *See* Kuo Sung-t'ao

lan-ling 藍翎

lao-fu-tzu 老夫子

lao-tung 老東

li 禮 (ceremonies)

li 吏 (clerks)

li 例 (Supplementary Laws; precedents)

Li Chao-ch'ing 李昭慶 (Yu-ch'üan 幼荃)

Li Chao-pin 李朝斌

Li Chao-t'ang 黎兆棠

Li Chi-ch'üan. *See* Li Ho-chang

Li Chi-kao. *See* Li Ching-mai

Li Chia-huang 李家煌

Li Ching-chin 李經進

Li Ching-fang 李經方 (Po-hsing 伯行)

Li Ching-mai 李經邁 (Chi-kao 季高)

Li Ching-p'u 李經璞

Li Ching-shu 李經述 (Chung-p'eng 仲彭)

Li Ching-yüan 李經遠

Li Chung-p'eng. *See* Li Ching-shu

Li Feng-chang 李鳳章

Li Fu-shan 李福山

Lo Ju-huai 羅汝懷
Lo Ping-chang 駱秉章
Lo Tse-nan 羅澤南
Lu-chiang 廬江
Lu-chou 廬州
Lu-kou-ch'iao 蘆溝橋
lü 律
Lü Hsi-yin. *See* Lü Hsien-chi
Lü Hsien-chi 呂賢基
　(Wen-chieh 文節 )
　(Hsi-yin 羲音 )
Lü Pu-wei 呂不韋
Lü Wen-chieh. *See* Lü Hsien-chi
*Lun-yü* 論語
Lung-men Academy 龍門書院

Ma Chien-chung 馬建忠
　(Mei-shu 眉叔 )
Ma Hsin-i 馬新貽
　(Ku-shan 穀山 )
Ma Ku-shan. *See* Ma Hsin-i
Ma Mei-shu. *See* Ma Chien-chung
*Ma-shih wen-t'ung* 馬氏文通
Mao Ch'ang-hsi 毛祉熙
　(Hsü-ch'u 旭初 )
Mao Hsü-ch'u. *See* Mao Ch'ang-hsi
Mei Ch'i-chao 梅啓照
　(Hsiao-yen 筱巖 )
Mei Hsiao-yen. *See* Mei Ch'i-chao
ming 名
Ming-chün 銘軍
Ming-tzu-ying 銘字營
Mo 莫
Mo Tzu-ssu. *See* Mo Yu-chih
Mo Yu-chih 莫友芝
　(Tzu-ssu 子偲)
Moho 漠河
mu-fu 幕府
mu-k'e 幕客
mu-liao 幕僚

mu-pin 幕賓
mu-yu 幕友

Nan-yang 南洋
Nanking (Nan-ching) 南京
Ni Pao-ts'en. *See* Ni Wen-wei
Ni Wen-wei 倪文蔚
　(Pao-ts'en 豹岑 )
Nien 捻
nien-chia-tzu 年家子
Nien-fei 捻匪
Ning 甯
Nurhaci 努爾哈赤

O 鄂

pa-kung-sheng 拔貢生
Pan Ch'ao 班超
Pan Ku 班固
P'an Ch'in-hsien. *See* P'an Ting-hsin
P'an Chün-te 潘駿德
P'an Ting-hsin 潘鼎新
　(Ch'in-hsien 琴軒 )
Pao Hua-t'an. *See* Pao Yüan-shen
Pao Shu 鮑叔
Pao-ting fu 保定府
Pao Yüan-shen 鮑源深
　(Hua-t'an 華潭 )
pei-te 悖德
Pei-yang 北洋
pei-yang t'ung-shang shih-wu ta-
　ch'en 北洋通商事務大臣
Peking (Pei-ching) 北京
P'eng Hsüeh-ch'in. *See* P'eng Yü-lin
P'eng Yü-lin 彭玉麟
　(Hsüeh-ch'in 雪琴 )
Pi Yüan 畢沅
pieh-chia 別駕
pien-hsiu 編修
ping-pu shang-shu 兵部尚書

p'in-ming tso-kuan 拼命做官
pu-cheng-shih 布政使
P'u-i 溥儀

san-yen hua-ling 三眼花翎
Seng-ko-lin-ch'in 僧格林沁
Shang 商
Shanghai 上海
Shang-wu chü 商務局
Shang Yang. *See* Kung-sun Yang
shao 哨
Shao-hsing fu 紹興府
Shen Ching-sheng. *See* Shen Kuei-fen
Shen Kuei-fen 沈桂芬
(Ching-sheng 經笙)
Shen Pao-chen 沈葆楨
(Yu-tan 幼丹)
Shen Pao-ching 沈保靖
Shen Yu-tan. *See* Shen Pao-chen
Sheng Hsing-sun. *See* Sheng Hsüan-huai
Sheng Hsüan-huai 盛宣懷
(Hsing-sun 杏蓀)
Sheng-tzu-ying 盛字營
*Sheng-yü kuang-hsün* 聖諭光訓
shih 士
*Shih-chi* 史記
shih-chiang hsüeh-shih 侍講學士
Shih K'e-k'uan 史克寬
shih-lang 侍郎
shih-ta-fu 士大夫
shih-yeh 師爺
shu 樹
Shu (Szechwan) 蜀
Shu-ch'eng 舒城
shu-chi-shih 庶吉士
shu-ch'i 書啟

Shu-tzu-ying 樹字營
shuang-yen hua-ling 雙眼花翎
Shun-chih 順治
Shun-ti 順帝
*Shuo-wen* 說文
Sian (Hsi-an) 西安
Soochow (Su-chou) 蘇州
ssu-tsui 私罪
Su 蘇
Su-sung-t'ai tao 蘇松太道
sui 歲
Sun Ch'iang-ming 孫鏘鳴
(Ch'ü-t'ien 蕖田)
Sun Ch'in-hsi. *See* Sun I-yen
Sun Ch'ü-t'ien. *See* Sun Ch'iang-ming
Sun I-yen 孫詒言
(Ch'in-hsi 琴西)
Sun Kuan 孫觀
Sun Shih-ta 孫士達
Sungkiang (Sung-chiang) 松江
sung-tu 訟蠹
Sung-tzu-chün 松字軍

*Ta-Ch'ing chin-shen ch'üan-shu*
大清搢紳全書
*Ta-Ch'ing lü-li* 大清律例
ta-hsüeh-shih 大學士
*Ta-Ming hui-tien* 大明會典
ta-shuai 大帥
Taiwan (T'ai-wan) 台灣
Tai Wang 戴望
Tai-Wŏn-Kun 大院君
Tai-yen men 代鴈門
T'ai-hu hsien 太湖縣
t'ai-shou 太守
T'ai-ting ti 泰定帝
t'ai-tzu shao-pao 太子少保
t'ai-tzu t'ai-fu 太子太傅
t'ai-tzu t'ai-pao 太子太保

T'ang Ching-hsing. *See* T'ang
  T'ing-shu

T'ang Hsün-fang 唐訓方
  (I-ch'ü 義渠 )

T'ang I-ch'ü. *See* T'ang Hsün-fang

T'ang Jen-shou 唐仁壽

T'ang Shao-ch'uan. *See* T'ang Shao-i

T'ang Shao-i 唐紹儀
  (Shao-ch'uan 少川 )

T'ang T'ing-shu 唐廷樞
  (Ching-hsing 景星 )

T'ang Yüan-pu 唐元圃

tao-i chin-shih chih chiao 道義
金石之交

Tao-kuang 道光

taotai (tao-t'ai) 道臺

T'ao Chu 陶澍

T'ao Kuang 陶桄

tien-shih 典史

Tientsin (T'ien-chin) 天津

T'ien-chin chi-ch'i chü 天津機器局

Ting Chih-huang. *See* Ting Pao-
  chen

Ting Jih-ch'ang 丁日昌
  (Yü-sheng 雨生 )

Ting Ju-ch'ang 丁汝昌

Ting Le-shan. *See* Ting Shou-ch'ang

Ting Pao-chen 丁寶楨
  (Chih-huang 稚璜 )

Ting Shou-ch'ang 丁壽昌
  (Le-shan 樂山 )

Ting-tzu-ying 鼎字營

ting-wei 丁未

ting-yu shih-lang 丁憂侍郎

Ting Yü-sheng. *See* Ting Jih-ch'ang

Tong King-sing. *See* T'ang T'ing-
  shu

t'ou-p'in ting-tai 頭品頂戴

Ts'ang-chou 滄州

Ts'ao Ts'an 曹參

Ts'ao Yen-yüeh 曹彥約

ts'ao-yün tsung-tu 漕運總督

Tseng Chi-hung 曾紀鴻
  (Li-hsien 栗諴 )

Tseng Chi-kang. *See* Tseng Chi-tse

Tseng Chi-tse 曾紀澤
  (Chi-kang 劼剛 )

Tseng Kuo-ch'üan 曾國荃
  (Yüan-p'u 沅浦 )

Tseng Kuo-fan 曾國藩
  (Ti-sheng 滌生 )

Tseng Kuo-pao 曾國葆
  (Shih-heng 事恆 )

Tseng Li-hsien. *See* Tseng Chi-hung

Tseng Shih-heng. *See* Tseng Kuo-
  pao

Tseng Ti-sheng. *See* Tseng Kuo-fan

Tseng Yüan-p'u. *See* Tseng Kuo-
  ch'üan

Tso Chi-kao. *See* Tso Tsung-t'ang

*Tso-chih yao-yen* 佐治藥言

tso-fu tu-yü-shih 左副都御史

tso-shih-lang 左侍郎

Tso Tsung-t'ang 左宗棠
  (Chi-kao 季高 )

Ts'o 撮

Tsungli Yamen 總理衙門

tu 篤

tu-liang-tao 督糧道

Tung Chung-shu 董仲舒

Tung-hsiang 東鄉

tung-weng 東翁

Tung-yang 東洋

t'ung 同

T'ung-ch'eng 桐城

T'ung-chih 同治

t'ung-chih 同知

t'ung-hsiang 同鄉

t'ung-hsüeh 同學

t'ung-ling 統領
t'ung-nien 同年
t'ung-sheng 同省
tzu 字
tzu-ch'iang 自強
Tz'u-an 慈安
Tz'u-hsi 慈禧

Wang An-shih 王安石
Wang Hui-tsu 汪輝祖
Wang Jen-ch'iu. *See* Wang K'ai-yün
Wang K'ai-yün 王闓運
  (Jen-ch'iu 壬秋)
Wang Mang 王莽
Wang Mao-yin 王茂蔭
Wang Shih-to 汪士鐸
Wang T'ang 王堂
Wang Tsun 王尊
Wei Ch'ing 衛青
Wei Wen-yün 魏溫雲
Weihaiwei (Wei-hai-wei) 威海衛
Wen-chung 文忠
Wen-ping 文彬
Weng Shu-p'ing. *See* Weng T'ung-ho
Weng T'ung-ho 翁同龢
  (Shu-p'ing 叔平)
Woosung (Wu-sung) 吳淞
Wuchang (Wu-ch'ang) 武昌
Wu Ch'ang-ch'ing 吳長慶
  (Hsiao-hsien 筱軒)
Wu Chih-fu. *See* Wu Ju-lun
Wu Chih-yung. *See* Wu T'ing-fang
Wu Chung-hsien. *See* Wu T'ang
Wu Hsiao-hsien. *See* Wu Ch'ang-ch'ing
wu-hsü 戊戌
Wu Ju-lun 吳汝綸
  (Chih-fu 摯甫)

Wu K'un-hsiu 吳坤修
  (Tzu-hou 子厚)
Wu Min-shu 吳敏樹
Wu Po-hua 吳伯華
Wu T'ang 吳棠
  (Chung-hsien 仲僎)
Wu-ti 武帝
Wu T'ing-fang 伍廷芳
  (Chih-yung 秩庸)
Wu Tzu-hou. *See* Wu K'un-hsiu
Wu-wei 無為

yamen 衙門
ya-men t'i-k'ung 衙門提控
Yang-chou fu 揚州府
Yang Hsiang-chi 楊象濟
yang-lien yin 養廉銀
Yang Shao-ming. *See* Yang Ting-hsün
yang-shih chih feng 養士之風
Yang Ting-ch'ing 楊鼎清
Yang Ting-hsün 楊鼎銘
  (Shao-ming 紹銘)
Yang Ting-nai 楊鼎載
Yang Tsai-fu 楊鼎福
Yeh Po-ying 葉伯英
yen-yün-shih 鹽運使
ying 營
ying-chü wen-jen 應舉文人
Ying-han 英翰
  (Hsi-lin 西林)
Ying Hsi-lin. *See* Ying-han
ying-kuan 營官
Ying Ssu 應嗣
Yu Chih-k'ai 游智開
yu-kung 優貢
yu-shih 遊士
yu-shih-lang 右侍郎
Yü Heng 余亨
Yü K'o 毓科

yü-shih 御史

Yü Yüeh 俞樾

Yüan Chia-san 袁甲三
  (Hsin-chai 新齋 )

Yüan Hsin-chai. *See* Yüan Chia-san

Yüan Pao-ch'ing 袁保慶
  (Tu-ch'en 篤臣 )

*Yüan-shih* 元史

Yüan Shih-k'ai 袁世凱
  (Wei-t'ing 慰庭 )

Yüan Tu-ch'en. *See* Yüan Pao-ch'ing

Yüan Wei-t'ing. *See* Yüan Shih-k'ai

Yüan Yüan 阮元

Yung-cheng 雍正

Yung-lo 永樂

Yung Wing. *See* Jung Hung

# Bibliography

(*Only those works cited directly in the text*)

Allen, Bernard M. *Gordon in China*. London: Macmillan and Co., Ltd., 1933.

Arlington, Lewis Charles. *Through the Dragon's Eyes. Fifty Years' Experience of a Foreigner in the Chinese Government Service*. London: Constable and Co., Ltd., 1931.

Bales, W. L. *Tso Tsung-t'ang: Soldier and Statesman of Old China*. Shanghai: Kelley & Walsh, Ltd., 1937.

Barnard, Chester I. *The Functions of the Executive*. Cambridge: Harvard University Press, 1956.

Bland, J. O. P. *Li Hung-chang*. Edited with a preface by Basil Williams. Makers of the Nineteenth Century. New York: Henry Holt and Co., 1917.

Bland, J. O. P., and E. Backhouse. *China Under the Empress Dowager, Being the History of the Life and Times of Tzu-hsi*. London: William Heinemann, 1911.

Bodde, Derk. "Authority and Law in Ancient China," *Journal of the American Oriental Society*, Supplement No. 17 (July/Sept., 1954), pp. 46–55.

Boulais, Guy, S.J., *Manuel du Code Chinois*. Variétés Sinologiques, No. 55. Shanghai: Imprimerie de la Mission Catholique, 1924.

Boulger, Demetrius C. *The Life of Gordon*. London: T. Fisher Unwin, 1896.

————. *The Life of Sir Halliday Macartney, K.C.M.G., Commander of Li Hung-Chang's Trained Force in the Taeping rebellion, Founder of the First Chinese Arsenal, for Thirty Years Councillor and Secretary to the Chinese Legation in London*. London and New York: J. Lane, 1908.

Bredon, Juliet. *Sir Robert Hart, The Romance of a Great Career*. London: Hutchinson and Co., 1909.

Brenan, Byron. "The Office of District Magistrate in China," *The Journal of the North China Branch of the Royal Asiatic Society,* New Series, XXXII (1897–1898), 36–65.

Brunnert, H. S., and V. V. Hagelstrom. *Present Day Political Organization of China.* Translated by A. Beltchenko and E. E. Moran. Taiwan reprint, 1961.

Carlson, Ellsworth C. *The Kaiping Mines (1877–1912).* Cambridge: Harvard University Press, 1957.

Chang Ch'un-ming. "The Chinese Standards of Good Government: Being a Study of the 'Biographies of Model Officials' in Dynastic Histories," *Nankai Social & Economic Quarterly,* VIII, No. 2 (July, 1935), 219–249.

———. "Ch'ing-tai ti mu-chih" (The *Mu* System of the Ch'ing Dynasty), *Ling-nan hsüeh-pao,* IX, No. 2 (June, 1949), 29–50.

Chang Chung-li. *The Chinese Gentry: Studies on Their Role in Nineteenth-Century Chinese Society.* Seattle: University of Washington Press, 1955.

Chang Te-ch'ang. "Li Hung-chang chih wei-hsin yün-tung" (Li Hung-chang's Reform Movement), *Ch'ing-hua chou-k'an,* XXXV, No. 2 (1931), 110–112.

Chang Tsung-i. "Ho-t'ung" (An Agreement [between the surviving sons and grandson as to the division of Li Hung-chang's property after his death]). *MS,* April 4, 1908, plus a codicil dated May 10, 1918. Photocopy of the original is in the author's possession. The original was in the possession of the late Li Kuo-ch'ao, San Francisco, California.

Chen, Gideon. *Tseng Kuo-fan, Pioneer Promoter of the Steamship in China.* Peiping: Yenching University, 1935.

Ch'en, Jerome. *Yuan Shih-k'ai, 1859–1916. Brutus Assumes the Purple.* Stanford: Stanford University Press, 1961.

Ch'en Shih-hsiang, Conversation, University of California, Nov. 21, 1963.

Chiang Shih-yung, ed. *Nien-chün shih-liao ts'ung-k'an* (A Collection of Historical Materials on the Nien Army). Shanghai: Shang-wu yin-shu-kuan, 1957. Vol. 2.

Chiang Siang-tseh. *The Nien Rebellion.* Seattle: University of Washington Press, 1954.

Ch'ien Shih-fu. *Ch'ing-chi chung-yao chih-kuan nien-pao* (A Table of the Important Officials at the End of the Ch'ing). Peking: Chung-hua shu-chü, 1959.

———. *Ch'ing-chi hsin-she chih-kuan nien-pao* (A Table of the Newly

Established Officials at the End of the Ch'ing). Peking: Chung-hua shu-chü, 1961.

China. Inspectorate General of Customs. *Decennial Reports on the Trade, Navigation, Industries, Etc., of the Ports Open to Foreign Commerce in China and Corea, and on the Condition and Development of the Treaty Port Provinces.* 2nd Issue, 1892–1901. Shanghai: Inspectorate General of Customs, 1904.

*Ch'ing shih* (History of the Ch'ing Dynasty). Compiled by the Ch'ing-shih pien-tsuan wei-yüan-hui. Taipei, Taiwan: Kuo-fang yen-chiu yüan, 1961. 8 vols.

*Ch'ing shih-kao* (Draft History of the Ch'ing Dynasty). Edited by Chao Erh-hsün, *et al.* Hong Kong: Hsiang-kang wen-hsüeh yen-chiu she [1960?]. 536 *chüan*, 2 vols.

*Ch'ing-shih lieh-chuan* (Biographies of the Ch'ing Dynasty). Compiled by the Ch'ing-shih kuan. Taipei, Taiwan: Chung-hua shu-chü, 1962. 10 vols.

*Ch'ing-tai cheng-hsien lei-pien.* Edited by Yang Chia-lo. Taipei, Taiwan: Shih-chieh shu-chü, 1961. 2 vols.

Ch'ü T'ung-tsu. "Chinese Class Structure and Its Ideology," *in* John K. Fairbank, ed., *Chinese Thought and Institutions.* Chicago: University of Chicago Press, 1957. Pp. 235–250.

————. *Law and Society in Traditional China.* The Hague: Mouton and Co., 1961.

————. *Local Government in China Under the Ch'ing.* Cambridge: Harvard University Press, 1962.

Ch'üan Tseng-yu. "Ch'ing-tai mu-liao chih-tu lun" (On the *Mu-liao* System of the Ch'ing Period), *Ssu-hsiang yü shih-tai yüeh-k'an*, No. 31 (Feb., 1944), pp. 29–35; No. 32 (Mar., 1944), pp. 35–43.

*Chung-kuo jen-ming ta-tz'u-tien* (Cyclopedia of Chinese Biographical Names). Compiled by Ts'ang Li-ho. Taipei, Taiwan: Shang-wu yin-shu-kuan, 1960.

Conger, Sarah Pike. *Letters From China.* London: Hodder and Stoughton, 1909.

Coser, Lewis A. *The Functions of Social Conflict.* Glencoe, Ill.: The Free Press, 1956.

Cunningham, Alfred. *The Chinese Soldier and Other Sketches with a Description of the Capture of Manila.* Hong Kong: The "Daily Press" Office, n.d.

De Bary, William T., "A Reappraisal of Neo-Confucianism," *in* Arthur F.

Wright, ed., *Studies in Chinese Thought*. Chicago: University of Chicago Press, 1953. Pp. 81–111.

De Bary, William T., ed. *Sources of Chinese Tradition*. New York: Columbia University Press, 1960.

Doolittle, Justus. *Social Life of the Chinese: With Some Account of Their Religious, Governmental, Educational, and Business Customs and Opinions*. New York: Harper & Brothers, 1865. 2 vols.

Douglas, Robert K. *Li Hungchang*. Public Men of To-Day. An International Series. London: Bliss, Sands and Foster, 1895.

————. "Some Peking Politicians," *The Nineteenth Century*, XL (Dec., 1896), 896–906.

Eastman, Lloyd Eric. "Reactions of Chinese Officials to Foreign Aggression: A Study of the Sino-French Controversy 1880–1885." Unpublished Ph.D. Dissertation, Harvard University, 1962.

*Erh-shih-ssu shih* (Twenty-Four Histories). Shanghai: T'ung-wen shu-chü, 1884. 711 *ts'e*.

Fairbank, John K., ed. *Chinese Thought and Institutions*. Chicago: University of Chicago Press, 1957.

Fan Yin-nan. *Tang-tai Chung-kuo ming-jen lu* (A Record of the Famous Men of Modern China). Shanghai: Liang-yu t'u-shu yin-shua kung-ssu ch'u-pan, 1931.

Fang Chao-ying and Tu Lien-che. *Tseng-chiao Ch'ing-ch'ao chin-shih t'i-ming pei-lu* (A Ranking of the *Chin-shih* of the Ch'ing Dynasty). Harvard-Yenching Institute Sinological Index Series, Supplement No. 19. Peiping: Harvard-Yenching Institute, 1941.

Fang, Lienche. "Chou Fu," draft *MS* prepared for the Men and Politics in Modern China Project, Columbia University, 1959.

Feuerwerker, Albert. *China's Early Industrialization: Sheng Hsuan-huai (1844–1916) and Mandarin Enterprises*. Cambridge: Harvard University Press, 1958.

Foster, John Watson. "The Great Chinese Viceroy and Diplomat," *International Monthly*, II (Nov., 1900), 584–596.

Franke, Wolfgang. *The Reform and Abolition of the Traditional Chinese Examination System*. Cambridge: Harvard University Press, 1960.

Freud, Sigmund. *Civilization and Its Discontents*. Translated by Joan Riviere. Garden City, N.Y.: Doubleday and Co., Inc., 1958.

Fried, Morton H. *Fabric of Chinese Society; A Study of the Social Life of a Chinese County Seat*. London: Atlantic Press, 1956.

Gervais, A.: "Diplomatie Chinoise: Li-Hung-Chang et le commandant

Fournier," *Revue Politique et Littéraire* (*Revue Bleue*), XXI, No. 15 (Oct. 11, 1884), 449–457.

Giles, Herbert A. *A Chinese Biographical Dictionary.* Taiwan reprint, 1962. 2 vols.

Giquel, Prosper. *The Foochow Arsenal and Its Results: From the Commencement in 1867, to the End of the Foreign Directorate, on the 16th February 1874.* Translated by H. Lang. Shanghai: The Shanghai Evening Courier, 1874.

Hail, William James. *Tseng Kuo-fan and the Taiping Rebellion.* Yale Historical Publications — Miscellany XVIII. New Haven: Yale University Press, 1927.

Hamilton, David. "Kuo Sung-tao; A Maverick Confucian," Harvard University, Center for East Asian Studies, *Papers on China*, Vol. 15 (1961), pp. 1–29.

Han Fei Tzu. *Han Fei Tzu, Basic Writings.* Transl. by Burton Watson. New York and London: Columbia Univ. Press, 1964.

Harris, Richard. "China Under the Empress Dowager," *History Today*, VII (Oct., 1957), 662–671.

Hart, Robert. "Letters to Various Westerners in the Chinese Customs Service," *MS.* Typed transcripts: 1865–1910, 1 box. Houghton Library, Harvard University.

Hinton, Harold C. *The Grain Tribute System of China (1845–1911).* Cambridge: Harvard University Press, 1956.

Hornby, Edmund G. *Sir Edmund Hornby, An Autobiography.* Boston and New York: Houghton Mifflin Company, 1928.

*Hou-Han shu in Erh-shih-ssu shih* (Twenty-Four Histories). Shanghai: T'ung-wen shu-chü, 1884. Vols. 59–86, 120 *chüan*.

Hsiao I-shan. *Tseng Kuo-fan chuan* (A Biography of Tseng Kuo-fan). Taipei, Taiwan: Chung-hua wen-hua ch'u-pan shih-yeh wei-yüan-hui ch'u-pan, 1955.

Hsiao Kung-ch'üan. *Rural China: Imperial Control in the Nineteenth Century.* Seattle: University of Washington Press, 1960.

————. "Rural Control in Nineteenth Century China," *Far Eastern Quarterly*, XII, No. 2 (February, 1953), 173–181.

————. "Weng T'ung-ho and the Reform Movement of 1898," *The Tsing Hua Journal of Chinese Studies*, New Series 1, No. 2 (April, 1957), pp. 111–243.

Hsieh Pao-chao. *The Government of China (1644–1911).* Johns Hopkins University Studies in Historical and Political Science, New Series, No. 3. Baltimore: The Johns Hopkins Press, 1925.

Hsü I-shih. "T'an Li Ching-fang" (On Li Ching-fang), *Kuo-wen chou-pao*, XI, No. 44 (Nov., 1934), 1–4.

Hsü, Immanuel C. Y. *China's Entrance into the Family of Nations: The Diplomatic Phase, 1858–1880.* Cambridge: Harvard University Press, 1960.

Hsüeh Fu-ch'eng. "Hsü Tseng Wen-cheng-kung mu-fu pin-liao" (A Discussion of the Members of Tseng Kuo-fan's *Mu-fu*), *in* Tso Shun-sheng, comp., *Chung-kuo chin-pai-nien shih tzu-liao ch'u-pien* (First Volume of Materials on the Last One Hundred Years of Chinese History). Taipei, Taiwan: Chung-hua shu-chü, 1958. Pp. 131–135.

———. "Li Fu-hsiang ju Tseng Wen-cheng-kung mu-fu" (Li Hung-chang Enters Tseng Kuo-fan's *Mu-fu*), *in* Tso Shun-sheng, comp., *Chung-kuo chin-pai-nien shih tzu-liao ch'u-pien.* Taipei, Taiwan: Chung-hua shu-chü, 1958. Pp. 160–162.

———. "Shu Ho-fei po-hsiang Li-kung yung Hu p'ing Wu" (How Li Hung-chang Used Shanghai to Pacify Soochow), *in* Tso Shun-sheng, comp., *Chung-kuo chin-pai-nien shih tzu-liao ch'u-pien.* Taipei, Taiwan: Chung-hua shu-chü, 1958, pp 163–167.

Hu Pin. *Mai-kuo-tse Li Hung-chang.* (The Traitor Li Hung-chang). Shanghai: Hsin chih-shih ch'u-pan she, 1955.

Huang Yün-hsiu. *Hsü-hsiu Lu-chou fu-chih* (Revised edition of the Lu-chou Prefecture Gazetteer). 1885. 100 *chüan.*

Kiernan, E. V. G. *British Diplomacy in China 1880 to 1885.* Cambridge: Cambridge University Press, 1939.

King, Paul. *In the Chinese Customs Service, A Personal Record of Forty-Seven Years.* Rev. ed. London: T. Fisher Unwin, Ltd., 1930.

Kramer, Samuel Noah. *History Begins at Sumer.* Garden City, N. Y.: Douobleday Anchor Books, 1959.

Ku Hung-ming. *Chang Wen-hsiang mu-fu chi-wen* (A Record of Chang Chi-tung's *Mu-fu*). Taipei, Taiwan: Shang-wu yin-shu-kuan, 1956.

Ku Yen-wu. *Jih-chih lu* (Diary). Shanghai: Shang-wu yin-sh-kuan, 1935. 2 vols.

Kung-sun Yang. *The Book of Lord Shang.* Transl. with an introduction by J. J. L. Duyvendak. Chicago: Univ. of Chicago Press, 1963.

La Fargue, Thomas E. *China's First Hundred.* Pullman, Wash.: The State College of Washington Press, 1942.

Lang, Olga. *Chinese Family and Society.* New Haven: Yale University Press, 1946.

Langer, W. L. *The Diplomacy of Imperialism, 1890–1902.* 2nd edition. New York and London: A. A. Knopf, 1951. 2 vols.

Legge, James. *The Chinese Classics: With a Translation, Critical and Exegtical Notes, Prolegomena and Copious Indexes.* Taiwan reprint, 1962. 7 vols.

Leroy-Beaulieu, Pierre. *La Rénovation de l'Asie.* Troisième édition. Paris: Armand Colin et Cie., 1900.

Levy, Marion Joseph, Jr. *The Family Revolution in Modern China.* Cambridge: Harvard University Press, 1949.

Li Chia-huang. Correspondence, Hong Kong, February 28, 1962.

Li Chia-wei. Interview, Hong Hong, November 2, 1961.

Li Chien-nung. *The Political History of China, 1840–1928.* Translated and edited by Teng Ssu-yü and J. Ingalls. Princeton: D. Van Nostrand Company, Inc., 1956.

Li Fang-ch'en. *Chung-kuo chin-tai shih* (Modern History of China). Taipei, Taiwan: Wu-chou ch'u-pan she, 1960. 2 vols.

Li Hung-chang. *Li Hung-chang chia-shu* (The Family Letters of Li Hung-chang). Shanghai: Chung-yang shu-tien, 1934.

———. *Li Wen-chung-gung ch'ih-tu* (The Letters of Li Hung-chang). Preface by Chou Fu. 1916. 32 *ts'e.*

———. *Li Wen-chung-kung ch'üan-chi* (The Complete Works of Li Hung-chang). Edited by Wu Ju-lun. Nanking, 1908. 100 *ts'e,* 165 *chüan.*

———. *Li Wen-chung-kung i-chi* (Posthumous Collection of the Writings of Li Hung-chang), *in* Li Kuo-chieh, ed., *Ho-fei Li shih san shih i-chi.* [No place]: The Li Family of Ho-fei, 1904. *Ts'e* 5–8.

Li Kuo-ch'ao. Interviews, San Francisco, California. February 21, April 4, June 7, and September 20, 1962; June 13, 1963; March 5, 1964.

Li Kuo-chieh, ed. *Ho-fei Li shih san shih i-chi* (Posthumous Collection of the Writings of Three Generations of the Li Family of Ho-fei). [No place]: The Li Family of Ho-fei, 1904. 12 *ts'e,* 24 *chüan,*

Li Shao-ling. *Tseng Kuo-fan.* Kao-hsiung, Taiwan: Ta-yeh shu-tien, 1955.

Li Shu-ch'un. "Li Wen-chung-kung Hung-chang nien-p'u" (A Chronological Biography of Li Hung-chang), *Shih-hsüeh nien-pao,* No. 1 (July, 1929), pp. 97–124.

Li Ting-i. Conversation, Taipei, Taiwan, July 20, 1961.

Liang Ch'i-ch'ao. *Lun Li Hung-chang* (On Li Hung-chang). Taipei, Taiwan: Chung-hua shu-chü, 1958.

Liang Fang-chung. *The Single-Whip Method of Taxation in China.* Chinese Economic and Political Studies. Cambridge: Harvard University Press, 1956.

Liang Ssu-kuang. *Li Hung-chang mai-kuo shih* (A History of the Traitor Li Hung-chang). Tientsin: Chih-shih shu-tien, 1951.

Little, Mrs. Archibald. *Intimate China. The Chinese as I Have Seen Them.* London: Hutchinson and Co., 1899.

———. *Li Hung-Chang. His Life and Time.* London: Cassell and Company, Ltd., 1903.

Liu, James T. C. *Reform in Sung China.* Cambridge: Harvard Univ. Press, 1959.

Liu Kwang-ching. "Steamship Enterprise in Nineteenth-Century China," *The Journal of Asian Studies*, XVIII, No. 4 (Aug., 1959), 435–455.

Liu Wang Hui-chen. "An Analysis of Chinese Clan Rules: Confucian Theories in Action," in David S. Nivison and Arthur F. Wright, eds., *Confucianism in Action*. Stanford, Calif.: Stanford University Press, 1959. Pp. 63–96.

———. *The Traditional Chinese Clan Rules.* Monographs of the Association for Asian Studies, VII. Locust Valley, N. Y.: J. J. Augustin, Inc., 1959.

Lo Erh-kang. "Ch'ing-chi ping wei chiang-yu ti ch'i-yüan" (The Origin of the Personal Armies at the End of the Ch'ing), *Chung-kuo she-hui ching-chi shih chi-k'an*, V, No. 2 (June, 1937), 235–250.

Lo Kuan-chung. *Romance of the Three Kingdoms.* Translated by C. H. Brewitt-Taylor. Rutland, Vt. and Tokyo: Charles E. Tuttle Co., 1959. 2 vols.

Ludwig, Albert Philip. "Li Hung-chang and Chinese Foreign Policy, 1870–1885." Unpublished Ph.D. Dissertation, University of California, 1936.

*Ma-kuan i-ho chung chih I Li wen-ta* (The Questions and Answers of Itō Hirobumi and Li Hung-chang During the Peace Negotiations at Shimonoseki). Compiled by the T'ai-wan yin-hang ching-chi yen-chiu shih. Taipei, Taiwan: T'ai-wan yin-hang, 1959.

Macgowan. "His Excellency Li Hung-chang," *The Far East*, Series 2, I, No. 3 (July, 1876), 73–75; No. 4 (October, 1876), 99–100.

Marsh, Robert M. *The Mandarins. The Circulation of Elites in China, 1600–1900.* Glencoe, Ill.: The Free Press, 1961.

Martin, W. A. P. *A Cycle of Cathay, or China, South and North.* London: Oliphant Anderson and Ferrier, 1896.

———. "Li Hung Chang," *The Independent*, LIII, No. 2763 (Nov. 14, 1901), 2686–2688.

Matignon, J. J. "La Grande figure de la vielle Chine: Li-Houng-Tchang," *La Nouvelle Revue* (1 août 1925), pp. 13, 211–220; (14 août 1925), pp. 323–341; (1 Sept. 1925), pp. 15–30.

Menne, Bernhard. *Blood and Steel; the Rise of the House of Krupp.* Translated by G. H. Smith. New York: L. Furman, Inc., 1938.

Michie, Alexander. *The Englishman in China During the Victorian Era, as Illustrated in the Career of Sir Rutherford Alcock.* Edinburgh: W. Blackwood and Sons, 1900. 2 vols.

————. "Li Hung-chang," *Blackwood's Edinburgh Magazine,* CLXX, No. 1034 (December, 1901), 836–851.

————. "Li Hung-chang," *The Nineteenth Century,* XL (August, 1896), 226–239.

Miller, James Martin. *China: Ancient and Modern: A History of the Chinese Empire from the Dawn of Civilization to the Present Time, Including Description of the People, Their Pursuits and Manner of Life, to Which Is Added a Complete Account of the Boxer Uprising.* Chicago: J. M. Miller, 1900.

*Ming shih, in Erh-shih-ssu shih.* Shanghai: T'ung-wen shu-chü, 1884. Vols. 600–711, 332 *chüan.*

Morse, Hosea Ballou. *The Gilds of China, with an Account of the Gild Merchant or Co-hong of Canton.* London: Longmans, Green and Co., 1909.

————. *In the Days of the Taipings, Being the Recollections of Ting Kienchang, Otherwise Meisun, Sometime Scoutmaster and Captain in the Ever-Victorious Army and Interpreter-in-chief to General Ward and General Gordon:An Historical Retrospect.* Salem, Mass.: The Essex Institute, 1927.

————. *The International Relations of the Chinese Empire.* Taiwan reprint, 3 vols.

————. "Letter-books of H. B. Morse Containing Copies of His Correspondence While Commissioner with the Chinese Maritime Customs, 1886–1907." *MS,* Houghton Library, Harvard University. 5 vols.

————. *The Trade and Administration of the Chinese Empire.* Shanghai: Kelly and Walsh, Ltd., 1908.

Nivision, David S. "Ho-shen and His Accusers: Ideology and Political Behavior in the Eighteenth Century," *in* David S. Nivison and Arthur F. Wright, eds., *Confucianism in Action.* Stanford, Calif.: Stanford University Press, 1959. Pp. 209–243.

Nivison, David S., and Arthur F. Wright, eds. *Confucianism in Action.* Stanford, Calif.: Stanford University Press, 1959.

Norman, Henry. *The Peoples and Politics of the Far East.* London: T. Fisher Unwin, 1900.

*The North China Herald and Supreme Court and Consular Gazette,* LXXXI, No. 2052, Shanghai, December 7, 1906.

Parker, Edward Harper. *China, Past and Present.* London: Chapman and Hall, Ltd., 1903.

————. *John Chinaman and a Few Others.* 2nd edition. London: John Murray, 1902.

Pirenne, Henri. *A History of Europe.* Translated by Bernard Miall. Garden City, N.Y.: Doubleday Anchor Books, 1956. 2 vols.

Powell, Ralph L. *The Rise of Chinese Military Power, 1895–1912.* Princeton: Princeton University Press, 1955.

Pulleyblank, Edwin G. "Neo-Confucianism and Leo-Legalism in T'ang Intellectual Life," *in* Arthur F. Wright, ed., *The Confucian Persuasion.* Stanford: Stanford Univ. Press, 1960.

Rawlinson, John Lang. "The Chinese Navy, 1839–1895." Unpublished Ph.D. Dissertation, Harvard University, 1959. 2 vols.

Richard, Timothy. *Forty-five Years in China: Reminiscences by Timothy Richard, D.D., Ltt.D.* New York: Frederick A. Stokes Co., 1916.

Sampson, Robert C. *The Staff Role in Management. Its Creative Uses.* New York: Harper and Brothers Publishers, 1955.

Schurmann, Franz. *Ideology and Organization in Communist China.* Berkeley: University of California Press, 1966.

Sergeant, P. W. *The Great Empress Dowager of China.* London: Hutchinson and Co., 1910.

*Shih-i ch'ao tung-hua lu.* Edited by Wang Hsien-ch'ien. Shanghai, 1911. 124 vols.

Simon, Herbert A. *Administrative Behavior.* 2nd ed. New York: The Macmillan Company, 1958.

Spector, Stanley. "Li Hung-chang and the Huai-chün." Unpublished Ph.D. Dissertation, University of Washington, 1953.

Ssu-ma Ch'ien. *Shih-chi.* Peking: Chung-hua shu-chü, 1959. 6 vols.

Stanley, C. John. *Late Ch'ing Finance: Hu Kuang-yung as an Innovator.* Cambridge: Harvard University Press, 1961.

————. "The *Mu-yu* in the Ch'ing Dynasty," *MS*, May 25, 1949. Seminar paper, Harvard University.

*Ta-Ch'ing chin-shen ch'üan-shu* (The Complete Record of the Officials of the Ch'ing). Quarterly editions. File for 1870–1874, 1884–1895 consulted.

*Ta-Ch'ing hui-tien shih-li.* Shanghai: Shang-wu yin-shu-kuan, 1908. 1220 chüan.

*Ta-Ch'ing li-ch'ao shih-lu* (Veritable Records of the Successive Reigns of the Ch'ing Dynasty). Tokyo, 1937–1938. 4485 *chüan*, 1220 *ts'e*. Photolithographic reproduction from the Mukden Archives.

T'ao-ch'i-yü-yen and Hsing-hsing-an-chu, eds. "Li Fu-hsiang yu-li ko-kuo jih-chi" (A Diary of Li Hung-chang's Journey to Various Countries), *in* Tso Shun-sheng, comp., *Chung-kuo chin-pai-nien shih tzu-liao hsü-pien*. Taipei, Taiwan: Chung-hua shu-chü, 1958. Pp. 387–415.

Teng Ssu-yü and John K. Fairbank. *China's Response to the West, A Documentary Survey, 1839–1923*. Cambridge: Harvard University Press, 1954.

Totman, Conrad D. "The Struggle for Control of the Shogunate (1853–1858)," Harvard University, Center for East Asian Studies, *Papers on Japan*, Vol. 1, pp. 42–88.

Tsao Hsüeh-chin and Kao Ngoh. *The Dream of the Red Chamber*. Translated by Florence and Isabel McHugh from the German translation of Franz Kuhn. Taiwan reprint.

Tseng Kuo-fan. *Tseng Wen-cheng-kung ch'üan-chi* (The Complete Works of Tseng Kuo-fan). Taipei, Taiwan: Shih-chieh shu-chü, 1952. 10 *ts'e*.

Tsiang, T. F. "Sino-Japanese Diplomatic Relations, 1870–1894," *Chinese Social and Political Science Review*, XVII, No. 1 (April, 1933), 1–106.

Tso Shun-sheng, comp. *Chung-kuo chin-pai-nien shih tzu-liao ch'u-pien* (First Volume of Materials on the Last One Hundred Years of Chinese History). Taipei, Taiwan: Chung-hua shu-chü, 1958.

————. *Chung-kuo chin-pai-nien shih tzu-liao hsü-pien* (Additional Materials on the Last One Hundred Years of Chinese History). Taipei, Taiwan: Chung-hua shu-chü, 1958.

Tyler, William Ferdinand. *Pulling Strings in China*. London: Constable and Co., Ltd., 1929.

*Tz'u-hai*. Taipei, Taiwan: Chung-hua shu-chü, 1959. 2 vols.

U. S. Department of State. *Despatches from United States Consuls in Tientsin, 1868–1906*. Washington, D.C.: The National Archives, 1947. 8 vols.

————. *Despatches from United States Ministers to China, June 27, 1843–August 14, 1906*. Washington, D.C.: The National Archives, 1946–1947. 131 vols.

U.S. Library of Congress. Asiatic Division. *Eminent Chinese of the Ch'ing Period (1644–1912)*. Edited by Arthur W. Hummel. Washington, D.C.: U.S. Government Printing Office, 1943. 2 vols.

van der Sprenkel, Sybille. *Legal Institutions in Manchu China. A Socio-*

*logical Analysis*. London School of Economics Monograph on Social Anthropology, No. 24. London: The Athlone Press, 1962.

van der Valk, Marc. *An Outline of Modern Chinese Family Law*. Monumenta Serica Monograph Series II. Peiping: H. Vetch, 1939.

Varé, Daniele. *The Last Empress*. Garden City, N.Y.: Doubleday, Doran and Co., Inc., 1936.

"The Visit of Li-Hung-Chang to England," *The Illustrated London News, Supplement*, CIX (August 15, 1896), 193, 195.

Waley, Arthur. *Yuan Mei, Eighteenth Century Chinese Poet*. London: George Allen and Unwin, Ltd., 1956.

Wang Hsien-ch'ien, ed. *Tung-hua lu*. Shanghai, 1911. 124 vols.

Wang Hui-tsu. *Hsü tso-chih yao-yen* (Additional Admonitions on Government). Shanghai: Shang-wu yin-shu-kuan, 1937.

———. *Hsüeh-chih i-shuo* (Learning to Govern). Ch'ang-sha: Shang-wu yin-shu-kuan, 1939.

———. *Tso-chih yao-yen* (Admonitions on Government). Shanghai: Shang-wu yin-shu-kuan, 1937.

Wei Hsi-yü. *Li Hung-chang*. Shanghai: Chung-hua shu-chü, 1931.

Wen Ching (Lim Boon-keng). *The Chinese Crisis From Within*. London: Grant Richards, 1901.

Williamson, H. R. *Wang An-shih . . . a Chinese Statesman and Educationalist of the Sung Dynasty*. London: A. Probsthain, 1935–1937. 2 vols.

Wilson, Andrew. *The "Ever-Victorious Army": A History of the Chinese Campaign under Lt.-Col. C. G. Gordon . . . and the Suppression of the Tai-ping Rebellion*. Edinburgh and London: W. Blackwood and Sons, 1868.

Wilson, James Harrison. *China: Travels and Investigations in the Middle Kingdom*. 3rd edition revised. New York: D. Appleton and Co., 1901.

Witte, Count. *The Memoirs of Count Witte*. Edited and translated by A. Yarmolinsky. London: William Heinemann, 1921.

Wittfogel, Karl. *Oriental Despotism; A Comparative Study of Total Power*. New Haven: Yale University Press, 1957.

Wright, Arthur F., ed. *The Confucian Persuasion*. Stanford: Stanford University Press, 1960.

———. *Studies in Chinese Thought*. Chicago: University of Chicago Press, 1953.

Wright, Mary Clabaugh. *The Last Stand of Chinese Conservatism. The T'ung-Chih Restoration, 1862–1874*. Stanford: Stanford University Press, 1957.

Wright, Stanley F. *Hart and the Chinese Customs*. Belfast: Wm. Mullan and Son, Ltd., 1950.

Wu Ching-tzu. *The Scholars*. Translated by Yang Hsien-i and Gladys Yang. Peking: Foreign Language Press, 1957.

Wu Ju-lun. "Li Wen-chung-kung mu-chih-ming" (Li Hung-chang's Tomb Inscription), *in* Li Hung-chang, *Li Wen-chung-kung ch'üan-chi*, chüan-shou, pp. 66a–67b. Edited by Wu Ju-lun. Nanking, 1908.

————. "Li Wen-chung-kung shen-tao-pei" (The Stone Tablet Before Li Hung-chang's Grave), *in* Li Hung-chang, *Li Wen-chung-kung ch'üan-chi*, chüan-shou, pp. 62a–65b. Edited by Wu Ju-lun. Nanking, 1908.

————. *Li Wen-chung-kung shih-lüeh* (An Outline of the Career of Li Hung-chang). Tokyo: Sanseidō Shoten, 1902.

Wu Wei-p'ing. "The Rise of the Anhwei Army," Harvard University, Center for East Asian Studies, *Papers on China*, Vol. 14 (1960), pp. 30–49.

Yang Chia-lo. *Min-kuo ming-jen t'u-chien* (A Survey of the Famous Men of the Chinese Republic). Nanking: Chung-kuo tz'u-tien kuan, 1937– . 18 *chüan*. *Chüan* 1–12 published, *chüan* 13–18 held by Library of Congress in galley-proof form.

Yang Lien-sheng. "The Concept of *Pao* as a Basis for Social Relations in China," *in* John K. Fairbank, ed., *Chinese Thought and Institutions*. Chicago: University of Chicago Press, 1957. Pp. 291–309.

Young, John Russell. *Around the World With General Grant*. New York: The American News Co., 1879. 2 vols.

Yü Yü-ti. "Tseng Kuo-fan mu-fu pin-liao nien-p'u" (A Chronological Record of Tseng Kuo-fan's *Mu-fu* and Its Members). Unpublished Bachelor's Thesis, National Taiwan University, Taipei, Taiwan, 1960.

*Yüan shih, in Erh-shih-ssu shih*. Shanghai: T'ung-wen shu-chü, 1884. Vols. 549–599, 210 *chüan*.

Yuan Tao-feng, "Li Hung-chang and the Sino-Japanese War," *T'ien Hsia Monthly*, III, No. 1 (1936), 9–17.

Yung Wing. *My Life in China and America*. New York: Henry Holt and Co., 1909.

# Index

Kuo-fan's student, 78–80, 93–94; official ranks of, 79, 80, 87, 89, 92, 97, 98, 99, 100, 166; career of, 79, 80, 97–103; poem "Entering the Capital," 79, 109–110; Tseng Kuo-fan's opinion of, 80–81; with Anhwei militia, 82, 98; as a *mu-yu*, 82, 98, 99; character of, 82, 83, 84, 88, 89, 94, 95, 96, 97, 99, 108–109, 109–120, 159; in Tseng Kuo-fan's *mu-fu*, 82–83, 85, 99; tension with Tseng Kuo-fan, 83–84, 85, 95, 119; and the *Huai-chün*, 85–86, 87, 90–92, 162–166; and Taiping Rebellion, 87–88; and family, 90, 103, 125–131, 129 n, 131–132, 147 n; and Nien Rebellion, 91; and Moslem Rebellion, 92; and foreign affairs, 92, 101–102, 182, 183–186, 187; and foreigners, 93–94, 157; practical nature of, 93–94, 113; debt to Tseng Kuo-fan, 93–94; comparison with Tseng Kuo-fan, 94–95, 190; debt to the *mu-fu* system, 95, 96, 99, 195; and the *mu-fu* system, 97, 150–151, 190, 195; as a leader, 100–101, 119, 120; and the nature of his *mu-yu*, 100, 120, 124, 125, 133, 146; and the Chinese Navy, 102, 177–179; wealth of, 103–109, 119; national position of, 103, 186–187; and ambition, 109–110; desire to be an official, 109–111, 194; and conduct of business, 113; and local populace, 114, 115; as a realist, 114, 189; as a stern ruler, 114–115; loyalty of, 116–119; and Anhwei, 117–118; and friends, 118, 142–143, 193–194; power of, 119, 158; and loyalty of his *mu-yu*, 119–120, 124; and the imperial authority, 123; and recruitment of *mu-yu*, 123, 124–125, 177, 194; and men of talent, 124–125, 152, 192; knowledge of the West, 131, 134, 136, 157, 186; and relatives as *mu-yu*, 132–133; and his Chinese *mu-yu*, 133–136, 138, 139–142, 144–145, 146; and his generals, 136–137; and merchants and compradores, 137–138; and "returned students," 138–141; and knowledge as power, 143, 157; and change, 143, 191–192; and Yüan Chia-san, 146–147; and Yüan Shih-k'ai, 148–150,

151; and T'ang Shao-i, 149–150; and his foreign *mu-yu*, 149, 152–157; and the right of recommendation, 150–151; and corruption in his *mu-fu*, 151–152; and foreign vs. Chinese *mu-yu*, 156; and China, 157, 158–159, 195; limitations on his power, 158; desire for power, 158–159; on the court, 159; new government of, 159, 160–161, 194; and centralization of power, 159–161, 194; as emperor, 161; *ad hoc* policies of, 161; provincial position of, 161–162; and Chihli, 166, 173–177; and *lien-chün*, 166; network of friends and acquaintances, 166–168, 172–173; and Manchu princes, 168, 171–172; and Tz'u-hsi, 168–171, 189; and conservative opposition, 170, 171, 186–189, 192–193; and inability to control friends, 173; and Tientsin Customs Taotai, 173–175; as Commissioner of Trade for the Northern Ports, 174, 183–184; and foreign financial entanglements, 181; and control of enterprises, 180–182; and protection of enterprises, 182; and patronage, 182–183; and Ch'ung-hou, 187; and Sino-Japanese War, 189; and Tso Tsung-t'ang, 189; and Confucian culture, 190–191; and the Confucian-Legalist controversy, 192–194; and professionalism, 194; and Chinese nationalism, 195

Li Hung-i, 75
Li Jung, 75
Li Keng Yun, 15
Li Kuo-ch'ao, 105
Li Kuo-chieh, 103–104
Li Mu, 33
Li Shan-lan, 75, 76
Li Shu-ch'ang, 74
Li Tsung-hsi, 74, 168, 172
Li Wen-an, 78, 79, 146, 147 n
*Li Wen-chung-kung i-chi*, 79
Li Yüan-tu, 75, 84–85, 118
Li Yün-chang, 128
Liang Ch'i-ch'ao, 94
Liangkiang governor-general, 166–167, 172
*Lien-ch'ih* Academy, 143
*Lien-chün*, 91, 165–166

234